ROUTLEDGE LIBRARY EDITIONS: SEMANTICS AND SEMIOLOGY

Volume 13

ISSUES IN THE SEMANTICS AND PRAGMATICS OF DISJUNCTION

ISSUES IN THE SEMANTICS AND PRAGMATICS OF DISJUNCTION

MANDY SIMONS

Routledge
Taylor & Francis Group
LONDON AND NEW YORK

First published in 2000 by Garland Publishing, Inc.

This edition first published in 2017
by Routledge
2 Park Square, Milton Park, Abingdon, Oxon OX14 4RN

and by Routledge
711 Third Avenue, New York, NY 10017

Routledge is an imprint of the Taylor & Francis Group, an informa business

© 2000 Mandy Simons

All rights reserved. No part of this book may be reprinted or reproduced or utilised in any form or by any electronic, mechanical, or other means, now known or hereafter invented, including photocopying and recording, or in any information storage or retrieval system, without permission in writing from the publishers.

Trademark notice: Product or corporate names may be trademarks or registered trademarks, and are used only for identification and explanation without intent to infringe.

British Library Cataloguing in Publication Data
A catalogue record for this book is available from the British Library

ISBN: 978-1-138-69750-8 (Set)
ISBN: 978-1-315-52029-2 (Set) (ebk)
ISBN: 978-1-138-69794-2 (Volume 13) (hbk)
ISBN: 978-1-138-69795-9 (Volume 13) (pbk)
ISBN: 978-1-315-52033-9 (Volume 13) (ebk)

Publisher's Note
The publisher has gone to great lengths to ensure the quality of this reprint but points out that some imperfections in the original copies may be apparent.

Disclaimer
The publisher has made every effort to trace copyright holders and would welcome correspondence from those they have been unable to trace.

ISSUES IN THE SEMANTICS AND PRAGMATICS OF DISJUNCTION

MANDY SIMONS

GARLAND PUBLISHING, INC.
A MEMBER OF THE TAYLOR & FRANCIS GROUP

Published in 2000 by
Garland Publishing Inc.
A Member of the Taylor & Francis Group
19 Union Square West
New York, NY 10003

Copyright © 2000 by Mandy Simmons

All rights reserved. No part of this book may be reprinted or reproduced or utilized in any form or by any electronic, mechanical, or other means, now known or hereafter invented, including photocopying and recording, or in any information storage or retrieval system, without permission in writing from the publishers.

10 9 8 7 6 5 4 3 2 1

Library of Congress Cataloging-in-Publication Data
Simmons, Mandy.
    Issues in the semantics and pragmatics of disjunction.
       p. cm. — (Outstanding dissertations in linguistics)
    Includes bibliographical references and index.
    ISBN 0-8153-3791-4 (alk. paper)
       1. Grammar, Comparative and general—Coordinate constructions.
  2. Semantics. 3. Pragmatics. I. Title. II. Series.
P293.S56 2000
415—dc21   00-026481

Printed on acid-free, 250-year-life paper
Manufactured in the United States of America

For Tom

Contents

1. INTRODUCTION — 3

1.1. Overview — 3
    1.1.1. What this dissertation is about — 3
    1.1.2. Context change: Pragmatic vs. semantic approaches — 9

1.2. The Stalnakerian Model of Presupposition and Assertion — 10

1.3. Dynamic Semantics — 16
    1.3.1. The Fundamentals — 16
    1.3.2. File Change Semantics (FCS) and the CCP proposal — 17
    1.3.3. Discourse Representation Theory (DRT) — 21
    1.3.4. Dynamic Montague Grammar (DMG) — 23

Notes to Chapter One — 25

2. DISJUNCTIVE SENTENCES IN DISCOURSE — 27

2.1. Introduction — 27

2.2. The Discourse Function and Felicity Conditions of Disjunction — 28
    2.2.1. The Basic Observations — 28
    2.2.2. Relation and Manner in the Stalnakerian Model — 30

2.3. The Enriched Context Change Framework — 35
    2.3.1. Presentation — 35

2.3.2.	Disjunction and the Relevant Informativity Condition	43
2.3.3.	Disjunction and Simplicity	46
2.3.4.	Disjunction and Rooth's Alternative Semantics	53
2.3.5.	Summary	56

2.4. Some Exceptions . . . 57
    2.4.1. Floutings . . . 57
    2.4.2. Reasoning contexts . . . 59
    2.4.3. Metalinguistic *or* . . . 60

2.5. The Exclusive Interpretation of *or* . . . 64
    2.5.1. Critique of the ambiguity account . . . 64
    2.5.2. Gazdar's (1979) account . . . 67
    2.5.3. Exclusivity from exhaustiveness . . . 72
    2.5.4. Exclusivity from alternativeness . . . 76
    2.5.5. Summary . . . 78

2.6. Conclusion . . . 78

Notes to Chapter Two . . . 79

3. PRESUPPOSITION PROJECTION   81

3.1. Introduction . . . 81
    3.1.1. The Basic Question . . . 81
    3.1.2. The Theoretical Issues . . . 82

3.2. The Data . . . 84

3.3. The Satisfaction Account of Presupposition Projection . . . 88
    3.3.1. Basics of the Satisfaction Account . . . 88
    3.3.2. CCPs for disjunction . . . 90
    3.3.3. Critique . . . 93

3.4. Towards a New Account . . . 102
    3.4.1. Gazdar's cancellation theory . . . 103
    3.4.2. The accommodation view: Van der Sandt (1992) . . . 105
    3.4.3. Translating DRSs into Stalnakerian contexts . . . 112

3.5. The Account in Action		114
3.5.1.	Basic cases	114
3.5.2.	Entailing disjunctions again	119
3.5.3.	Beaver's counterexample	120
3.6. Conclusion		122
Notes to Chapter Three		123
4. INTERNAL ANAPHORA		**125**
4.1. Introduction		125
4.2. Anaphora-based Accounts in Dynamic Semantic Theories		127
4.2.1.	DMG: Groenendijk and Stokhof (1990)	128
4.2.2.	DRT: Kamp and Reyle (1993)	131
4.2.3.	A second DRT proposal: Krahmer and Muskens (1994)	134
4.2.4.	Van der Sandt (1992) revisited	138
4.3. A Felicity-based Approach		140
4.3.1.	Introduction to the account	140
4.3.2.	The E-type account of anaphora	145
4.3.3.	A felicity-based solution to the internal anaphora puzzle	154
4.3.4.	Summary	157
4.4. Further Data		158
4.4.1.	Narrow scope antecedents	158
4.4.2.	Non-E-type unbound anaphora	160
4.4.3.	Pleonastic pronouns	166
4.5. Conclusion		175
Notes to Chapter Four		177

5. EXTERNAL ANAPHORA — 181

5.1. Introduction — 181

5.2. The Basic Data — 183
    5.2.1. Anaphora to a disjunction of NPs — 183
    5.2.2. Clausal disjunction — 186

5.3. A First Reformulation of the E-type Account — 188

5.4. A Compositional Structural E-type Account — 194
    5.4.1. Presentation — 194
    5.4.2. Comparison with Chapter Four account — 197
    5.4.3. Narrow scope antecedents — 198

5.5. Application to the External Anaphora Data — 203
    5.5.1. Anaphora to a disjunction of NPs — 203
    5.5.2. Anaphora to clausal disjunctions — 205
    5.5.3. Summary — 217

5.6. The Single-antecedent Reading — 217
    5.6.1. Derivation of single-antecedent readings — 218
    5.6.2. Maximal quantifier antecedents — 220
    5.6.3. Summary — 224

5.7. Other Approaches to External Anaphora — 224

5.8. Further Issues for the E-type Account — 230
    5.8.1. Inference-based anaphora — 230
    5.8.2. Interpretation of plural pronouns — 230
    5.8.3. Anaphora to NP disjuncts and conjuncts — 233

5.9. Conclusion — 234

Notes to Chapter Five — 236

CONCLUDING REMARKS — 239
    Grice, Stalnaker and Dynamic Semantics

Appendix **243**

Bibliography **247**

Index **257**

Preface

This book is a slightly revised version of my 1998 Cornell University doctoral dissertation. I have made small corrections throughout the text and tidied up some of the discussion, but have made no major changes. The analyses presented here remain unchanged from the original. These analyses do not in all cases represent my current thinking, as I have continued to work on these topics since my dissertation was written. However, I remain committed to the central premise of this work, namely, that in accounting for the interpretation of language it is crucial to distinguish between pragmatic and semantic factors. The general principles which govern rational interaction have significant explanatory power, and this power should be exhausted before we attribute unnecessary semantic complexity to lexical items or syntactic constructions.

In this book, I try to show that some of the behavior of disjunctive sentences can be accounted for quite straightforwardly by taking pragmatic principles into consideration. After a brief introduction to the data and basic assumptions (Chapter One), I offer an account of the felicity conditions to which clausal disjunctions are subject in terms of general principles of information update (Chapter Two). I then go on to demonstrate that these conditions provide a basis for an account of the presupposition projection properties of disjunction (Chapter Three) and of the possibilities of anaphora across disjunction (Chapter Four). In the final chapter, which digresses somewhat from my central theme, I discuss anaphora involving disjoined NP antecedents and antecedents contained in clausal disjunctions. This account requires the development of a new E-type account of anaphora.

This dissertation would never have been written without the help, guidance, encouragement (and occassional bullying!) of many people. First and foremost, I would like to thank Sally McConnell-Ginet, the chair of my dissertation committee, advisor, confidante and role model throughout my graduate student career and now beyond. Thanks also to the other members of my (extended) dissertation committee, Molly Diesing, Zoltán Gendler Szabó, and Sandro Zucchi, whose insights, comments and criticisms inform this work. This work also reflects the influence of teachers and fellow students who talked to me about semantics in general and disjunction in particular during my graduate student years. In particular, I wish to thank Angelika Kratzer, Barbara Partee, Jason Stanley and Tom Werner. Finally, my sincere thanks to Jeremy Avigad and again to Tom Werner for giving up time to proofread parts of this manuscript when they had much better things to do.

Leaving best for last, as is customary, I dedicate this book to Tom, with love and appreciation.

Issues in the Semantics and Pragmatics of Disjunction

CHAPTER 1
Introduction

1.1. OVERVIEW

1.1.1. What this dissertation is about

This dissertation is about sentences containing the word *or*. In the sentences I discuss, *or* occurs in a main clause and is not embedded under any other operators. I will deal primarily with sentences in which *or* conjoins clauses, but also some cases in which it conjoins expressions of other categories.

The starting point of the dissertation was the observation that not all clauses can sensibly be disjoined. Sometimes, the disjunction of two independently acceptable clauses produces an unacceptable result. Sentence (1), below, is acceptable, but (2) is not. (3) is also odd, but in a different way from (2). (I use the symbol "#" to indicate that a sentence is unacceptable in some non-syntactic way.)

(1)   Jane owns a red truck or she owns a blue truck.
(2)   #Jane owns a truck or she owns a red truck.
(3)   #Jane owns a truck or it is raining in Tel-Aviv.

I began with the intention of characterizing the permissible relations that may hold between disjuncts, and of explaining why disjunction is constrained in this way. At the same time, I began to think about other constraints on the assertion of disjunctions. (4) and (5) are also very odd things to say in a normal conversation.

(4)   Jane owns a truck. #Either she owns a truck or she owns a station wagon.
(5)   Jane doesn't own a truck. #Either she owns a truck or she owns a station wagon.

The oddity of these sentences seems to have something to do with their being redundant, but I wondered whether there could be a connection between the infelicity of these and the infelicity of (2) and (3).

While working on these questions, I began to think that if I could answer them, then I would also be able to resolve some other puzzles about disjunction. One of these has to do with the way presuppositions project in clausal disjunctions. Usually, a disjunction inherits all of the presuppositions of its disjuncts. The exception is when the presupposition of one disjunct is incompatible with the content of another. So (6) inherits from its second disjunct the presupposition that Jane is in town, but (7) does not.

(6)   Either George had a particularly good day, or he knows that Jane is in town.
(7)   Either Jane isn't in town or George knows that she is.

The question is why presuppositions should be "filtered" or "canceled" in just these conditions.

In the framework which I adopt, a presupposition is a proposition that must be assumed as part of the background context in which the presupposing sentence is uttered. So when a speaker asserts a presupposing sentence, what she does is, in a way, equivalent to what she would do by asserting the presupposition, and then asserting the sentence (or a non-presupposing version of it). If I say out of the blue:

(8)   George knows that Jane is in town

the communicative effect is equivalent to my saying:

(9)   Jane is in town, and George knows that she is.

Now, suppose that (7) were to inherit the presupposition. Then to say (7) would be equivalent to saying:

Introduction

(10)   Jane is in town. Either Jane isn't in town, or George knows that she is.

But this is something a speaker would never say. So if we adopt a view of presupposition which allows presupposition projection to be sensitive to considerations of felicity, then the presupposition projection problem for disjunction comes down to explaining when and why a disjunction can be felicitously asserted.

Another puzzle about disjunction has to do with possible anaphoric relations between an indefinite in one disjunct and a pronoun in another. The problem is illustrated by the contrast between (11) and (12), a contrast originally observed by Barbara Partee and already much discussed in the literature:

(11)   Either there's no bathroom in this house, or it's in a funny place.
(12)   #Either there's a bathroom in this house, or it's in a funny place.

Researchers working on unbound anaphora have been puzzled by the question of why anaphora is possible across disjunction in (11), but not in (12). This seems to have something to do with the presence of negation in the first disjunct. But this just makes the matter more mysterious, for normally negation itself blocks anaphora:

(13)   There's no bathroom in this house. #It's in a funny place.

It seemed to me, however, that the infelicity of (12) does not indicate that the pronoun cannot be anaphoric on the NP in the previous clause. The observed infelicity arises because, as the pronoun in fact is anaphoric on that NP, the disjunction (12) has an interpretation equivalent to:

(14)   #Either there's a bathroom in this house, or the bathroom in this house is in a funny place.

(14) itself is infelicitous in the same way as (2) above, but this has nothing to do with anaphora. It is a consequence of the constraints which determine the allowable relations between disjuncts. Thus, if this approach is right, then the solution to the anaphora puzzle is the same as the answer to the question about why certain pairs of clauses cannot be disjoined. But to give this answer, I also had to have a way of explaining

how the pronoun in (12) comes to be interpreted as "the bathroom in this house," that is, I needed some theory of cross-clausal anaphora.

The project undertaken here is thus to give an account of the discourse properties and felicity conditions of disjunction, and to use this account in explaining the behavior of presupposition projection and of anaphora in disjunctive sentences. This project, then, would seem to have as its goal the formulation of some set of special properties pertaining to the word *or*.

However, the project has led in a quite different direction. At the heart of my account is the claim that there is nothing very special about *or*, and that the only semantic information that must be specified about this lexical item is that it functions as a logical operator equivalent to Boolean join (inclusive disjunction). I will argue that the properties observed can be accounted for in terms of very general principles governing assertoric contributions to discourse, and their interaction with the truth conditional properties of *or*.

This position echoes the familiar views of Paul Grice. Grice (1967) argued that many of the properties of logical operators in natural language are to be explained in terms of general principles governing all cooperative rational interaction, including conversation. The general principle, which he dubs the Cooperative Principle, he formulates as follows:

> *The Cooperative Principle*
> Make your conversational contribution such as is required, at the stage at which it occurs, by the accepted purpose or direction of the talk exchange in which you are engaged.

This principle subsumes four Maxims of Conversation: the Maxims of Quality, Quantity, Relation and Manner. The brief formulation of these maxims is as follows:

> *Quality*: Try to make your contribution one that is true.
> *Quantity:* Make your contribution as informative as is required (for the current purposes of the exchange), and no more informative than is required.
> *Relation*: Be relevant.
> *Manner*: Be perspicuous.

Grice urged that those aspects of the behavior of an expression which can be explained in terms of speakers' compliance with the Cooperative Principle not be treated as part of the semantic content of an expression.

Grice's proposal in part informed the model of presupposition and assertion developed by Robert Stalnaker in a series of papers written in the 1970's. The central idea of this model is that every discourse takes place against the background of the assumptions shared by the participants: their common ground. The purpose of an assertion is to change the common ground, to add to the set of shared assumptions. This purpose determines the appropriateness of a given utterance in a given discourse context. Following Grice, Stalnaker suggests that the kinds of information update allowed may be constrained by certain general principles. The Stalnakerian model thus suggests a reframing of the Gricean Maxims as conditions on information update, and also provides a framework for a precise formulation of these conditions. Stalnaker's model will provide the central framework for the development of the ideas in this dissertation.

In Chapter Two, I will use the Stalnakerian model to give a formal characterization of the Gricean Maxims of Quantity and Relation, and will use these as the basis of an account of the discourse properties and felicity conditions of disjunction. The characterization of Relation will require an extension of Stalnaker's original model, with which some of that chapter will be concerned. The conclusions reached in that chapter will provide the foundations for the discussion of presupposition projection and anaphora which follow.

I turn to the presupposition projection problem in Chapter Three. The account is, essentially, that the presuppositions of disjuncts are inherited by the disjunction whenever this does not lead to infelicity. The kinds of infelicity that may be caused by inheritance of presuppositions are just those which are described and explained in Chapter Two. To spell out the account, of course, some theory of presupposition is needed. This is provided, again, by the Stalnakerian model, but makes crucial use of proposals due to Van der Sandt (1992). I argue that the projection properties of disjunction provide evidence for the pragmatic approach to presupposition advocated by Stalnaker, for on this approach it is to be expected that general considerations of felicity will constrain presupposition.

In Chapter Four, I move to the anaphora puzzle. Following Groenendijk and Stokhof (1990), I dub the data discussed in this chapter *internal anaphora*, as what is involved is anaphora between disjuncts. Once again, the goal is to account for the data in terms of the felicity conditions of disjunction, but in order to do this, I must give an account of the anaphora itself. I thus present a version of the E-type account of cross-clausal anaphora, based closely on that of Neale (1990), and apply it to the disjunction data. This view of anaphora will support the felicity-based account of the basic data which I sketched above. I will argue that disjunction imposes no special constraints on anaphora, but that certain cases of anaphora across disjunction result in infelicity. The usefulness of the E-type account, though, will go beyond its facilitation of this kind of explanation. In discussing some more complex instances of internal anaphora, we will find cases in which it is indeed not possible to establish an anaphoric link between an indefinite in one disjunct and a pronoun in another, as in (15).

(15)   #Either most people own a car$_i$, or it$_i$'s in the shop.

This failure of anaphora is predicted by the E-type account adopted, and is entirely parallel to the failure of anaphora in (16):

(16)   Most people own a car$_i$. #It$_i$'s in the shop.

So the E-type view will enable me to maintain my principal claim, namely, that disjunction imposes no special constraints on anaphora.

In Chapter Five, I depart somewhat from my main theme to pursue further the interaction of disjunction and anaphora. In that chapter, I will discuss the *external anaphora* data. These data involve anaphora between a disjunction of NPs and a pronoun in a following sentence (as in (17)), and anaphora between NPs contained inside a clausal disjunction and a pronoun in a following sentence (as in (18)).

(17)   A soprano or an alto will sing. She will be accompanied on the piano.
(18)   A soprano will sing Mozart, or an alto will sing Schubert. She will be accompanied on the piano.

The account of these data will not rely on the felicity conditions of disjunction, as do the accounts in Chapters Three and Four. But these data will provide an opportunity to investigate further the E-type account introduced in Chapter Four. In fact, the external anaphora data will lead me to propose a new version of the E-type account, in which the interpretations of E-type pronouns are derived compositionally from the content of the antecedent clause. This proposal constitutes a significant departure from existing formulations of the E-type strategy.

1.1.2. Context change: Pragmatic vs. semantic approaches

The Stalnakerian model in terms of which I will frame my account was originally conceived as a pragmatic model, intended to provide a basis for stating "some general rules of conversation" (Stalnaker 1973: 450). This is how I shall understand the model, and how I shall use it.

In other frameworks, the Stalnakerian idea is transmuted into a semantic theory. These *dynamic semantic theories* are developments of the proposals of Kamp (1981) and Heim (1982). The central thesis of these theories is that the meaning of an expression resides in its potential to change the information state of a hearer. The theories are thus closely related to the pragmatic Stalnakerian model, but differ from it in seeing context change as a semantic phenomenon. In Dynamic Semantics, the potential context change effect of an expression constitutes its semantic value. Consequently, the job of the semantics is to specify context change operations as values for expressions.

Dynamic semantic theories have been proposed primarily to account for cross-clausal anaphora and for presupposition projection, two issues on which this dissertation focuses. The dissertation thus offers an opportunity for a critical discussion of the semantic view of context change. Throughout the dissertation, I will discuss dynamic semantic accounts of the data, and will compare and contrast my own accounts with them. I will focus on the difference between the kinds of explanation offered by dynamic semantic theories, and the kinds of explanation which can be given on the basis of a pragmatic view of context change. I will argue that the pragmatic view provides more satisfactory accounts of the phenomena in question.

In the remainder of this introduction, I will present the theoretical background that will be assumed in the coming chapters. I begin, in section 1.2., with an expanded presentation of the Stalnakerian model of presupposition and assertion. In section 1.3., I present the outlines of the major theories of dynamic semantics, to facilitate the later discussion of proposals made in these frameworks.

1.2. THE STALNAKERIAN MODEL OF PRESUPPOSITION AND ASSERTION

I have already explained the basic idea of the Stalnakerian model: that in any discourse situation there is a set of propositions whose truth is taken for granted as part of the background to that discourse. These propositions are what the discourse participants *presuppose*. For Stalnaker, presupposition is not a property of sentences, but of speakers, which can be defined roughly as follows:

> A proposition P is a pragmatic presupposition of a speaker in a given context just in case the speaker assumes or believes that P, assumes or believes that his addressee assumes or believes that P, and assumes or believes this his addressee recognizes that he is making these assumptions, or has these beliefs (1974: 200).

This definition generally suffices for simple cases where speakers are completely sincere, and no pretense of any kind is involved. In my later discussion, I will generally talk in terms of this definition of presupposition. However, strictly speaking Stalnaker does not view presupposition as a "mental attitude," but as a "linguistic disposition" (1974: 202). A speaker presupposes a proposition P if

> the speaker is disposed to act as if he assumes or believes that the proposition is true, and as if he assumes or believes that his audience assumes or believes that it is true as well. . . .The propositions presupposed in the intended sense need not really be common or mutual knowledge; the speaker need not even believe them. He may presuppose any proposition that he finds it convenient to assume for the purpose of the conversation, provided he is prepared to assume that his audience will assume it along with him (1978: 321)

The fundamental idea, though, is that presuppositions are propositions that are in some sense taken for granted in a discourse by a discourse

Introduction 11

participant. The set of presuppositions of an individual constitutes what Stalnaker calls her *context*.

Stalnaker assumes a "rational ideal" with respect to contexts: that the set of presuppositions of an individual is consistent and deductively closed (1973:450). Given this, contexts can be characterized as sets of possible worlds: those worlds at which all of the individual's presuppositions are true. These sets, which Stalnaker calls *context sets*[1], represent all of the possible ways things might be which are consistent with what that individual takes to be the common beliefs of the participants in the discourse.

Stalnaker often adopts a further idealization: that the context sets of all participants in a discourse are the same. He dubs such a situation a *non-defective context*. This idealization is convenient, in particular because it allows us to speak of the context set of the discourse, rather than the context sets of individuals. Moreover, it reflects an important aspect of Stalnaker's notion of presupposition, namely, that the participants in a discourse themselves assume that everyone's context set is the same. This is to say that discourse participants assume that they have correctly identified the beliefs which are commonly shared. When discrepancies between presuppositions are identified, participants will try to rectify this. Those participants who do not have the relevant proposition in their context will either challenge those who do and insist that they remove it, or will simply add it to their own set of presuppositions. For example, suppose a speaker says, "I have to pick up my daughter from school," thereby indicating that she presupposes that she has a daughter. (In Chapter Three, I will discuss the question of how it is that certain utterances indicate that their speakers hold a presupposition.) Suppose further that some of her hearers did not know that the speaker had a daughter, or did not take it to be common knowledge, and so their own contexts did not contain this proposition. If they take the proposition to be uncontroversial, they will simply modify their contexts, bringing them in line with what the speaker indicates her context to be like. This process of context modification was first discussed by Lewis (1979b). The process, which he calls *accommodation*, has come to play an important role in theories of presupposition projection.

The function of assertion can now be defined in terms of the notion of presupposition. The goal of an assertion is to add to the presuppositions of the discourse participants, that is, to increase the set of propositions which they can assume to be commonly held beliefs. As an individual adds propositions to her context, she eliminates from her context set any worlds incompatible with these propositions. Formally, then, the function of an assertion is to eliminate worlds from the context sets of hearers. Context sets thus represent the possibilities among which speakers are expected to distinguish by their assertions (1978:322), for if an assertion does not distinguish between these possibilities it will not lead to any alteration of the context set. A successful assertion takes an initial context set c to a new context c', which consists of the intersection of c with the asserted proposition.

Here, a further idealization is introduced. In order to formalize the effect of assertion as intersection of the context and the asserted proposition, we must ignore the possibility of hearers accepting an assertion which is incompatible with their presuppositions. Clearly, though, participants in a discourse may change their beliefs, and so their presuppositions, in a way which requires the introduction of *additional* worlds into the context set. This is quite clear in a defective context. Suppose that I believe, mistakenly, that New York City is the capital of New York state. This seems to me to be something I can take for granted, so I presuppose it. You, on the other hand, know that Albany is the capital of New York state. At some point in our conversation, you become aware of my mistake and correct me. Being aware that you are more likely than I to know what the capital of New York state is, I accept your correction, and, presumably, modify my context set accordingly (thus moving closer towards a non-defective context). To do this, I must eliminate all worlds incompatible with Albany being the capital of NY state, but must also *introduce* worlds compatible with this proposition, as previously my context set included no such worlds.

Even accepting the idealization of a non-defective context, we must still allow for this kind of revision. Suppose that you and I both presuppose that George is out of town, when suddenly we see him through the window. We both know that the other has seen George, and so both abandon the presupposition.

The point is simply that an adequate model of how assertions (and environment) change a context set must allow for cases such as these[2]. However, this is a complication which is peripheral to my main interests, so I will set it aside in my discussion, and maintain the assumption that one cannot successfully assert something incompatible with the context set.

Another collection of problems which I shall set aside are the well known difficulties of treating propositions as sets of possible worlds. This treatment is central to Stalnaker's model, but is problematic in a number of respects, principally in that it is not sufficiently fine-grained to capture our intuitive notion of proposition. The view commits one, for instance, to saying that there is only one logically true proposition. This is because every logical truth holds at every possible world, and hence any expression of any logical truth will denote the same set of possible worlds, that is, the universal set.

Although I will adopt the Stalnakerian framework, I do not wish to suggest that I am committed to this view of propositions for all purposes, or even to this highly unstructured view of context. However, the framework I am setting out here has the advantage of extreme simplicity, which will allow me to bring out certain generalizations about discourse and the nature of information update in discourse in a rather straightforward way. For other purposes, we may well need to adopt a more complex, structured notion of proposition, and a more complex and structured notion of context itself. But for the data I am discussing here, this treatment of propositions and context sets as sets of possible worlds is useful. In fact, introducing further complexity at this stage would merely obscure the points which I want to use the framework to illustrate. I trust that the generalizations I make will be unaffected by refinements of the framework. So despite its well known drawbacks, I will maintain this very simple picture: contexts as sets of possible worlds, updated by assertions[3].

Let us return now to the question of how Stalnaker's model can be used to provide solutions to the problems that will be addressed in this dissertation. As I mentioned earlier, Stalnaker's original conception has Gricean underpinnings. This is made clear in passages such as the following:

> I want the definition [of presupposition] to provide justification for some general rules of conversation. The kind of justification that I want is an argument that shows the rules to be, not just arbitrary stipulations or conventions, but maxims which derive from general principles of rational cooperative behavior. If we

have such a justification for certain maxims, and can use the
maxims to explain some of the linguistic facts about
presuppositions that have been noted, then we will be able to
show that there is no need to postulate specific syntactic or
semantic rules in order to explain the facts (1973: 450).

Here, Stalnaker is explicit in suggesting the model as one in which Gricean conversational maxims can be formulated and indeed explained. The point of developing these general rules of conversation is to use them, rather than "specific syntactic or semantic rules" to explain observations about presupposition and other linguistic phenomena.

The idea that the model can be used to give a pragmatic account of facts pertaining to presupposition is further brought out in the following:

The pragmatic account [of presupposition] makes it possible to
explain some particular facts about presuppositions in terms of
general maxims of rational communication rather than in terms
of complicated and *ad hoc* hypotheses about the semantics of
particular words and particular kinds of constructions (1974:
198). Where [pragmatic explanations] can be given, there is no
reason to build specific rules about presuppositions into the
semantics (206).

My own approach is the one that Stalnaker advocates here. When a linguistic phenomenon is amenable to an account in terms of general conversational principles, I advocate such an account over a semantic one.

Perhaps the first example of how the context change model can provide a pragmatic account of a fact to do with presupposition projection is given in Stalnaker (1974). There, Stalnaker offers an explanation for the presupposition projection properties of conjunction[4]. Before I get to the facts, let's clarify what it means, in this framework, for a sentence to presuppose. In the pragmatic model of presupposition, the notion of sentence presupposition is derivative: a sentence S presupposes P just in case the use of that sentence would *for some reason* normally be inappropriate unless the speaker presupposes P. A simpler way to say this is to say that a sentence S presupposes P just in case the use of S indicates that the speaker presupposes P. So to say that a complex sentence S inherits the presuppositions of one of its constituent clauses, φ, is to say that whatever presuppositions the speaker would need to have in order to felicitously utter φ, she also needs in order to felicitously utter S.

Now, with respect to conjunction, the inheritance facts are as follows: In general, a conjunction *A and B* inherits the presuppositions of its conjuncts. However, any presuppositions of B which are entailed by A are not inherited. This behavior is illustrated in (19)-(20). Sentence (19) inherits the presupposition of the second conjunct, that George has children. Sentence (20) does not inherit this presupposition. In other words, a speaker who does not believe that her hearers assume that George has children could utter this sentence felicitously:

(19)   George is skiing in Colorado and his children are camping in Vermont.
(20)   George has several children, and his children are camping in Vermont.

Here is Stalnaker's explanation for these observations. When a speaker says something of the form *A and B*, the proposition that A is added to the context – the set of presuppositions – before the speaker asserts that B. Now, suppose that B presupposes A, or something entailed by A. Even if A is not presupposed initially, a speaker may still assert *A and B*, "since by the time one gets to saying that B, the context has shifted, and it is by then presupposed that A" (1974:211). Hence, utterance of the conjunction as a whole does not indicate that A was included in the speaker's original set of presuppositions.

Notice that this explanation does not require any special assumptions about the semantics of *and*. It does rely on the assumption that in the case of conjunction, context update is incremental. But this is a fairly harmless assumption about how language is processed, not about any lexical properties. The approach contrasts with that currently pursued in theories of dynamic semantics, which incorporate into the semantics at least part of what, in the original conception, was to be derived from general rules of conversation. In the next section, I present the outlines of these dynamic theories, with emphasis on the kind of explanations they offer.

1.3. DYNAMIC SEMANTICS

1.3.1. The Fundamentals

The central idea of dynamic semantics is that the semantic value of an expression is its contribution to information update, or context change. Some of these theories utilize a more structured notion of context than we have seen so far. The components of dynamic semantic contexts are a domain of special variables called *discourse referents* and a set of conditions on these referents.

The theories of Kamp (1981) and Heim (1982) were originally proposed as theories of NP meaning and of anaphora, and they depart significantly from earlier assumptions about the semantics of NPs. Both argue that indefinites are non-quantificational, and that both indefinite NPs and pronouns are represented by discourse referents. The two types of NP are distinguished in that indefinites must introduce new discourse referents, while pronouns must be translated using a discourse referent already in the domain. (Indefinites also require the introduction of conditions on the new referents, which represent the descriptive content of the NP.) On these theories, cross-clausal anaphora between indefinites and pronouns is a reflection of variable-sharing. An anaphoric relation is established by using the discourse referent introduced by the indefinite to translate the pronoun.

Much of the account of anaphora in dynamic semantics involves specification of the structural conditions under which two NPs can share a discourse referent. The different versions of the theory express these conditions in different ways, but the basic conception is the same in all cases. Dynamic Montague Grammar differs from the other two frameworks to be discussed in that it maintains a quantificational view of indefinites. But in that theory too, anaphora is expressed as a kind of variable-sharing, and the account is parallel to those given in File Change Semantics and in Discourse Representation Theory in the respects relevant here.

I begin the following presentation with Heim's (1982) File Change Semantics, and its evolution into Context-Change semantics (Heim 1988). I discuss this in the most detail, and then compare it with Kamp's (1981) Discourse Representation Theory (DRT), and Groenendijk and Stokhof's (1990) Dynamic Montague Grammar (DMG). The reason for presenting

Introduction 17

all three frameworks is that I will be interested in proposals made about disjunction in each of them, so the reader will need some understanding of the basic components of each theory. However, in Chapter Three, I will "translate" the DRT and DMG proposals into Heim's context change terminology, which allows the simplest exposition. This is possible because of the fundamental similarities between the frameworks. The discussion that follows is intended to clarify these similarities. It will also bring into focus the difference between the semantic and the pragmatic view of context change.

1.3.2. File Change Semantics (FCS) and the CCP proposal
1.3.2.1. Files and File Change

Heim (1982) adopts the metaphor of a file to talk about the way in which information is accumulated in a discourse. A file consists of a domain of discourse referents and a set of conditions which provide information about the members of the domain. Speaking somewhat imprecisely, we can say that the discourse referents represent the individuals that have been introduced in the discourse, and the conditions represent the information which has been given about those individuals. For instance, the sentence *a woman$_1$ is stroking a cat$_2$* will give rise to a file with a two-member domain $\{x_1, x_2\}$ and a three-membered set of conditions: $\{woman(x_1), cat(x_2), is\text{-}stroking(x_1, x_2)\}$.

The theory does not aim to provide a complete specification of the formal properties of files, but rather characterizes them in terms of two defining properties. One of these properties is the domain of the file. The other is what Heim calls the *satisfaction set* of the file. Satisfaction sets are sets of *sequences*, which are functions from discourse referents to individuals in the world. The sequences in the satisfaction set of a file are those which satisfy it, where the conditions under which a sequence satisfies a file depend upon properties of the sentences whose content the file represents. A file constructed on the basis of an atomic sentence containing no quantifiers or operators is satisfied by any sequence which maps each discourse referent in the file to an individual in the world which meets the conditions associated with that referent. So, for example, the file defined in the previous paragraph will be satisfied by any sequence mapping x_2 to a cat and x_1 to a woman who is stroking that cat.

The satisfaction set of a file is the set of all sequences which satisfy that file.

When an existing file is "updated" with a new sentence, its domain and its satisfaction set will change. The precise nature of the change depends upon what Heim calls the *file change potential* of the sentence: the particular effect which that sentence will have on any file updated with it. The central task of the theory is thus to assign file change potentials to all sentences. This "can be seen as amounting to the task of defining 'F+p' [the result of updating F with p] for files F and [sentences] p of arbitrary composition and complexity" (Heim 1983a: 173)[5]. Where p is atomic, the domain of F+p is the union of the domain of F with (roughly speaking) the discourse referents introduced by NPs in p; the satisfaction set of F+p is the intersection of the satisfaction set of F with (roughly speaking) the set of sequences that satisfy p itself. For non-atomic p, Heim offers recursive definitions, with the file change potential of the complex sentence determined by the file change potentials of its atomic parts. Consider for instance the file change potential for conjunctive sentences, which is given in (21)[6]:

(21) Where p is of the form [φ and ψ]:
Dom(F+p) = Dom((F+φ)+ψ)
Sat(F+p) = Sat((F+φ)+ψ)

This we can read as an instruction: To determine the domain of the file that results from updating with [φ and ψ], first find the domain of the file that you get by updating with φ, and then find the domain of the file that you get by updating that intermediate file with ψ. The same procedure gives you the satisfaction set of the updated file.

Notice that the conjunction rule encapsulates the assumption made by Stalnaker that updating a context with a conjunctive sentence involves updating it first with the content of the first conjunct, and then with the content of the second. The difference is that for Stalnaker, this is a pragmatic principle which derives from assumptions about sentence processing, whereas here it has the status of a semantic rule.

It is the interaction of these file change procedures with the treatment of indefinites and pronouns which gives rise to predictions about possible anaphoric links in complex sentences. Heim assumes that in calculating a cumulative update procedure such as (21), each step must be an admissible update. In particular, at each step, any definite NP must have a possible

Introduction

antecedent. Consider, then, why it should be the case that an indefinite in one conjunct can serve as antecedent to a pronoun in a following conjunct, as in (22), but not in a preceding conjunct, as in (23).

(22) A cat$_i$ came in and it$_i$ lay down.
(23) #It$_i$ came in and a cat$_i$ lay down.

The answer is that the update procedure for a conjunction requires the starting file to be updated with the first conjunct, and then for the resulting file to be updated with the second. So in the case of (22), by the time we look for an existing referent with which to identify the pronoun *it*, the one introduced by *a cat* is already in the domain. But in (23), we have to find an old referent for *it* before we have introduced the referent for *a cat*.

The form of this explanation directly parallels Stalnaker's account of the projection properties of conjunction. But whereas Stalnaker's account relies on a fairly intuitive processing principle, this account relies on the dynamic semantics of *and*. Similarly, for all other cases of possible cross-clausal anaphora, the theory must define the file change potential of sentences containing the relevant connective in such a way that the clause containing the antecedent is added to the file before the clause containing the pronoun. As will become clear in Chapters Three and Four, it is much less straightforward to apply this technique to disjunction.

1.3.2.2. From Files back to Contexts: Presupposition Projection

So far, we have seen how cross-clausal anaphora is handled in the original version of FCS. Heim (1982) also alludes to the possibility that her semantic framework could provide a general solution to the presupposition projection problem, along the lines of the Stalnakerian treatment. A solution is developed in Heim (1983b), using a slightly modified version of the original semantics.

Heim (1983b) extends the account of anaphora discussed above to presupposition projection. The basic idea, just as formulated in Stalnaker for the conjunction case, is that the presuppositions of a constituent clause C fail to project to the sentence S containing it just in case the required proposition is introduced by another constituent of S which is added to the file, or context, before C.

Instead of taking sentences to act upon the kind of structured entities which she called *files* in Heim (1982), Heim (1983b) adopts the Stalnakerian view that sentences act upon contexts, construed as sets of possible worlds[7]. She carries over to this model the idea that the semantic value of an expression consists in its potential effect on a context: what she now calls its *context change potential (CCP)*. Just like file change potentials, context change potentials define a procedure for updating a context with the content of the sentence. The CCP of 'It is raining,' for instance, is the instruction to eliminate from the starting context any worlds in which it is not raining. That is, the context which results from updating a starting context c with an atomic proposition p (c+p) is the intersection of c with p. (Note that whereas files were characterized "indirectly," in terms of their domains and satisfaction sets, contexts are characterized directly.)

As before, the CCPs of complex structures are to be defined recursively, in terms of the CCPs of their constituents. The CCP of a conjoined sentence *A and B*, given in (24), is an instruction to first update the context with *A* and then to update the intermediate context with *B*:

(24)   c+[A and B] = [c+A]+B

Also as before, Heim assumes that each stage in an update procedure is required to be well-formed. This requirement, combined with the specification of CCPs, will be used to explain both the possibilities of anaphora within a complex structure, and the presupposition projection properties of the structure. The question that remains, though, is why the update procedure of a given expression is as it is claimed to be. Heim (1983b) suggests that the truth conditions of an expression determine its CCP, but as Soames (1989) points out, and Heim (1990) acknowledges, there are multiple ways to define a CCP for an expression which reflect its truth conditional content. And indeed, a number of different suggestions have been made as to the appropriate CCP for disjunction. These proposals will be discussed in detail in Chapters Three and Four.

1.3.3. Discourse Representation Theory (DRT)
1.3.3.1. Discourse Representation Structures (DRSs)

DRT utilizes an even more structured notion of context than does File Change Semantics. The theory posits a level of representation called a Discourse Representation Structure (DRS) which, like a file, consists of a domain of discourse referents and a set of conditions. The additional structure arises from the fact that the DRS conditions may themselves be DRSs, giving rise to a hierarchically structured representation. In particular, the constituent clauses of complex sentences introduce sub-DRSs, which are subordinate to the main DRS in which they are contained. The schematic representation usually used makes this quite easy to see. On the following page, I provide an example. The diagram in (26) gives a slightly simplified version of a DRS for the sentence sequence in (25), using one way of representing disjunction in DRT. Notice that each of the disjuncts is represented as a subordinate DRS[8]

(25)   Jane is unhappy. Either she had a bad day, or she argued with George.

(26)

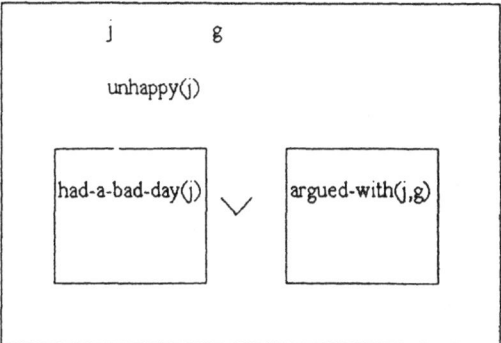

Just as files are evaluated for truth in File Change Semantics, it is DRSs which are evaluated for truth in DRT. A DRS is true in a model iff there is a mapping from the domain of the principle DRS to the domain of the model which verifies all of the conditions of the DRS. Where the DRS contains only atomic conditions of the form $\varphi(x)$, the definition of verification of a condition is straightforward. The complexity arises in stating the verification conditions of complex DRS conditions, which themselves contain DRSs. As in FCS, the verification conditions of complex conditions are given recursively, in terms of the verification conditions of the sub-DRSs.

In File Change Semantics, the central task was to define context (file) change procedures for sentences of arbitrary complexity. In DRT, the parallel task is two-fold. The first step is to state DRS construction algorithms for sentences of arbitrary complexity. These algorithms are instructions as to how to modify an existing DRS to represent the content of a new sentence. The second step is to state accessibility relations between the constituent DRSs of a main DRS. Accessibility relations determine when a discourse referent in one sub-DRS is "accessible" as an antecedent for a pronoun in another. The construction algorithms together with the accessibility relations serve the same function as the procedural CCPs in FCS. Suppose, for instance, that a complex sentence S allows anaphoric relations between an indefinite in a constituent clause φ and a pronoun in a constituent clause ψ. In FCS, this is explained by giving a procedural CCP which ensures that the starting context (or file) is updated with φ before it is updated with ψ. In DRT, the accessibility relations must be stated in such a way that the discourse referent introduced by the indefinite is accessible to the sub-DRS containing the pronoun.

It is interesting to note that even though DRT does not in general utilize procedural rules in accounting for cross-clausal anaphora, it does in the case of conjunction. The distinction between (22) and (23), repeated here, is captured by assuming that the conjuncts are incorporated serially into the DRS (see Kamp and Reyle 1993: 214-228).

(22)　A cat$_i$ came in and it$_i$ lay down.
(23)　*It$_i$ came in and a cat$_i$ lay down.

A number of different proposals have been made in the DRT literature as to how to represent disjunction in a way which explains its properties with respect to anaphora. I will discuss these together with the CCP proposals. The thrust of my argument in each case will be the same: the phenomena do not reflect a complex context update property of

Introduction 23

disjunction, but the effects of pragmatic constraints on the context update process.

1.3.4. Dynamic Montague Grammar (DMG)

Groenendijk and Stokhof (1990) proposed Dynamic Montague Grammar as a way of incorporating the insights of dynamic semantics into a more standard semantic model. The formal machinery is complicated and largely irrelevant for my purposes, so I will not attempt to review it here. Let me simply note the major points of difference and similarity between DMG and the two theories already discussed.

The most significant difference is that in DMG, indefinites are treated as existential quantifiers, in something like the standard manner. The quantifiers, though, are redefined in such a way as to allow them to bind variables which lie outside of their syntactic scope. As in the other systems, pronouns are uniformly treated as variables. Thus, in the sentence sequence in (27), the pronoun *it* is treated as a variable bound by the indefinite introduced by *a cat*, as shown in (28):

(27) A cat$_i$ came in. It$_i$ lay down.
(28) $\underline{\exists}$x[cat(x)] $\underline{\&}$ lay down(x)

The lines under the operators "$\exists$" and "&" indicate that they are dynamic operators. The semantic scope of the dynamic existential operator in (28) extends over the dynamically conjoined clause.

We have seen how possible anaphoric relations are predicted in FCS by giving procedural update rules, and in DRT by construction algorithms and a statement of accessibility relations. These predictions are made in DMG by defining operators in such a way as to ensure that in constructions where anaphora is possible, the variable which represents the pronoun falls within the dynamic binding domain of its antecedent. The formal machinery of the theory is powerful, and various different means are used to ensure the correct results. I will discuss the specific strategies used for disjunction in Chapter Four, and delay further discussion of the theory until then. What should be evident is that although some of the assumptions of the theory are different from those of FCS and DRT, the central task is essentially the same: to define the semantics of the logical operators in such a way as to predict the observed patterns of possible anaphoric relations.

NOTES

1. In Stalnaker (1973, 1974), Stalnaker uses the term "presupposition set." He changes to the term "context set" in Stalnaker (1978). I use the latter term because that is the one which is current in the linguistic literature.
2. There is an extensive literature on the representation of belief revision. See, for example, Gärdenfors (1988).
3. For discussion and defense of the possible world treatment of propositions, see Stalnaker (1976, 1984). Kripke (ms.) offers some remarks on a more structured view of context, suggesting in particular that a distinction is needed between the "active context," perhaps a complex entity, and "the passive context," consisting of general background information. Heim (1983b) suggests that contexts be viewed as sets of assignment-world pairs.
4. Karttunen (1974) makes a proposal much like Stalnaker's. In later work, though, Karttunen goes back to a much more semantic approach to presupposition projection. See, in particular, Karttunen and Peters (1979).
5. Heim actually assigns File Change Potentials to the syntactic Logical Forms (LFs) of sentences. She assumes a syntactic theory in which LF is the level of syntactic representation which provides the input to the interpretative component. I will be making the same assumption throughout, but this will not become relevant until Chapter Four.
6. This is actually the rule which Heim gives for a cumulative molecular formula with φ and ψ as immediate constituents. Heim (1982) is concerned primarily with quantificational structures and with conditionals, and does not discuss sentential connectives except for a few remarks in her conclusion (p. 397). However, it is apparent from these remarks, and certainly from her treatment of conjunction in Heim (1983b), that she would treat conjoined clauses as cumulative molecular formulae, that is, as indicated in (21).
7. Heim (1983b) begins by construing contexts as sets of possible worlds, but argues that they should properly be construed as sets of world-sequence pairs in order to deal with the presuppositions of quantified structures. This construal of context has the advantage of introducing additional fine-grainedness to the notion, but this is tangential to my interests here. In further work on presupposition projection within the context change framework, both by Heim and others, contexts continue to be construed as sets of possible worlds (see, for instance, Heim 1992).

8. Here and throughout, I will follow the conventions introduced in Kamp (1981) for the representation of proper names and of pronouns, although these conventions have been modified in current formulations of the theory (e.g. Kamp and Reyle 1993). In current formulations, both proper names and pronouns introduce new discourse referents. The first introduction of a proper name introduces a discourse referent, and a condition of the form [x = NAME]. Each further use of the name introduces a new referent, along with a condition of the form [y = x]. Similarly, pronouns are now assumed to introduce a new discourse referent, and a condition equating the new referent with an old one. To simplify the representations, I use constants throughout for proper names, and just re-use old discourse referents for pronouns. These simpler conventions have no bearing on the matters at issue here.

CHAPTER TWO
Disjunctive Sentences in Discourse

2.1. INTRODUCTION

In this chapter, I establish the foundations of my discussion of disjunction. The main task is to understand how disjunctive sentences function in discourse, why they function in this way, and how their use is constrained by various pragmatic principles. I begin in section 2.2. by reviewing the basic observations and offering a somewhat informal account of them. This informal account will motivate an enrichment of the Stalnakerian framework, which I present in section 2.3. In the remainder of that section, I use the enriched framework to formulate a more precise account of the felicity conditions on disjunction in terms of general constraints on context update.

In section 2.4., I turn to some apparent exceptions to the constraints I identify. In the final section of this chapter, section 2.5., I give an account of the exclusive reading of disjunctive sentences. This discussion will be a slight digression from my main theme, but will complete the characterization of the pragmatics of *or*. The pragmatic properties identified in this chapter will provide a basis for the accounts of presupposition projection and internal anaphora data to be discussed in the following chapters.

2.2. THE DISCOURSE FUNCTION AND FELICITY CONDITIONS OF DISJUNCTION

2.2.1. The Basic Observations

In "Indicative Conditionals," Grice (1989: 68) observes that:

> A standard (if not *the* standard) employment of "or" is in the specification of possibilities (one of which is supposed by the speaker to be realized, although he does not know which one), each of which is relevant in the same way to a given topic. 'A or B' is characteristically employed to give a partial answer to some [wh]-question, to which each disjunct, if assertible, would give a fuller, more specific, more satisfactory answer.

As illustration, consider sentence (1):

(1) Either you have dirt in your fuel line or your carburetor is gummed.

This sentence might naturally be said by one's mechanic as a way of listing the possibilities as to what is wrong with one's car. It could be given in answer to the explicitly asked question, "What is wrong with my car?" with each disjunct representing what, from the mechanic's perspective, is a possibly true answer to the question.

It is not only typical for disjunctions to be used in this way, but apparently necessary. A disjunction which cannot be interpreted as listing related possibilities is generally quite unacceptable, as illustrated by the following:

(2) #Either you have dirt in your fuel line or it is raining in Tel-Aviv.

This suggests that disjunctions not only may be used to list possible answers to a question, but indeed must be so used.

Grice provides an argument as to why disjunctions should be used in giving interim answers to *wh*-questions, rather than any other truth conditionally equivalent form. He observes that the appropriate answer to a *wh*-question is usually, although not invariably, an affirmative and not a negative statement: "We ask 'who killed Cock Robin?' not 'Who didn't kill Cock Robin?'"(p.69). Consequently, he argues, it will be "more economical" to use a disjunction *A or B* to give an interim answer to a *wh*-question than to use the equivalent forms *It is not the case that not A and not B* or *If not A then B*, because the subordinate clauses of the disjunction have the form of the desired answer. This state of affairs gives rise to a "habit or practice" of using disjunctive sentences for the purpose of giving interim answers to *wh*-questions. Given this convention, use of a disjunction by a speaker "implicates or suggests ... that he is addressing himself to some explicit or implicit *wh*-question." By this argument, it is the violation of a convention of linguistic practice which gives rise to the oddity of (2). I will show that there are more compelling reasons for the use of *or* to list possibilities, and for the oddity of (2).

The infelicity of (2) indicates that in a felicitous disjunction, the disjuncts must be related to each other in some way yet to be specified. On the other hand, disjuncts must not be too closely related. As Hurford (1974) observes, disjunctions in which one disjunct entails another are infelicitous, as illustrated by[1]:

(3)   #Either Jane owns a truck, or she owns a red truck.

Note that what is relevant here is what Chierchia and McConnell-Ginet (1990) call *contextual entailment*. Infelicity arises whenever one disjunct, in conjunction with any assumptions which are part of the background knowledge of the speakers, entails another. For example, suppose that the participants in the discourse assume that graduate students live on a very tight budget and also that people on a very tight budget can't afford to eat out at expensive restaurants. In such a situation, the assertion of (4) would be very odd:

(4)   #Either she's a graduate student, or she can't afford to eat out at expensive restaurants.

Of course, if things were different, and the speakers thought that graduate students are generally better off financially than other people, then (4) would be perfectly acceptable.

In (2-4) we have examples of disjunctions which are infelicitous because the relationship between the disjuncts is, apparently, not one which admits of disjunction. Speaking quite informally, we might say that in (2), the problem is that the disjuncts are not related to each other, and in (4), the problem is that they are too closely related. Infelicities also arise when disjuncts are inappropriately related to the content of the context. As a number of authors have observed (see, inter alia, Stalnaker (1975), Grice (1989)), a felicitous disjunction may not contain a disjunct whose truth value is already established in the context. Thus, if the context already entails that Jane is not at home, it would generally be infelicitous to assert either (5) or (6):

(5)   Either Jane isn't at home or she's ignoring her telephone.
(6)   Either Jane is at home or she forgot to turn the lights off.

In the next section, I will introduce the Gricean principles in terms of which these infelicities will be explained, and provide an informal outline of the explanations.

2.2.2.   Relation and Manner in the Stalnakerian Model

As defined by Stalnaker, the context set of a conversation represents all those possibilities which are compatible with what the speakers presuppose. The purpose of conversation, Stalnaker says, is to eliminate possibilities from this set, in order to bring the participants closer to a shared view of how things are. The goal of an assertion is to reduce the context set in a particular way, eliminating those possibilities incompatible with the content of the assertion. One obvious constraint on assertions, then, is that they express something true at some but not all possible worlds in the context set (1978: 325)[2]. It is only in this case that an assertion can have the desired effect of eliminating possibilities.

In Stalnaker's picture, participants in a conversation are supposed to have a very general interest in the way things are. All that is needed for an assertion to be successful is for it to bring them a little closer to knowing how things are, by excluding at least some world from the context set. But in the normal case, participants have much more parochial concerns. At any given point, there are usually certain aspects of the world that people are interested in knowing about, and others that they are not interested in. If I am trying to find out what time the semantics seminar begins, I will not appreciate your telling me about the population of China. You might thereby give me new information, and so bring about a reduction of my (or our) context set, but you will not have reduced the context set in a way that is currently of interest to me. What I want is to reduce the possibilities with respect to the starting time of the seminar. Other reductions of my context set are currently irrelevant. And if you insist on telling me about the population of China, I am likely to be quite bewildered by what you are telling me.

Even in a casual conversation, some kinds of contributions will be accepted as relevant, and some will not. If we are in the middle of talking about the baseball scores, and you make an assertion about the completeness proof for modal logic, something will have gone wrong. What you have said may be informative, but it is not relevantly so: it does not eliminate any possibilities which we are currently (jointly) interested in eliminating. And even at a point in the conversation where a new topic can appropriately be raised, some assertions will be relevant, and some will not. In most casual conversations, any assertion about the completeness proof for modal logic will fail to be relevantly informative at any point in the conversation. Thus, not all reductions of the context set are equally acceptable as conversational moves.

Grice's Maxim of Relation (see Chapter One, section 1.1.1.), states the requirement that assertions be relevant to the purposes of conversational participants. To say exactly what it is for an assertion to be relevant is not easy. As Grice himself says, "the formulation [of the Maxim of Relation] conceals a number of problems...: questions about what different kinds and focuses of relevance there may be, how these shift in the course of a talk exchange, how to allow for the fact that subjects of conversation are legitimately changed, and so on" (1975:46).

A number of researchers have attempted, in one way or another, to provide answers to these questions. Perhaps the most extensive attempt is that of Sperber and Wilson (1986), who propose a theory of communication based on a much elaborated version of the principle of Relation. More recently, several proposals have been made in the linguistic literature for formal models of discourse (Ginzburg 1997, Groenendijk 1997, Roberts 1996) which are intended to capture the requirement that assertions address some topic of interest to the participants, some issue which they are interested in resolving. All of these authors characterize issues of current interest as questions currently under discussion in the discourse. The questions under discussion may have been asked explicitly, or may be implicit in the discourse.

The idea of Question Under Discussion provides a simple way to characterize the notion of an assertion being relevantly informative, as opposed to informative *simpliciter*. An assertion is informative *simpliciter* just in case its incorporation into the context set results in the elimination of some world from that set. Now we can say that an assertion is *relevantly* informative just in case it provides at least a partial answer to some question under discussion in the discourse. In the context change model, that means that the assertion must eliminate some possibility (subset of the context) as to the answer to the question. Let us then assume that felicitous assertions are required to achieve this effect. I will call this requirement the Relevant Informativity condition, and will for now state this condition informally, as follows:

(7) Relevant Informativity condition
An assertoric contribution to a discourse is required to provide at least a partial answer to some Question Under Discussion in the discourse.

Even this informal characterization suffices to show that the notion of Relevant Informativity provides an explanation for the infelicity of disjunctions like (2), repeated here in slightly modified form:

(8) Either this car has dirt in its fuel line or it is raining in Tel-Aviv.

What effect does this disjunction have on a context set? It results in the elimination of worlds in which the car does not have dirt in its fuel line and in which it is not raining in Tel-Aviv. In other words, we eliminate any worlds which do not belong to the union of the propositions expressed by each disjunct. Now, what question might be partially resolved by excluding just those worlds? It is hard to think of one. The first disjunct would obviously be a potential answer to a question like "What is wrong with this car?" and the second, to a question like, "What is the weather like in Tel-Aviv?" But with our ordinary assumptions about the world in place, it is hard to think of any single question to which the disjunction as a whole could give even a partial answer. Now, the Relevant Informativity condition requires that every assertion, including disjunctive assertions, provide at least a partial answer to some question under discussion. The point here is that we cannot think of any question to which the disjunction provides an answer, and so cannot think of any context in which the disjunction could be relevantly informative. This is the source of the judgment that (8) is infelicitous.

Suppose, however, that we change the background assumptions, that is, we change the entailments of the context set. Suppose that the car in question is in Jerusalem, that when it rains in Tel-Aviv it is humid in Jerusalem, and that humidity causes the same kind of car malfunctions as dirt in the fuel line. Once we accept all of these premises, then each disjunct of (8) constitutes a possible answer to the question "What is wrong with the car?" and thus so does the disjunction as a whole. The initial judgment of infelicity reflects the fact that in making "out of the blue" judgments, speakers evaluate the disjunction with respect to their ordinary assumptions. We will see further examples of this kind later on.

It might seem that one way to construct a question to which the disjunction in (8) would be an answer is to conjoin the two questions mentioned above, giving something like: "What is wrong with this car and what is the weather like in Tel-Aviv?" Intuitively, though, this is two questions conjoined, and not one single question. It does not seem to be possible to conflate issues by conjoining questions. This raises the issues of what counts as a question, and what kinds of formal relations exist between questions. I will not be able to address these issues here, although I will say a little more when I give the formal model. For the time being, I merely observe that the conjunction of two acceptable questions does not necessarily result in a new, single, acceptable question.

I claim, then, that it is the requirement that assertions be relevantly informative which accounts for the ill-formedness of (8). I will claim further that this requirement accounts generally for Grice's observation that disjunctions are used to list possibilities each of which is relevant in the same way to a given topic. I will show that disjoining propositions which are not related to each other in this way will always result in a failure to be relevantly informative. Hence, it is only when disjuncts are so related that a disjunction can be felicitously asserted. To argue for this more convincingly, I will formalize the Relevant Informativity condition in the enriched Stalnakerian framework in section 2.3.1.

The Relevant Informativity condition constrains the content of contributions made at particular points in a discourse. Grice's Maxim of Manner indicates that the felicity of an assertion is not determined solely by its content, but also by the form which is used. Sentences (9) and (10) are synonymous, but (9) is a much more felicitous expression of this content, in most contexts, than (10):

(9) I will arrive on Monday or Tuesday.
(10) It's not the case that I will not arrive on Monday and will not arrive on Tuesday.

What is required is, essentially, to express the proposition in the simplest way possible. This, I will call the Simplicity condition. In terms of the context change model, in which assertions are understood as instructions to hearers to update the context set in a particular way, the condition can be characterized as follows: A speaker should give her hearers the simplest context update instruction she can while still achieving the desired context update effect.

Consider now how this requirement relates to the case of entailing disjunctions (11):

(11) #Either Jane owns a truck or she owns a red truck.

Suppose that (11) is given in partial answer to the question: "What kind of vehicle does Jane own?" (11) certainly provides a partial answer to this question, as it entails that Jane owns a truck. But just the same answer would be provided by asserting the first disjunct alone. So the speaker has violated the Simplicity condition by using a more complex form than is necessary to effect the context change which is achieved. This will be true in any context in which (11) is uttered. As there is no context in which the sentence could be straightforwardly felicitous, it is judged ill-formed.

Now, what about examples like (12)?

(12) #Either Jane owns a red truck or she owns a truck and she's happy.

Here, neither disjunct entails the other, but the disjunction is still unacceptable. The explanation for this will come from an interaction between the Relevant Informativity condition and the Simplicity condition. But to characterize this interaction, I will have to state the conditions more rigorously in terms context change.

2.3. THE ENRICHED CONTEXT CHANGE FRAMEWORK

2.3.1. Presentation

The basic idea is to take the Stalnakerian context as one part of a more complex structure, which I will call a Discourse Context (DC). A DC will be a pair, ⟨c, QUD⟩, where c is a Stalnakerian context set and QUD is the set of Questions Under Discussion at the point in the discourse where c is the context set. Formally, QUD will be modeled as a set of question denotations, so we must begin by adopting a semantic treatment of questions.

I adopt here the semantics for questions developed in Groenendijk and Stokhof (1984). In this semantics, a question denotes a set of propositions. Each proposition in the denotation is a possible and exhaustive answer to the question. A proposition is a possible answer to a question Q if it is a true answer at some possible world. For example, the question *Is it raining in Tel-Aviv?* denotes the set containing the proposition that it is raining in Tel-Aviv and the proposition that it is not raining in Tel-Aviv. These two propositions are the only two (direct) answers to this question.

In general, a yes/no question will have as denotation a two-membered set of propositions: basically, the "yes" answer and the "no" answer. (The exception to this is where the question is tautological or contradictory, when there will be only one possible answer to it.) The denotation of a *wh*-question, on the other hand, will generally have many members, as there are generally many possible exhaustive answers to a *wh*-question.

Groenendijk and Stokhof identify propositions with sets of possible worlds, so instead of thinking of the denotation of a question as a set of propositions, we can think of it as a set of sets of possible worlds. Moreover, because each answer in the denotation is an *exhaustive* answer, the sets of possible worlds are non-overlapping. To see why this is so, consider two possible answers to the question *Who came?*: George came (and no one else did), George and Jane came (and no one else did). The qualifications in parentheses are needed because the answers we are interested in are exhaustive answers. Now, if it is true that George and Jane and no one else came, then it is not true that George and no one else came. If the first of these propositions is true at some world, then the second is false, and vice versa. The same will be true for any two exhaustive answers to a given question.

The denotation of a question, then, divides up the set of possible worlds into a number of non-overlapping subsets, with each subset representing a possible exhaustive answer to the question. Such a division of a set is called a *partition*; the members of the partition are called *cells*. The formal definition of a partition is given in (13).

(13) Let A be a set. A partition of A is a set P such that:
    (i) $P \subseteq pow(A)$ and $\emptyset \notin P$
          (P is a set of non-empty subsets of A)
    (ii) $A = \cup\{B: B \in P\}$
          (The union of the members of P equals A, i.e. every member of A is in some cell of P.)
    (iii) $\forall X, Y \in P: X \cap Y = \emptyset$ or $X = Y$
          (The cells of P do not overlap.)

Formally, then, the denotation of a question is a partition on the set W of possible worlds, each cell of which corresponds to a possible and exhaustive answer to the question. For any question Q, the denotation of Q is written as W/Q, the partition imposed by Q on W.

Figure 1 represents one possible partition for a very small set of possible worlds W = {a,b,c,d,e,f,g}.

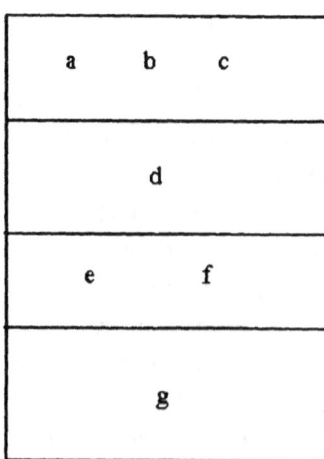

Figure 1

Groenendijk and Stokhof are concerned with the relationship between question denotations and states of information of speakers, or, in our terms, context sets. They define a number of notions relating questions and contexts which will be useful in what follows.

First, we define the set of possible answers to Q which are compatible with a context c, W/Q^c:

(14) $W/Q^c = \{X : X \in W/Q \ \& \ X \cap c \neq \varnothing\}$

W/Q^c is the set of answers to a question which have a non-empty overlap with the context, those answers which are compatible with what participants in the discourse assume. For instance, suppose that it is already established in the context that the only people who might have come are George and Jane. (We have eliminated all other possibilities). Then W/*who came*^{c} will have only three members: the set of worlds in which only George came, the set of worlds in which only Jane came, and the set of worlds in which only George and Jane came. No other members of W/*who came* are compatible with c.

Using this definition, we can define two further notions: the notion of being a *proper question* in a context, and the notion of a question being *resolved* in a context. A question Q is proper in a context c iff more than one possible answer to Q is compatible with c. Formally:

(15)   Q is a *proper question* in c iff $|W/Q^c| > 1$

(15) says that Q is a proper question in c iff W/Q^c (the set of answers compatible with c) has more than one member. This situation is illustrated in Figure 2.

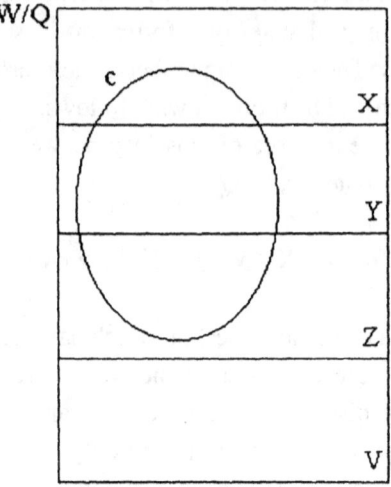

Figure 2
Q is a proper question in c
$W/Q^c = \{X,Y,Z\}$

In this figure, as before, the large rectangle represents the set of worlds W, partitioned as determined by the question Q. Each cell in the partition corresponds to a possible answer to Q. The circle c is the context set (a subset of W). Note that the context overlaps with three of the cells of W/Q, the cells X, Y and Z. In other words, three possible answers to Q are compatible with what is assumed at this point in the discourse. So Q is a proper question in c.

The next notion to define is that of a question being *resolved*. I will say that a question Q is resolved in c when only one possible answer to Q is compatible with c. Formally:

(16)   Q is *resolved* in c iff $|W/Q^c| = 1$

This situation is illustrated in Figure 3.

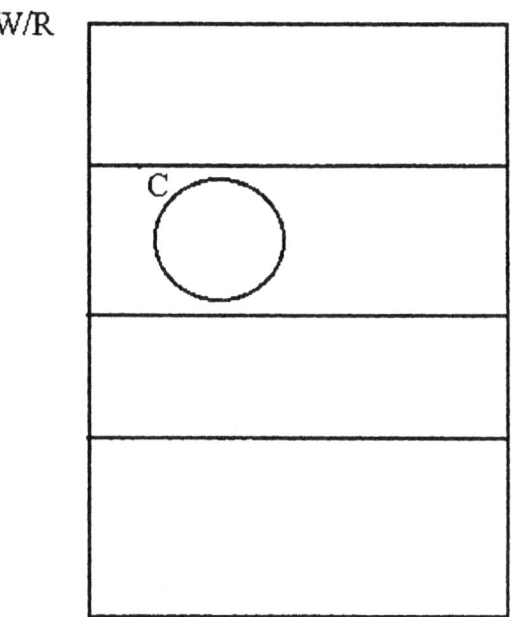

Figure 3
R is resolved in c

Note that when c is the empty set, then for any Q, W/Q^c is the empty set too. Given my definitions, Q is neither proper nor resolved in such a context. This is as it should be, for the empty context is the formal correlate of complete communicative breakdown, in which situation no questions can be considered. I will set aside as irrelevant any consequences pertaining to the possibility of an empty context.

With the help of the definitions above, I can now characterize partial and complete answers to Q. To give a partial answer to Q is to eliminate some potential answer to it. This corresponds to reducing the context set in such a way that its intersection with some cell of the partition becomes empty. A proposition φ thus partially answers a question Q in c iff fewer possible answers to Q (i.e. fewer cells of W/Q) are compatible with the result of updating c with the content of φ than are compatible with c. To denote the context update operation, I will adopt Heim's "+" notation, which I introduced in Chapter One. The result of updating c with φ is written "c+φ." The formal definition of a partial answer is as follows:

(17) A proposition φ *partially answers* a question Q in c iff
$W/Q^{c+\varphi} \subset W/Q^c$

To give a complete answer to a question is to eliminate all but one of the possible answers to that question i.e.

(18) A proposition φ *completely answers* a question Q in c
iff Q is proper in c and is resolved in c+φ.

Note that answerhood is here defined relative to a context c. Whether or not a proposition counts as an answer to a question may depend on what the hearer already takes to be true. We have already seen that this is indeed the case. We observed above (section 2.2.2.) that given an appropriate set of background assumptions, the proposition that it is raining in Tel-Aviv could be an answer to the question "What is wrong with this car?" even though, with a more ordinary set of assumptions, it would not do so. This variability in answerhood will carry over to the judgments of felicity of disjunctions.

The treatment of answers adopted here is somewhat rudimentary, and ignores many of the intricacies of actual discourse. Speakers do not always respond to a question with a direct answer. Groenendijk and Stokhof discuss, in particular, what they call indirect answers. Consider, for example, the following exchange:

(19) Abe: What color is the new car?
Bud: If Jane picked it out, it's red.

Bud's conditional answer does not eliminate any possible answer to the question. It does not, by itself, get Abe any closer to knowing the correct answer. But, as Groenendijk and Stokhof point out, it suggests a strategy for discovering the answer. Abe now knows that finding out whether Jane picked out the car is a possible way to find out what color the car is. Bud's response is certainly an acceptable answer, although it does not meet the simple condition given in (17). Groenendijk and Stokhof formulate a definition of pragmatic answerhood which allows for indirect answers like these. I will set these aside and treat only direct answers.

Note that there is another kind of answer which is in a sense indirect, but falls under definition (17). This is exemplified in (20):

(20)   Abe: Where is Jane?
       Bud: She's working.

Bud's reply does not name a location, so is in a sense indirect. However, it is a felicitous reply only if Jane's working contextually entails her being in a particular place, or at least rules out certain places where she might be. Having been told that Jane is working, Abe can eliminate some possible answers to the question: that she's not at the movies, for instance. So, given certain contextual assumptions, Bud's response does provide a partial direct answer to the question asked.

Using the definitions of questions and answers set out above, I can now give the formal definition of the notions that will play a role in the remainder of the discussion. (21) gives the formal definition of Discourse Context:

(21)   DC = $\langle c, QUD \rangle$ where
       c is a Stalnakerian context set
       QUD $\subseteq$ {W/Q: Q is a proper question in c}

The definition of QUD states the minimal requirement on the questions in the set: that they be proper questions in the context. It does not, though, give any idea as to which of the questions that have this property will count as members of QUD. For any possible context set c there are many – perhaps infinitely many – questions whose denotation is a partition containing more than one cell with a non-empty intersection with c. Clearly, only a very limited subset of these will belong to QUD at a given point. The definition given does not constitute a characterization of this subset, or of what it is for a question to be a question under discussion. Crucially, I rely on the intuitive idea that there is in every conversation a recognized set of open issues, and that discourse participants can identify what is an open issue and what is not. The formalization does no more than characterize open issues as proper questions.

Recall also from the informal discussion that the logical structure of QUD is not straightforwardly definable. QUD appears not to have a Boolean structure. Although we may define operations on partitions which correspond to conjunction and disjunction (see Landman 1991), it is not clear that these operations correspond to any linguistic operation on questions. As I observed above, the result of conjoining two questions does not necessarily produce a linguistic object which is intuitively a single question, as illustrated by (22):

(22)   What is wrong with this car and what is the weather like in Tel-Aviv?

But whether or not questions in general admit of Boolean operations, we must assume that QUD does not have a Boolean structure: it is not closed under conjunction and disjunction. In other words, even if each of the conjuncts of (22) is in QUD, (22) itself is not necessarily also in QUD.

Having defined Discourse Contexts, we must now state how these contexts are updated. This is straightforward. To update a Discourse Context in response to an utterance, we first update the Stalnakerian context set in the usual way, that is, replace it with its intersection with the proposition asserted. Second, we eliminate from QUD any questions which are not proper questions in the new context. This means simply that we eliminate any questions which have been resolved by the assertion.

In some cases, an assertion may resolve a question without the participants in the discourse realizing that this is the case. This parallels the case in which participants in a discourse fail to realize that their set of presuppositions entails some proposition P. In such a case, P is true at every world in the context set and so is strictly presupposed, even though no participant in the discourse realizes this. I set this complication aside.

There is always the possibility that a given assertion may introduce a new question into QUD. Consequently, I do not define the update of QUD only as the elimination of resolved questions. Although I do not address here the question of how new issues are raised in discourse, I do not wish the model to exclude this possibility. Let QUD+φ denote a set from which any questions in QUD resolved by φ are eliminated, but which may contain additional questions not in QUD. Then we can define the update of a Discourse Context as follows:

(23) Let DC = ⟨c, QUD⟩
DC updated with φ, DC[φ] = ⟨c+φ, QUD+φ⟩

Recall that one of the reasons for developing this refinement was to give a formal definition of Relevant Informativity. The definition states in the terms of the new model the informal characterization which I gave earlier: an assertion of φ is relevantly informative iff it provides a partial answer to some question under discussion, i.e.:

(24) φ is relevantly informative with respect to DC iff
$\exists Q \in QUD$ s.t. $W/Q^{c+\varphi} \subset W/Q^c$

I now use this to define an appropriateness condition on DC update:

(25) *The Relevant Informativity Condition*
If φ is asserted in a talk exchange whose purpose is the exchange of information, then DC[φ] is appropriate only if φ is relevantly informative w.r.t. DC.

I take (25) to be a partial formalization of Grice's Maxim of Relation. It is partial in that, although every contribution to a discourse must be relevant, not every contribution must meet the Relevant Informativity Condition. Exceptions to the condition include contributions which function to add a new question to QUD. The definition of relevance for such utterances will be quite different from this. Similarly, in talk exchanges whose purpose is primarily phatic, the Relevant Informativity Condition probably does not apply. (Stalnaker (1974:201) offers his conversations with his barber as such a case.) I will restrict my attention to contributions which are intended to be informative. To these, the Relevant Informativity Condition applies.

2.3.2. Disjunction and the Relevant Informativity Condition

In section 2.2.2., I argued that the reason that disjunctions generally list possibilities relevant to the same topic is that this is the only way in which they can be Relevantly Informative. In terms of the new model I have constructed, this is the claim that for any discourse context DC, a sentence S_1 *or* ... *or* S_n can be Relevantly Informative (i.e. provide a partial answer to some Q∈QUD) only if there is some Q∈QUD such that all of $S_1 \ldots S_n$ are partial answers to Q. This can be proved to follow from the definitions given. For simplicity, I give the proof for the specific case of a two disjunct disjunction. I show:

(26)　For any context c and any question Q:
$W/Q^{c+\{A \text{ or } B\}} \subset W/Q^c$ only if
$W/Q^{c+A} \subset W/Q^c$ and $W/Q^{c+B} \subset W/Q^c$

This result falls out from the definitions given, by virtue of the fact that the result of updating a context c with a sentence *A or B* is the intersection of c with the union of (the set of worlds denoted by) A and (the set of worlds denoted by) B. In giving the proof, I use the lemma in (27), which is itself a straightforward consequence of the definition of W/Q^c and set theory:

(27)　Lemma:
$W/Q^{c+\varphi} \subset W/Q^c$ iff $\exists X \in W/Q$ s.t. $X \cap c \neq \emptyset$ and $X \cap c \cap \varphi = \emptyset$

(28)
1. Show: for any Q, any c:
$W/Q^{c+[\varphi \text{ or } \psi]} \subset W/Q^c$ only if
$W/Q^{c+\varphi} \subset W/Q^c$ and
$W/Q^{c+\psi} \subset W/Q^c$

2. Suppose that for some arbitrary Q and c,
$W/Q^{c+[\varphi \text{ or } \psi]} \subset W/Q^c$

3. Then $\exists X \in W/Q$ s.t. $X \cap c \neq \emptyset$ and $X \cap c \cap [\varphi \text{ or } \psi] = \emptyset$
　　　　　　　　　(by lemma, L to R)

4. $X \cap c \cap [\varphi \text{ or } \psi] = X \cap c \cap (\varphi \cup \psi)$

5. So $\exists X \in W/Q$ s.t. $X \cap c \neq \emptyset$ and $X \cap c \cap [\varphi \cup \psi] = \emptyset$
　　　　　　　　　(rewrite of line 3)

6. So $\exists X \in W/Q$ s.t. $X \cap c \neq \emptyset$ and $X \cap c \cap \varphi = \emptyset$ and $X \cap c \cap \psi = \emptyset$

7. Hence:
   $\exists X \in W/Q$ s.t. $X \cap c \neq \emptyset$ and $X \cap c \cap \varphi = \emptyset$ and
   $\exists X \in W/Q$ s.t. $X \cap c \neq \emptyset$ and $X \cap c \cap \psi = \emptyset$

7. Hence:
   $W/Q^{c+\varphi} \subset W/Q^c$ and
   $W/Q^{c+\psi} \subset W/Q^c$ (by two applications of lemma, R to L)

This theorem provides the explanation for Grice's (1989: 68) observation, that "a standard ...employment of *or* is in the specification of possibilities ... each of which is relevant in the same way to a given topic". It is only when the disjuncts are related in this way that the disjunction as a whole will be Relevantly Informative with respect to some context. For suppose that *A or B* meets the Relevant Informativity condition w.r.t. DC = ⟨c, QUD⟩. Then there is some question in QUD s.t. *A or B* provides a partial answer to it. Call this question Q. By (26), it follows that both A and B will also provide partial answers to Q. But an assertion of *A or B* must always meet the Relevant Informativity condition. So whenever *A or B* is asserted, there will be some question under discussion to which both disjuncts provide partial answers.

When a disjunction is given in answer to an explicit question, the disjunction must provide an answer to that question. Hence, by (26), each disjunct must provide a possible answer to it. This is what Grice observes when he says that disjunctions are "characteristically employed to give a partial answer to some *wh*-question, to which each disjunct, if assertible, would give a fuller ... answer" (1989:68). The case of disjunctions asserted in an informative discourse but not in answer to an explicit question is simply an extension of this. We have assumed that in such a case there is some implicit question to which the disjunction provides an answer, and thus each disjunct must provide a possible answer to that same implicit question.

We noted above that disjunctions in which the disjuncts cannot be interpreted as possible answers to a single question are infelicitous. This was the explanation for the oddity of (8), repeated here:

(8) #Either this car has dirt in its fuel line, or it is raining in Tel-Aviv.

The claim, then, is that when speakers judge (8) odd, their judgment reflects their inability to think of a context in which the sentence would be relevantly informative, and therefore assertible. This, in turn, is a claim that speakers judge there to be no "askable" question to which each disjunct constitutes a possible answer.

Verification for this claim comes from the fact that judgments change when informants are offered a context which does provide such a question. Consider the following example:

(29)   Either several linguists went to the party, or some philosophers stayed all night.

Presented with this sentence out of the blue, my informants have invariably found it infelicitous. But now, here is a situation in which to locate it. Suppose that our friend Cleo has given a party, and is upset about something that happened. We are speculating as to what that might be. As we know Cleo well, we have a clear idea as to what the possible causes of her upset might be. We know that these include, but are not limited to:
   (i)   the possibility that several linguists went to the party
   (ii) the possibility that some philosophers stayed all night
If, in the course of our conversation, we exclude all possibilities but these, we can certainly conclude it felicitously by saying: "Either several linguists came to the party, or some philosophers stayed all night. That's why she's upset." In other words, once we have established a context in which there is a question under discussion to which each disjunct is a possible answer, the disjunction becomes felicitous. The context we came up with, though, is hardly one that anyone is likely to think of "out of the blue." Hence, the sentence is usually judged infelicitous in the absence of any context.

2.3.3. Disjunction and Simplicity
2.3.3.1. Entailing Disjunctions

Let's turn now to cases of disjunctions in which one disjunct entails another, which, as we observed above, are quite strongly infelicitous. Recall example (3):

Disjunctive Sentences in Discourse 47

(3) #Either Jane owns a truck or she owns a red truck.

An assertion of (3) would meet the Relevant Informativity condition in a context in which the question of what kind of vehicle Jane owns is under discussion. Updating the Discourse Context with this assertion would result in a new context in every world of which Jane owns a truck. The assertion thus eliminates many possible answers to the question, and so is relevantly informative. But note that the second disjunct entails the first. Consequently, the proposition expressed by the second is a subset of that expressed by the first, i.e.:

(30) {w: Jane owns a red truck in w} $\subseteq$ {w: Jane owns a truck in w}

This means that the result of updating c with the disjunction as a whole is just what we would get if we updated c with the first disjunct alone:

(31) c + *Jane owns a truck or she owns a red truck* =
c + *Jane owns a truck*

Consequently, an assertion of (3) in any context would violate the Simplicity Condition introduced earlier. In any context, the context update effect which is achieved by asserting (3) could also be achieved by asserting one of the constituents of (3), which would surely be simpler.

In light of our discussion of Relevant Informativity, there is a slightly different way to characterize the failure to abide by Simplicity. Because of the entailment between the disjuncts, it is the case that for any Discourse Context, and for any Q∈QUD, the answer to Q provided by the disjunction as a whole could just as well have been provided by asserting the first disjunct alone. Let's describe this by saying that the disjunction as a whole has the same degree of Relevant Informativity as the first disjunct alone:

(32) For any Discourse Context DC and any Q∈ QUD:
$W/Q^{c \;+ \textit{Jane owns a truck or she owns a red truck}}$ =
$W/Q^{c \;+ \textit{Jane owns a truck}}$

It will turn out that viewing the violation in terms of Relevant Informativity is crucial for understanding certain cases where there is no entailment between the disjuncts.

Before I turn to these cases, let me just review an example in which the relation between the disjuncts is not strict logical entailment, but contextual entailment. Recall example (4):

(4)   #Either she's a graduate student, or she can't afford to eat out at expensive restaurants.

I pointed out that in a context in which it is assumed that graduate students are on tight budgets, and that people on tight budgets can't afford to eat out at expensive restaurants, this sentence has the same effect as (3), repeated here:

(3)   #Either Jane owns a truck or she owns a red truck.

The reason the two have the same effect is that whether or not a particular proposition provides an answer to a given question, and thus whether or not a proposition is Relevantly Informative, depends on what the hearer already takes to be true. Suppose c entails the two assumptions. Then c+ *she's a graduate student* will entail that she is on a tight budget and can't afford to eat out at expensive restaurants. This set will be a subset of c+*she can't afford to eat out at expensive restaurants*. So once again, the context update effect of the disjunction as a whole will be identical to the context update effect of the second disjunct alone. Hence, the Simplicity condition is violated.

2.3.3.2. Non-entailing cases

Because of the way in which Relevant Informativity and Simplicity interact, it turns out that disjunctions can violate the Simplicity Condition in terms of their degree of Relevant Informativity, even when no disjunct entails another. Consider example (33) which, out of the blue, is infelicitous.

(33)   #Either Jane owns a big truck, or she owns a truck and George owns a stationwagon.

Disjunctive Sentences in Discourse

No disjunct in this example entails another, so the explanation given for the infelicity of the entailing disjunctions cannot be applied here straightforwardly. But consider what possible questions the disjunction could provide an answer to. Suppose the disjunction is to address the question of what kind of vehicle George owns. Because the first disjunct does not eliminate any possible answers to this question (assuming no contextual assumptions about connections between the kinds of vehicles the two people own), neither will the disjunction as a whole. So with respect to this question, the disjunction is uninformative.

Suppose, alternatively, that the disjunction is to address the question of what kind of vehicle Jane owns. Now we derive an interesting result. Although the context update effected by the disjunction as a whole is distinct from that effected by either disjunct, the disjunction as a whole gives the same answer to this question as the second disjunct alone, i.e.:

(34) $W/Q^{c+J \text{ owns a big truck or she owns a t. and G owns a s.w.}} =$
$W/Q^{c+J \text{ owns a t. and G owns a s.w.}}$

The easiest way to see this is from the diagrams in Figures 4 and 5. Look first at Figure 4.

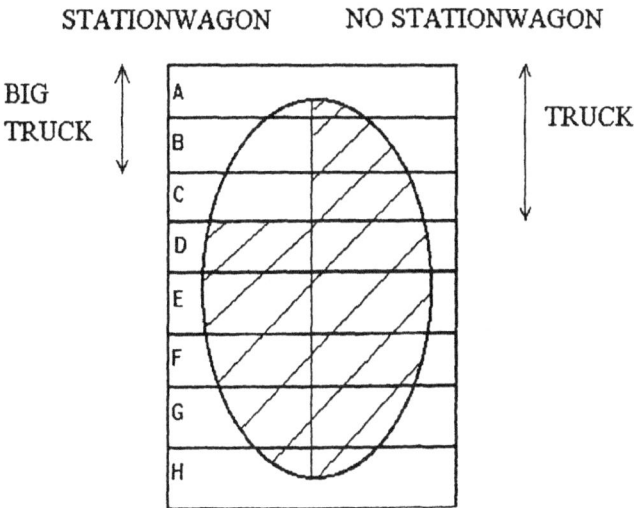

Figure 4
$c + J.$ *owns a truck and G. owns a stationwagon* $= c'$
$W/Q^{c'} = \{A,B,C\}$

As usual, the large rectangle with its divisions represents the partition imposed on W by the question. The three cells A, B and C contain worlds in which Jane owns a truck. The cells A and B contain worlds in which Jane owns a big truck. The oval represents the starting context set. As the question of whether George owns a stationwagon is unresolved in this context, and is unrelated to the kind of vehicle Jane owns, I assume that in half of the worlds in the context (the left hand side of the picture) George owns a stationwagon, and in the other half (the right hand side of the picture) he doesn't. The diagram shows the effect of updating this context with the content of the second disjunct, *Jane owns a truck and George owns a stationwagon*. The shaded area represents the worlds incompatible with this proposition, which will be eliminated. The unshaded area represents the updated context. Notice that this new context is compatible with three cells of the partition, A, B and C: those cells containing worlds in which Jane owns a truck.

Now look at Figure 5:

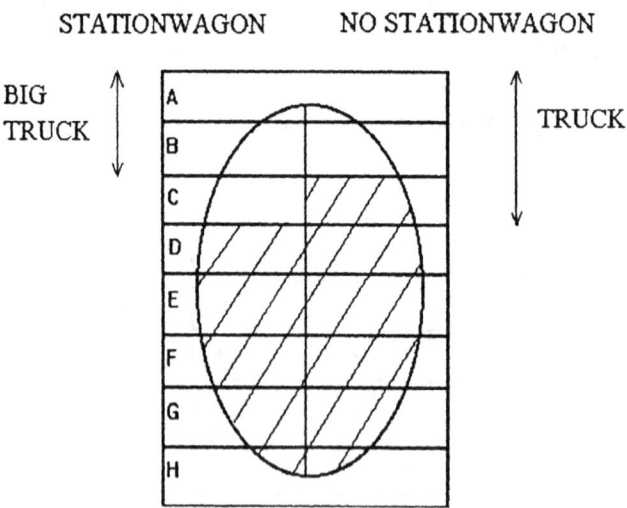

Figure 5
c + *J. owns a big truck or she owns a truck and G. owns a stationwagon* = c''
$W/Q^{c''} = \{A,B,C\}$

Disjunctive Sentences in Discourse 51

Figure 5 represents the effect of updating the context with the disjunction as a whole. Notice first that the resulting context set is different from that in Figure 4: the disjunction as a whole is differently informative, overall, than the second disjunct alone. But now notice that nonetheless, this context set is compatible with the same three cells of the partition: A, B and C. In other words, the disjunction gives the same answer to the question under discussion as would its second disjunct alone. So, although the disjunction is relevantly informative with respect to the question of what kind of vehicle Jane owns, its use to answer the question violates the Simplicity Condition, viewed in terms of Relevant Informativity, rather than in terms of informativity *simpliciter*. The interaction of Relevant Informativity and Simplicity thus accounts for the infelicity of sentence (33) out of the blue.

Once again, though, an appropriate Discourse Context – one in which there is a QUD to which each disjunct provides a possible and distinct answer – renders the disjunction felicitous. Suppose, then, that Jane and George are house mates, and that they are moving house together. Abe is wondering about the mechanics of their move:

(35)   Abe: How are they going to move all their stuff?
           Bud: Well, either Jane has a big truck, or she has a truck and George has a stationwagon. Either way, they can get everything into their own cars.

In response to this question, the disjunction is acceptable. Assuming that Bud's context set includes some ordinary assumptions about how much stuff you can get into trucks and stationwagon, each disjunct will constitute an answer to the question with respect to his context set, ensuring that the disjunction satisfies Relevant Informativity. Moreover, the partial answer provided by the disjunction differs from the answer offered by either disjunct alone, ensuring that Simplicity is not violated. The felicity of the disjunction relative to this Discourse Context is thus predicted.

There is one final felicity condition which is also to be explained in terms of the two context-update conditions. The observation is that a felicitous disjunction may not contain any disjuncts whose truth value is determinate in the context (Stalnaker 1975, Grice 1989). It is quite simple to show that a disjunction in which any disjunct is known to be true violates the Relevant Informativity condition, while a disjunction in which any disjunct is known to be false violates the Simplicity condition.

Suppose that A is assumed in the context to be true, that is, it is entailed by c. Then updating c with any disjunction which has A as a disjunct will have no effect i.e.:

(36)   c + A or B = c

But then the resulting context cannot be any closer to an answer to any question than c itself, as the resulting context is identical with c, i.e.:

(37) $\neg\exists Q \in$ QUD s.t. $W/Q^{c+\{A \text{ or } B\}} \subset W/Q^c$

Thus, the Relevant Informativity condition is violated.

Suppose now that A is assumed to be false, that is, is not true at any world in c. Then A will make no contribution to the informativity of any disjunction of which it is a disjunct, i.e.:

(38)   c + A or B = c + B

So in this case, the Simplicity condition is violated.

In conclusion, we can summarize the felicity conditions on disjunction in terms of the enriched Stalnakerian model in the following way:

(39)   *Summary of felicity conditions*
A disjunction S_1 or ... or S_n is felicitous only if there is a question Q in QUD s.t.
(i) Each disjunct S_1 ... S_n is a partial answer to Q and
(ii) Each disjunct S_1 ... S_n provides a more informative answer to Q than does the disjunction S_1 or ... or S_n.

(i) is required in order for the disjunction to satisfy Relevant Informativity. (ii) is a minimal requirement for the disjunction to satisfy Simplicity. Together, these requirements have the effect that disjunctions are generally used in the manner described by Grice (1989): "in the specification of possibilities ... each of which is relevant in the same way to a given topic."

2.3.4. Disjunction and Rooth's Alternative Semantics

In this section, I want to discuss briefly a connection between the issues raised here and the Alternative Semantics proposed by Rooth (1985, 1992) in his account of focus constructions. In Alternative Semantics, linguistic expressions are assigned two semantic values. One is the ordinary denotation ($[\alpha]^o$), and the second is what Rooth calls the *focus semantic value* ($[\alpha]^f$). When an expression contains no focused constituents, its focus semantic value is identical to its ordinary denotation. The interesting case is the case of expressions which do contain a focused constituent. In this case, the focus semantic value of the expression is a set of semantic objects of the same type as the expression. For example, the focus semantic value of a sentence which contains a focused constituent is a set of propositions, each one a proposition derived from the ordinary denotation of the sentence by substituting into the position corresponding to the focused phrase. So, for example, the focus semantic value of [$_S$Jane likes [George]$_F$] is the set of propositions of the form "Jane likes x," where x is some individual. Similarly, the focus value of [$_S$[Jane]$_F$ likes George] is the set of propositions of the form "x likes George." Intuitively, the focus semantic value of a sentence, or its focus set, is "a set of alternatives from which the ordinary semantic value is drawn, or a set of propositions which potentially contrast with the ordinary semantic value" (Rooth 1992:76). So the members of the focus semantic value of a sentence look a lot like propositions which could potentially be disjoined.

Given that there is already evidence for the utility of positing a focus semantic value, could we not use this to characterize those propositions which can be disjoined and those which cannot? It appears that what is required for a felicitous clausal disjunction is that the propositions disjoined all be drawn from a single focus semantic value. We might formulate this as a constraint in the following way:

(40) For any clausal disjunction [d_1 or d_2 or ... or d_n], for each d_i, i>1, $[d_i]^o \, \varepsilon \, [d_1]^f$

This says that in a clausal disjunction, the proposition expressed by each disjunct after the first must belong to the focus semantic value of the first.

This seems like an accurate characterization of some simple cases. So, for instance, (41) is a felicitous disjunction, but (42) is not.

(41)   Either Jane likes [George]$_F$, or she likes [Henry]$_F$.
(42)   #Either Jane likes [George]$_F$, or [Henry]$_F$ likes George.

Now, the first thing to note is that (40) states a constraint on disjunction, but does not derive the constraint from any other principles, as I have done above. Second, note that the characterization in (40) is really no different from saying that each disjunct must be a possible answer to the same question. As Rooth has shown, there is a correlation between *wh*-questions and the position of focus in answers. Essentially, the position of focus corresponds to the base position of the *wh*-expression. All potential direct answers to a *who* or *what* question share the same focus structure; any potential answer will belong to the focus set of all other potential answers. To put it another way, the members of the focus set of a possible answer to a question Q are also possible answers to Q. So to say that in a disjunction, the disjuncts must all be members of a single focus set is just to say that all of the disjuncts must be possible answers to the same question.

The problem with trying to use focus sets to characterize possible disjunctions is, simply, that although any disjunction which conforms to (40) will be a felicitous disjunction, not all felicitous disjunctions conform to (40). In other words, (40) gives a sufficient but not a necessary condition for a disjunction to be felicitous. Consider, for instance, the very first example of this chapter, repeated here:

(1)   Either you have dirt in your fuel line or your carburetor is gummed.

Whatever bears the focus in the first disjunction, there is no way to construct a focus semantic value for it which would include the proposition expressed by the second disjunct.

(1), and other cases which do not conform to (40), tend to be sentences that would be given as answers to *why*-questions (*Why isn't my car running?*), or to rather general questions like *What is wrong with my car?* or *What happened?* The correlation between questions like these and the focus properties of their answers is much less clear than with simple constituent questions like *Who came?* For instance, the constraint on question-answer pairs formulated in Rooth (1992), given in (43), clearly does not apply to these questions.

(43)   Question-Answer constraint: The ordinary semantic value of a question must be a subset of the focus semantic value of a corresponding answer.

The problem seems to have to do with the unavailability of a definition of focus set for sentences which have the broadest possible focus. In the case of (1), for instance, the second disjunct could be seen as a candidate for substitution into the position of the complement clause in the following:

(44)   What is wrong with your car is that you have dirt in your fuel line.

Perhaps for (?), we need to require that the disjuncts following the first be clauses which appear in the complement position of the propositions in the focus semantic value of (44). But if what is focused in (44) is the whole clause *that you have dirt in your fuel line*, then, following the usual strategy for generating focus sets, what we get is the (infinite) set of propositions of the form of (44). In other words, the strategy offers no systematic way of constraining which propositions will appear in the complement position. This, then, brings us back to where we started. To say what should be in the focus set of (44), we need to be able to say what constitutes a possible or allowable answer to *What is wrong with my car?* or to say which propositions could felicitously be disjoined in answer to this question. But what we were using focus sets for was to state a constraint on answers to questions, or on felicitous disjunctions.

In a similar vein, Tomioka (1998) has suggested that the focus set of a sentence should not contain all propositions derived by substituting into the focused position, but only propositions which are in some sense contrasting alternatives. The problem, he points out, is how to characterize the required notion of alternative. He suggests that an informal way to do this is to say that propositions count as alternatives just in case they can be disjoined.

What emerges is a rather tantalizing interconnection between the notion of focus sets, the denotations of questions and the question-answer relation, and the felicity conditions on disjunction. In the account I have given of the felicity conditions of disjunction, I have taken the question-answer relation to be basic. In effect, disjunctions are required to be felicitous answers to some question, and from this their felicity conditions follow. But the connections between these issues remain to be explored further.

2.3.5. Summary

Using the augmented Stalnakerian model, I have given an explanation for the discourse function and felicity conditions of disjunction on the basis of two pragmatic principles: the Relevant Informativity Condition and the Simplicity Condition. The former principle, which plays the chief explanatory role, is stated as a condition on context update. There is thus an assumption implicit in the account that to understand pragmatic processes, we must make reference to a process of context update. However, the account makes no reference to any particular procedure for updating a context with a disjunction. Reference is made only to the *result* of updating a context with a disjunction, which is the elimination from the starting context of any world at which no disjunct is true. More formally, it is the result of intersecting the context with the union of the denotations of each disjunct. This is the minimal assumption one can make, assuming that disjunction in English has the truth conditions of logical inclusive disjunction and that the context update process reflects truth conditional content.

The basic point, then, is that the context update induced by a disjunction will be allowable only when the elimination of just this set of worlds contributes information which the participants in the discourse are interested in. This, I characterized as answering some question in the set of Questions Under Discussion. I showed that for this to be possible, each disjunct must constitute a possible answer to that same question. I then showed that the Simplicity Condition has the effect of requiring each disjunct to constitute a *distinct* answer to the question. If the answer offered by any disjunct includes (i.e. entails) the answer given by another, then the degree of Relevant Informativity of the disjunction will be identical to that of a constituent of the disjunction, in violation of Simplicity.

In my model, I have not attempted any formal definition of QUD. The notion is useful only to the extent that we can imbue it with intuitive content. However, using questions to characterize felicitous disjunctions brings out the fundamental connection between the two forms. In some sense, both questions and disjunctions are sets of answers. Questions denote sets of all possible answers. Disjunctions give a list of some subset of possible answers. Crucially, what we seem to find is that a disjunction is felicitous just in case the union of the disjuncts equals the union of some subset of a possible, or perhaps "askable," question.

2.4. SOME EXCEPTIONS

2.4.1. Floutings

There are two sorts of disjunctions in which the felicity conditions I have named are blatantly violated, but which can nonetheless be used appropriately in certain circumstances. Consider the discourse in (45):

(45)   Alex: Do you think I'm going to pass this exam?
              Bill: Either you will or you won't.

Bill's response is a tautology. A tautology is by definition uninformative *simpliciter*, and so can never be Relevantly Informative. Hence, we would expect the disjunction to be infelicitous.

But the very obviousness of the non-informative nature of Bill's response indicates that he is doing what Grice calls "flouting" the condition. She is obviously failing to abide by the usual requirements of felicitous discourse. Utterances such as these, according to Grice, generate *conversational implicatures*. Conversational implicatures are inferences made by hearers when they observe that what a speaker actually said was in violation of some conversational maxim. If the hearer assumes that the speaker intends to be cooperative, she will attempt to construct some additional proposition which the speaker meant to convey, which would render her utterance cooperative. The inference is always based on the truth-conditional content of the speaker's utterance.

Bill's utterance in (45) is so obviously uninformative that it indeed does seem intentionally uncooperative. But there are a number of additional propositions that Bill could intend to convey by his utterance: that he can't answer the question, that he is uninterested in answering the question, that there is nothing now to be done about passing the exam, and so on. Alex may not be able to arrive at a specific proposition, but she will certainly derive some information about Bill's attitude from his utterance. Thus, although *you will or you won't* is not itself informative, its utterance is. What is needed is to allow the model of Discourse Context update to include update with the implicatures generated by assertions, and thus to register the informativity of examples like (45B).

This does not quite resolve the issue however. For note that the tautologous disjunction, even out of the blue, is not judged infelicitous in the same way as some of our earlier examples, such as:

(46)   #Either this car has dirt in its fuel line or it is raining in Tel-Aviv.

Moreover, uninformative examples like (46) cannot be rendered felicitous by virtue of conversational implicatures to which they give rise.

The failure of (46) to give rise to conversational implicatures which would "rescue" it is due, I think, to the fact that its uninformativity is not obvious. In general, conversational implicatures arise when it is clear that the speaker has intentionally violated some maxim.

But why is the tautologous disjunction not infelicitous in the same way as (46), even out of the blue? It will not do here to say that it always gives rise to conversational implicatures, as conversational implicatures are contextual inferences, and do not attach to particular forms. What seems to be the case is that the fact that the disjuncts are each possible answers to the question under discussion suffices to make the sentence acceptable. I suggest, then, something along these lines: As we've now seen, for a disjunction to be Relevantly Informative, each disjunct must constitute a possible answer to a given question. Consequently, in judging whether or not a disjunction is felicitous, speakers attempt to construct a question to which each disjunct could be a possible answer. It is the possibility of constructing such a question which is the principal criterion of felicity. When speakers fail to construct such a question, they judge the sentence anomalous. When they succeed, they judge the sentence acceptable, even if its utterance might give rise to a violation of Relevant Informativity for some other reason.

Another kind of flouting is illustrated by (47):

(47)   Either George is in love, or I'm a duck-billed platypus.

Clearly, the second disjunct is false. Assertion of the disjunction is thus equivalent to assertion of the first disjunct alone, in violation of the Simplicity condition. However, once again the violation is blatant, and an implicature is generated. Here, what is implicated is that the speaker is absolutely certain that George is in love. Thus, the disjunction as a whole is differently informative than the first disjunct alone, as long as the effect of the implicature is taken into account.

2.4.2. Reasoning contexts

The felicity conditions I have stated apply only in situations in which the normal rules of conversation are in force. One case in which these rules are typically suspended is in the presentation of a logical argument, where explicit statement of all premises and all reasoning steps is required. In a logical argument, one might say:

(48)   George is at home. Therefore, George is at home or he is in the library.

Clearly, one of the disjuncts in the conclusion is known to be true in the context, but the disjunction is allowable in the context of the argument. Similarly, suppose that one had constructed two independent logical arguments, one of which led to the conclusion that Jane has a dog, and the other of which led to the conclusion that Jane has a brown dog. One could then continue:

(49)   Either Jane has a dog or she has a brown dog. Therefore, Jane has a dog.

Logical arguments are judged only for their validity; statements used in making them are not required to avoid redundancy. Given that the normal conversational rules are not in effect, the normal felicity conditions constraining disjunctive utterances are suspended.

2.4.3. Metalinguistic *or*

There is a use of *or* in which it may conjoin clauses one of which entails the other. Consider, for example:

(50) Henry lives in the South of France, or at least he lives somewhere in Europe.

Notice, first, that eliminating *at least* from this example renders it infelicitous, just like the other examples of entailing disjunctions[3].

(51) #Henry lives in the South of France or he lives somewhere in Europe.

Even with *at least* left in, the sentence is made infelicitous by the addition of *either* at the beginning of the first disjunct:

(52) #Either Henry lives in the South of France or at least he lives somewhere in Europe.

Finally, notice that *or* can be eliminated from the original example without any real change in the sense of the string.

(53) Henry lives in the South of France. At least, he lives somewhere in Europe.

In (53), the expression *at least* indicates that the second proposition is offered as some kind of correction of the first. The effect of the string as a whole is to convey that Henry perhaps lives in the South of France, but certainly somewhere in Europe. The same is true of the *or* sentence in (50). *Or* does not appear to make a truth conditional contribution here, as shown by the fact that we can just as well do without it. Despite its form, (50) is not a disjunction of propositions, although it has something in common with true disjunctions. As in true disjunctions, each disjunct constitutes an answer to the same question. The difference is that one answer – the second – wholly or partially replaces the first, and hence there is no constraint on entailment between the disjuncts. Here are some more examples, these not involving entailment between clauses, which illustrate the same phenomenon:

(54) Harriet isn't coming to the party, or at least she didn't say she was.
(55) George has got a job offer, or at least that's what Harriet told me.

Horn (1985) suggests that in examples like these, *or* expresses what he calls *metalinguistic disjunction*. This suggestion is part of an extended argument that many natural language operators are "pragmatically ambiguous" between standard truth functional interpretations and metalinguistic interpretations. His discussion centers on negation, which, he argues, is semantically unambiguous but has an extended metalinguistic use. In this use, negation does not negate the propositional content of the embedded clause, but rather indicates non-acceptance of some implicature of what is said, or the form used to express that content. In (56), for example, negation indicates the speaker's non-acceptance of a particular pronunciation. In (57), it indicates non-acceptance of a particular locution, and its associated implications. (The examples are from Chierchia and McConnell-Ginet 1990:196). Italics indicate intonational prominence.

(56) I don't like to/*mah*/toes but to/*mey*/toes.
(57) No, I didn't have lunch with the *girls*. We *women* ate together.

Horn goes on to suggest that disjunction also has a metalinguistic use. As with negation, he argues against treating disjunction as semantically ambiguous. Rather, he says, we should recognize that not all uses of *or* are truth functional. Following Du Bois (1974), he notes that "a principal source of non-logical disjunction is the phenomenon of intentional mid-sentence correction" (p.151). These self-corrections appear commonly in written prose, where they have "survived presumably careful editing," as in:

(58) I can only very briefly set forth my own view, or rather my general attitudes. (Sapir, Language)

In their discussion of metalinguistic negation, Chierchia and McConnell-Ginet suggest that its use may indicate that the speaker is distancing herself from the illocutionary act that would be performed by utterance of the embedded clause. Metalinguistic disjunction might also be understood as indicating a relation between illocutionary acts, rather than a relation between asserted content. Thus, in examples like (50) and (54-55), *or* perhaps indicates that each disjunct is intended to fill the same "discourse slot." *Or* indicates that the two clauses are to be treated in parallel, not in sequence. Just as a true disjunction offers parallel possible answers to a given question, so metalinguistic disjunction indicates that two distinct but parallel illocutionary acts are being performed.

In order for *or* to be understood as metalinguistic disjunction, it must be accompanied by some qualifying expression. In the examples given so far, the expression is *at least*. This expression contributes here whatever it contributes in the sentence sequence without *or*. *Rather* may also accompany metalinguistic *or*, and carries with it a stronger implication than *at least* that the second "disjunct" is a correction of the first:

(59) Harriet isn't coming to the party, or rather she didn't say she was.
(60) George has got a job offer, or rather Harriet told me that he has.

Other qualifying expressions are *I should say* and *should I say*, as in:

(61) Good afternoon Ms. Brown, or should I say Dr. Brown.
(62) Good afternoon Ms. Brown, or, I should say, Dr. Brown.

Metalinguistic disjunction cannot be used to go from a weaker to a stronger claim, even though such moves are allowed in sentence sequences. Compare:

(63) Henry lives in Europe. In fact, he lives in the South of France.
(64) #Henry lives in Europe, or in fact he lives in the South of France.

In (63), the second sentence makes a stronger assertion than the first. The second assertion does not replace the first, but adds to it; the assertions are not parallel, but serial. Consequently, they cannot be metalinguistically disjoined.

Ball (1986) discusses a use of metalinguistic disjunction which she calls "equivalent *or*," exemplified in (65-66). (Ball's examples 21 and 29.)

(65) You'll need 7-inch (18-cm) and 12-inch (30-cm) skillets or frying pans (they mean the same thing).
[Farmer, F.M. The Fannie Farmer Cookbook 1984:29]

(66) Created to provide energy for hikers, trail mix or "gorp" has become an all-purpose snack.
[Fannie Farmer. 1984:72]

In these cases, *or* conjoins two synonymous terms, one of which is presumably unfamiliar. This is made explicit in example (65). Such examples need not, though, be treated as distinct from the corrective uses of metalinguistic or. Both uses extend the truth functional use of *or* in a similar way, capitalizing on the fact that in interpreting a disjunction, the disjuncts are interpreted in parallel, rather than serially. In the case of corrective *or*, the hearer is to understand that the two terms could be used interchangeably, and from this can infer that they are synonymous.

The parallel between metalinguistic negation and metalinguistic disjunction seems robust. In sentences like (67), if the negation is interpreted truth-functionally the result is contradictory, and unacceptable:

(67) It isn't warm in here. It's stiflingly hot!

With the negation understood metalinguistically, the sequence is perfectly sensible. The sensible interpretation, though, requires the hearer to attribute to the speaker illocutionary acts other than simple assertion. Similarly with sentences like (68):

(68) Henry lives in the South of France or at least somewhere in Europe.

This can easily be given a sensible interpretation, but only if we understand the disjunction metalinguistically, and understand that the speaker intends to execute a correction of some kind.

Metalinguistic disjunction is no doubt subject to felicity conditions of its own. The subject matter of this study, though, is logical disjunction, as used in natural language, and the felicity conditions I have identified apply to this primary use of *or*.

2.5. THE EXCLUSIVE INTERPRETATION OF *OR*

One of the apparent discrepancies between English *or* and logical "∨" is the tendency of the former to receive what is often described as an exclusive interpretation. In the current linguistic literature there is quite general agreement that exclusivity should be given a pragmatic explanation. However, the explanation most standardly given, due to Gazdar (1979), is flawed. In this section, I will review, first, some of the arguments against a semantic account of the exclusive reading of disjunction, and will then present and critique Gazdar's pragmatic account, and some variants on it. I will then argue that what we are used to calling an exclusive reading of the disjunction is really an exhaustive reading of each disjunct, and that this is due to the observation discussed at length in this chapter: that disjuncts are interpreted as answers to a question under discussion.

2.5.1. Critique of the ambiguity account

The exclusive interpretation of disjunction is evident in examples like the following:

(69)   Either I will eat dinner at home or I'll eat out with Cleo.

Everyone agrees that for (69) to be true, at *least* one of the disjuncts must be true. There is also general agreement that a speaker who uses (69) will usually be understood to imply that at *most* one of the disjuncts is true. The hearers of (69) would be surprised to find out later that the speaker both ate dinner at home and ate out with Cleo. And should they discover that the speaker intended all along to do both, they will probably feel that she misled them by uttering (69).

These intuitions led many authors, including Tarski (1941: 21), Rescher (1964: 178), Massey (1970: 9) and Salmon (1984: 40), to claim that English *or* is semantically ambiguous. (These citations, and many others, are given in Jennings 1994.) The claim is that *or* sometimes has the truth conditions of *inclusive disjunction*, and sometimes those of *exclusive disjunction*. An inclusive disjunction, as we have seen, is true if and only if at least one of the disjuncts is true; this does not rule out the possibility of more than one disjunct being true. An exclusive disjunction is true if and only if one and only one disjunct is true. Thus, according to the ambiguity claim, sentence (69) is sometimes true when both disjuncts are true, and sometimes false.

The claim that *or* can be equivalent to exclusive disjunction is based, of course, on the intuition that disjunctions are sometimes interpreted this way. However, there is evidence that *or* cannot always be ascribed the truth conditions of exclusive disjunction. First, even in unembedded cases like (69), it is not clear that the sentence is strictly false when both disjuncts are true. Second, there are cases where assigning *or* the truth conditions of exclusive disjunction makes clearly incorrect predictions. One such case involves disjunctions embedded under negation, as in (70):

(70)   I won't eat dinner at home or go out with Cleo. [I'll go out with you instead.]

(70) has only one interpretation, which can be paraphrased as:

(71)   I won't eat dinner at home and I won't go out with Cleo.

The equivalence between (70) and (71) parallels that of the following logical equivalence:

(72) $\neg(p \vee q) \equiv \neg p \& \neg q$

The disjunction in this equivalence is *inclusive* disjunction. If we substitute for it *exclusive* disjunction, represented by "$\veebar$," the equivalence becomes:

(73) $\neg(p \veebar q) \equiv (\neg p \& \neg q) \vee (p \& q)$.

This is because there are two cases in which $(p \veebar q)$ is false: when both disjuncts are false, and when both disjuncts are true.

Given (73), if the *or* in (70) had the truth conditions of exclusive disjunction, the sentence should be true if I both eat dinner at home and go out with Cleo i.e. if both disjuncts are true. This is an obviously incorrect prediction. So the *or* here must be equivalent to inclusive disjunction. Hence, anyone who wishes to maintain that the exclusive reading of (69) is due to *or* having the truth conditions of exclusive disjunction is forced to assume that *or* is ambiguous between inclusive and exclusive disjunction. This, though, is an odd kind of ambiguity, which is apparently sometimes suppressed. (69) might be argued to be ambiguous between an inclusive and an exclusive reading of *or*, but (70) certainly is not. The ambiguity theorist ought therefore to explain why exclusive *or* is ruled out under the scope of negation.

The job of the ambiguity theorist is complicated further by disjunctions of more than two clauses, like (74):

(74)   Either I will eat dinner with you, or I will go out with Cleo, or I'll stay at home.

An utterance of (74), like (69), would normally imply that (the speaker believes that) one and only one of the disjuncts is true. However, if each of these *or*'s were equivalent to $\vee$, (74) would be predicted to be true just in case either only one or all three of its disjuncts were true, as we can see by looking at the truth-table in (75).

(75)

p	q	r	(p$\vee$q)$\vee$r	p$\vee$(q$\vee$r)
T	T	T	T	T
F	T	T	F	F
F	F	T	T	T
T	T	F	F	F
T	F	T	F	F
F	T	F	T	T
T	F	F	T	T
F	F	F	F	F

Thus, by treating the *or*'s in this sentence as exclusive disjunction, we predict a reading which the sentence lacks, and fail to predict the exclusive reading which it has, namely, that only one of the disjuncts is true. Hence, the ambiguity theorist would be forced to assume some additional mechanism to account for the interpretation of multi-clausal disjunctions. The multiple disjunct case makes clear that what we call the exclusive reading of disjunctions is not the assignment to *or* of the truth conditions of exclusive disjunction. It is, rather, an inference that only one of the disjuncts is true. Alternatively, we could describe it as an inference that the truth of any disjunct rules out the truth of any other. From this point on, this is what I will mean by the term "exclusive reading."

Arguments against the ambiguity view appear *inter alia* in Cann (1993), Chierchia and McConnell-Ginet (1990), Gazdar (1979), Horn (1989), Levinson (1983), and Pellettier (1977). Barrett and Stenner (1971) and Pellettier also point out that examples given to exemplify apparent uses of semantically exclusive disjunction frequently fail to demonstrate what they are supposed to. Most of these authors argue that *or* is truth-conditionally equivalent to inclusive disjunction, and that some pragmatic account should be given of the tendency to interpret disjuncts as mutually exclusive.

2.5.2. Gazdar's (1979) account

An often-cited account of the exclusive reading of disjunction is given by Gazdar (1979). However, a number of authors, including Soames (1982), Groenendijk and Stokhof (1984) and Horn (1989) have pointed out that Gazdar's explanation is flawed, predicting a stronger inference than is actually licensed by the premises. In this section, I will present Gazdar's account and the objection to it, and will also discuss a modification suggested by Soames and Horn.

Gazdar derives the exclusive interpretation of *or* as a *scalar implicature*, a notion originally due to Horn (1972). This notion is a generalization of certain kinds of implicatures generated by the first part of Grice's Maxim of Quantity:

Quantity I
Make your contribution as informative as is required (for the current purposes of the exchange).

Scalar implicatures are so called because they involve what Horn and Gazdar call *quantitative scales*. These scales are ordered n-tuples of expressions which have the following property:

Quantitative Scale:
Let Q be an n-tuple of expressions such that $Q = \langle e_0, e_1,...e_{n-1}\rangle$ where $n > 1$. Let $S[e_i]$ be a sentence containing the expression $e_i \in Q$, and let $S[e_{i+1}\backslash e_i]$ be a sentence just like $S[e_i]$ except that e_i is replaced by the subsequent element of Q, e_{i+1}. Then if Q is a quantitative scale, $S[e_i] \supset S[e_{i+1}\backslash e_i]$, as long as e_i and e_{i+1} are not within the scope of an operator[4].

This says that if you take a sentence *S* containing some element *e* of a quantitative scale, and replace *e* with the subsequent element in the scale to form *S'*, then *S* will entail, but will not be entailed by, *S'*. (So every element in a quantitative scale is stronger than the element which follows it.)

According to Gazdar, scalar implicatures are generated as follows: Take a sentence *S'* as defined in the previous paragraph. *S'* scalar-quantity-implicates that the speaker knows that it is not the case that *S*.

We now have all the ingredients of Gazdar's derivation of the exclusivity implicature. First, we note that $\langle and, or\rangle$ is a quantitative scale: any sentence of the form *A and B* entails, but is not entailed by *A or B*, assuming *or* to have the truth conditions of inclusive disjunction. We then have the following (Gazdar, p.59):

(76)   i.   *A or B.*
          ii. Speaker knows that it is not the case that *A and B*. (by scalar implicature)
          iii. NOT(*A and B*)   (by entailment from ii)
          iv. *A or B* & NOT(*A and B*) (= exclusive disjunction) (from i and iii)

Gazdar thus claims that *A or B* scalarly implicates that it is not the case that *A and B* because the *and* sentence is stronger than the *or* sentence.

The flaw in this argument lies in the strength of the scalar implicature which is generated. Recall our two sentences *S* and *S'*, identical except that where *S* contains $e_i \in Q$, *S'* contains the weaker expression $e_{i+1} \in Q$,

Disjunctive Sentences in Discourse 69

and thus S entails S'. Gazdar claims that an utterance of S' (the weaker sentence) licenses the inference that the speaker knows that it is not the case that S. Let's represent this as $K_s(\neg S)$. Gazdar indicates that this inference is licensed by the Maxim of Quantity, which requires speakers to make the most informative contribution they can. But this Maxim is qualified by the requirement to abide by the Maxim of Quality: say only what you know to be true. Hence, from an utterance of a sentence *A or B*, the hearer can infer that the speaker is not in a position to assert *A and B*. This does not mean, though, that the speaker knows that *A and B* is false, but only that she does not know that *A and B* is true i.e $\neg K_s(S)$. The scalar implicature crucial to Gazdar's argument is thus stronger than that licensed by Quantity alone.

It is worth comparing what Gazdar takes to be the scalar implicature of a disjunction with the clausal implicatures he assumes. The rule for clausal implicatures is that if a speaker asserts a sentence S with constituent φ, and S entails neither φ nor ¬φ, then S clausal-implicates that the speaker does not know that φ and that the speaker does not know that ¬φ: $\neg K_s(\varphi)$ and $\neg K_s(\neg \varphi)$. Following this rule, a disjunction *A or B* clausal-implicates that the speaker does not know that A, does not know that not A, does not know that B and does not know that not B i.e.:

(77) *A or B* clausal-implicates $\neg K_s(A)$, $\neg K_s(\neg A)$, $\neg K_s(B)$, $\neg K_s(\neg B)$

In this case, Gazdar does assume that what is implicated is merely absence of knowledge. Notice further that in this case we cannot possibly "push the negation through" in these inferences, and go from, for instance, $\neg K_s(A)$ to $K_s(\neg A)$. If we did, then disjunctions would carry implicatures inconsistent both with each other and with the asserted content of the disjunction.

The point made here has been noted by a number of authors. Groenendijk and Stokhof (1984) note the difference in strength of scalar and clausal implicatures, and object that the move to the stronger inference is unmotivated. Levinson (1983: 135), while accepting the argument given in (76) above, notes that "it equivocates between the inference ... 'Speaker does not know that [*S*]' and 'Speaker knows that not [*S*].'" He claims that scalar implicatures generally license the stronger inference, while other Quantity implicatures license only the weaker, and concludes that "why this should be remains one of the many mysteries in this area." Horn (1989:543 n.5), in his presentation of the derivation of scalar implicatures, objects to "the institutionalization of the move from ¬K(p) (speaker does not know for a fact that p...is true) to K¬(p) (speaker knows that p ...is not true)." In the sample derivation that he gives, this move is licensed by a further assumption on the part of the hearer that the speaker has all the information she would need to determine whether or not p is true. Soames (1982: 455-6), apparently the first to object in print to Gazdar's scalar implicature rule, also points out that the Maxim of Quantity licenses only the weaker implicature (¬K(p)). He goes on to say, like Horn, that the stronger implicature, K(¬p), is derivable only when the context of utterance and the content of the assertion justify the presumption that the speaker knows the truth value of p.

Combined with this presumption, the Maxim of Quantity does indeed predict that from an utterance of *A or B*, the hearer may infer that either A is false or B is false. Suppose that the hearer has evidence that the speaker knows the truth value of the stronger *A and B*. If the speaker knows *A and B* to be true, then she ought to say this, by Quantity. As she has not, she must know *A and B* to be false. *A and B* is false just in case either A is false or B is false. Hence, it must be the case that only one of A and B is true. This is the exclusive interpretation.

One objection to this account of the exclusive reading is that the situations in which a hearer could legitimately assume the speaker to know the truth value of the conjunction seem rather limited, while the exclusive interpretation is very common. A more straightforward objection is that the inference strategy suggested does not generalize to disjunctions with more than two disjuncts. However many disjuncts there are, if we interpret the disjunction exclusively, we infer that one and only one disjunct is true. The exclusive interpretation never surfaces as an inference that, say, at most two of the disjuncts are true. Now, suppose a speaker has uttered a three-disjunct disjunction, *A or B or C*. We observe that she has chosen this form, rather than the stronger *A and B and C*. Suppose further that we have reason to believe that the speaker knows the truth value of the stronger proposition. Again, by reason of Quantity, we can infer that she knows the stronger proposition to be false. What we can infer then, is the following:

(78)   (A or B or C) & ¬(A and B and C)

But (78) does not entail that only one of A, B and C is true. It entails merely that at least one of A, B and C is false. So this reasoning still brings us to a weaker conclusion than is generally reached.

There are six other sentences isomorphic to *A or B or C* which lie on the scale between it and *A and B and C*:

(79) a. A and (B or C)   d. (A and B) or C
      b. C and (A or B)   e. (B and C) or A
      c. B and (A or C)   f. (A and C) or B

Suppose that it is one of these that the hearer believes the speaker to know to be false. Could this assumption in any case lead to the inference that only one of A, B and C is true?

The answer again is no. Any of (79a-c) can be rendered false by virtue of only one of their constituent clauses being false. So if we take the utterance of *A or B or C* as evidence of the falsehood of one of these sentences, we still cannot infer that only one of the three propositions is true.

All of (79d-f) can be rendered false only if at least two of their constituents are false. However, a speaker who knew one of these to be false would be in a position to make a stronger assertion than *A or B or C*. For instance, anyone who knew that (some instance of) (79d) was false would have to know that C was false. If she then said *A or B or C*, she would generally be in violation of Quantity, as she could have said ¬*C and (A or B)*, which is more informative. The same argument holds, mutatis mutandis, for (79e-f). Hence, none of these could form the basis of a Gricean argument from an utterance of *A or B or C* to the conclusion that only one of A, B and C is true.

Applied to a two-disjunct disjunction, the kind of Gricean argument proposed by Horn and by Soames does lead, validly, to the conclusion that only one disjunct is true. Perhaps, in the two disjunct case, and where all the necessary assumptions can be made, this is the reasoning that underlies the exclusive interpretation. But the exclusive interpretation also arises in multiple disjunct cases, where it cannot be licensed by the same kind of reasoning. So some other account is needed for these cases.

2.5.3. Exclusivity from exhaustiveness

Let me begin by reviewing some well known effects of the first part of the Maxim of Quantity. Suppose you ask me:

(80)   Where did Jane go for her vacation?

and I reply:

(81)   Sweden.

You will most likely understand me to mean that, to the best of my knowledge, Sweden was the only place Jane went. Grice's Maxim of Quantity provides an explanation for this. As a cooperative participant in this exchange, I should give you all the information which I have which is relevant to the purposes of the exchange. If I know that Jane went to Sweden and also somewhere else, I should tell you. As I didn't, you can assume that as far as I know, Jane went only to Sweden. What is more, because I know that you will make this assumption, then, if I am less than certain that Sweden was the only place Jane went, I should say so. Now, if you later find out that Jane went to both Sweden and Greenland, you will conclude one of two things: either I didn't have complete information, or I was, for some reason, not being as informative as I could have been, and so was misleading you. You won't, I think, conclude that what I said was *false*. I said that Jane went to Sweden, and indeed she did.

Now, suppose that when you asked me your question, I wasn't quite sure where Jane had been, and replied:

(82)   I'm not sure. Either Sweden or Greenland.

You are now most likely to understand me to mean that either Jane went to Sweden and not to Greenland, or that she went to Greenland and not to Sweden. In other words, you will interpret the disjunction exclusively. Again, should you later find out that in fact Jane went to both Sweden and Greenland, I think you will hold what I said to be strictly true, but will think that I was either not fully informed, or was being intentionally misleading.

Much of this chapter has been concerned with establishing the relation between disjuncts and answers. I have shown that in order for a disjunction to be felicitous, it must be possible to interpret each disjunct as a possible answer to a single question. If a disjunction is used to list a series of possible answers to a question, it seems reasonable to assume that each potential answer must in fact satisfy just the same requirements as an actual answer would have to, in particular, the requirement that it be maximally informative. In my reply to your question, I have offered two possible answers. One is "Jane went to Sweden," and the other is "Jane went to Greenland." By Quantity, you can assume that the first answer is equivalent to "Jane went to Sweden and nowhere else," and that the second is equivalent to "Jane went to Greenland and nowhere else." Given this interpretation of each disjunct, you are forced to understand that the truth of either one excludes the truth of the other, not because you assign to *or* the truth conditions of exclusive disjunction, but simply because the two disjuncts, under the given interpretation, are incompatible[5].

Now, suppose I do think it possible that Jane went to both Sweden and Greenland. Then, by Quantity, I should say so. In order to add this information, should I have it, I would say:

(83)   Sweden or Greenland, or both.

Note that *both* is given as an additional disjunct, that is, as an additional alternative, or an additional possibly correct answer to the question asked. This contrasts with the response:

(84)   Sweden or Greenland, but not both.

Not both is added as a conjunct, that is, as a further piece of information distinct from the disjunction.

One might wonder why it would ever be necessary to add *but not both*, if the disjuncts are always interpreted as I have suggested. I think that the added conjunct serves to reinforce, by explicit assertion, what is otherwise there only by implicature. This is not uncommon. Consider:

(85)   I can take three people in my car, but not more.

(86) I have visited some, but not all, of the major capitals of the world.

(87) Jane turned up for the meeting, but no-one else did.

Notice that in all of these examples, the conjunction used is *but*, just as in (84).

If exclusivity is indeed a function of completeness, then in any context in which completeness of information is not expected, disjuncts should not be understood exclusively. This seems to be the case. Suppose I am telling you about my plan to go somewhere possibly dangerous. Concerned about my safety, you say that you hope I will have at least one person with me. I reply:

(88) Oh, yes, Jane will come with me for sure.

This doesn't seem to exclude the possibility that other people will come with me too. The point of my response is not to give you complete information about who is coming with me, but merely to assure you that I will not be alone. The Maxim of Quantity does not, in this case, demand completeness of information. Similarly, if I reply:

(89) Oh, yes, Jane or George will come with me for sure.

I don't imply that Jane and no one else or George and no one else will come with me. The reason, I think, is the same. The question did not demand an exhaustive answer, and so the disjuncts are not interpreted exhaustively[6].

Here, I have relied on an intuitive appreciation of when a question requires an exhaustive answer and when not. Eventually, we will want a developed theory of when and why questions demand exhaustive answers. The point I wish to make here is that there is a correlation between the requirement of exhaustivity, and the interpretation of a disjunction as exclusive.

Groenendijk and Stokhof (1984) give a similar account of the exclusive reading of disjunction. Their account differs from mine in a crucial particular: while I have suggested that each disjunct is interpreted pragmatically as exhausting a given option, they argue that this interpretation is part of the semantics. Their account is part of a general theory of linguistic questions and answers. One observation which they wish to account for is the observation made above, that in the context of a question, a sentence is generally interpreted as giving a complete specification of the answer. Thus, for instance, in the context of (80), (81) is interpreted as (81a). (I repeat the examples here.)

(80) Where did Jane go for her vacation?
(81) Sweden.
(81a) Jane went to Sweden and nowhere else.

I have suggested that this observation is best accounted for as a Gricean effect. On this view, (81) and (81a) are truth conditionally distinct. Groenendijk and Stokhof, however, choose to account for this semantically, that is, they assign to (81) the truth conditions of (81a). They accomplish this using a semantic function which they call *exhaustivization*, and represent as *exh*. *exh* is a function which applies to a set of sets and gives back the smallest member of that set. It can thus be applied to anything which denotes a set of sets. As an example, consider the generalized quantifier interpretation of proper names, under which names denote sets of sets of individuals. So, for instance:

(90) *Jane* ==> $\lambda P[P(j)] = \{X : jane \in X\}$

Application of the exhaustivization function to this set gives back the unit set of the set containing Jane.

What is relevant for our purposes here is that the exhaustified form of a disjunction is always the disjunction of the exhaustified form of each disjunct. Thus, in the context of (80), (91) is interpreted as in (92):

(91) Jane went to Sweden or Greenland
(92) Jane went to *exh*(Sweden) $\vee$ *exh*(Greenland)

Just as I have proposed, the disjunction is understood exclusively, in the sense that the two disjuncts are understood as mutually incompatible. For Groenendijk and Stokhof, though, this interpretation is truth conditional. If it is in fact the case that Jane went to both Sweden and Greenland, then what I said will be literally false on their account.

Groenendijk and Stokhof themselves note that answers are not always interpreted as exhaustive, and they assume that pragmatic factors are responsible for determining when they are so interpreted, and when not. They propose that where the context indicates that complete information is not expected or required, a sentence serving as an answer receives its usual, unstrengthened interpretation. In other words, hearers must use pragmatic inferences to determine whether or not the semantic interpretation of an answer should include the exhaustivization operation. This seems somewhat redundant. The semantic account needs all of the elements of the pragmatic account, but does not seem to make any welcome predictions which are not made by the pragmatic account. Moreover, the exhaustive inference has some of the hallmarks of implicature: it can be reinforced without redundancy and defeated without contradiction, as in (93) and (94):

(93)   Jane went to Sweden and nowhere else.
(94)   Jane went to Sweden and perhaps somewhere else.

These are properties which distinguish implicatures from entailments.

I will continue to assume that the pragmatic account of exhaustiveness is correct. But whether exhaustiveness is treated as a product of semantics or of pragmatics, the fundamental idea is the same: disjunctions are interpreted exclusively because disjuncts are interpreted exhaustively. Interpreted in this way, they are necessarily mutually exclusive, and so the truth of one excludes the truth of any other.

2.5.4. Exclusivity from alternativeness

Another source of the exclusive reading of disjunctions is the assumption that disjunctions meet their felicity conditions: that each disjunct provides an answer to the same question, and that the answers are distinct in the sense discussed above.

Consider (95) (due to Barbara Partee, p.c.):

(95)   Either Jane is working or she's in the library.

Given this disjunction out of the blue, we undoubtedly infer from it that it is not the case that Jane is working in the library. In other words, we interpret the disjunction exclusively. Moreover, we would tend to infer further from this that it is generally the case that Jane does not work in the library. But it isn't clear how exhaustiveness applies here. Even if the first disjunct is interpreted as "Jane is working and doing nothing else," it does not rule out the possibility of her being in the library.

Consider, though, the questions which this disjunction could most obviously be used to address. One is "What is Jane doing?" and the other is "Where is Jane?" Suppose that the disjunction is intended to give an answer to the first of these. Then it must be the case that Jane's being in the library entails that she is doing something in particular (or at least excludes some possibilities). But if it entails that she is working, then the information conveyed by the second disjunct would be identical to that conveyed by the first with respect to the question under discussion. This would incur a violation of Simplicity, and render the disjunction infelicitous. Hence, if the disjunction is to be an acceptable answer to "What is Jane doing?" it must be the case that where Jane works is not the library.

Similarly, if the disjunction is to provide an answer to the question "Where is Jane?" it must be the case that Jane's working entails that she is in a particular place, or excludes some possibilities. But if it entails that she is in the library, then again, the disjunction would be in violation of Simplicity. Consequently, for the disjunction to constitute an acceptable answer to either of the two questions it could most obviously be used to answer, it must be the case that Jane does not work in the library.

Thus, the exclusive reading of this disjunction appears to be a consequence of the fact that the two questions we have considered are the most obvious candidates for questions which the disjunction would be used to answer. Evidence for this is provided by the observation that in the context of other questions, the disjunction is less likely to be read as exclusive. For example, offered in answer to the question:

(96)   Why isn't Jane answering her telephone?

our disjunction does not seem to imply that Jane is not working in the library.

2.5.5. Summary

What emerges from this discussion is that the exclusive reading of disjunctions may have different sources in different cases. The reasoning suggested by Soames and Horn is valid for the two disjunct case, as long as it can indeed be assumed that the speaker knows the truth value of the stronger assertion. However, in any case in which disjuncts are interpreted as exhaustive answers, this reasoning will be redundant, as the disjuncts will simply be interpreted as mutually exclusive. In cases like (95) above, the exclusivity inference is motivated by the assumption that the speaker is not violating Simplicity, which requires the disjuncts to be differently informative with respect to some issue. But in no case does the exclusive interpretation arise from assigning to *or* the truth conditions of exclusive disjunction [7].

2.6. CONCLUSION

In this chapter, I have identified a number of conditions which disjunctions must satisfy in order to meet general Gricean requirements of informativity. First, I've shown that it must be possible to identify a question to which each disjunct provides a possible answer. The answers offered by the disjuncts must be differently informative with respect to the question. This rules out entailing disjuncts. It also rules out non-entailing disjuncts where the answer provided by one disjunct entails the answer provided by another. In addition, I've shown that each disjunct must contribute to the overall informativity of the disjunction. No disjunct may be either entailed by or inconsistent with the context in which it is uttered.

In the chapters that follow, I will continue to make reference to these felicity conditions. I will show that once we assume that interpretation is constrained by felicity, much of the behavior of disjunction with respect to presupposition projection and cross-clausal anaphora can be explained without attributing to *or* any semantic complexity.

NOTES

1. Hurford in fact claims that "the joining of two sentences by *or* is unacceptable if one sentence entails the other; otherwise, the use of *or* is acceptable." As we have already seen, this biconditional formulation of the generalization is too strong.
2. As discussed in Chapter One, Stalnaker's model makes no provision for belief revision.
3. This generalization holds as long as the normal intonation pattern of a disjunctive assertion is maintained. If *somewhere* is given focal stress and the rest of the second disjunct is given rising intonation (something like question intonation), then *at least* can be omitted.
4. The definition is actually a little more complicated than this, to deal with embedded clauses, but we can set this aside here.
5. Barrett and Stenner (1971) and Pellettier (1977) both make the point that we should not confuse disjunctive sentences in which the disjuncts are incompatible with disjunctions which are interpreted as exclusive disjunction.
6. This example came up in conversation with Ed Gettier.
7. Just for the record, note that Grice himself does not discuss the exclusive interpretation of *or*. He is concerned, in *Further Notes on Logic and Conversation*, with a different purported ambiguity of *or*, between a truth functional and a "strong" non-truth functional meaning.

CHAPTER THREE
Presupposition Projection

3.1. INTRODUCTION

3.1.1. The Basic Question

I introduced the notion of presupposition, and the related question of presupposition projection, in Chapter One. Let me begin by reviewing these notions. The view of presupposition I adopt is the pragmatic view advocated by Stalnaker. On this view, to say that a speaker presupposes a proposition p is to say that a speaker is disposed to act in her linguistic behavior as if p is commonly assumed by all participants in the discourse. A sentence presupposes p if utterance of that sentence by a speaker would normally be inappropriate unless the speaker presupposed p, in the sense just defined. As we can assume that speakers generally intend to speak appropriately, we can say that a sentence presupposes p if its utterance by a speaker indicates that the speaker presupposes p.

The question of presupposition projection arises from the observation that complex sentences often, but not always, presuppose whatever would be presupposed by their constituent clauses, if those clauses were uttered in isolation. Adopting some terminology from Van der Sandt (1988), let's use the term *elementary presuppositions* for those presuppositions that a simple clause usually has when uttered in isolation. When the elementary presuppositions of the constituents of a complex sentence are also presuppositions of the complex sentence itself, we say that the presuppositions are *projected* to the complex sentence, or are *inherited* by it. For example, the sentence in (1) has as an elementary presupposition the proposition that Jane has a sister, and this presupposition projects to the disjunctions in (2) and (3), of which (1) is a constituent.

(1)   Jane's sister lives in Seneca Falls.
(2)   Either Jane's sister lives in Seneca Falls, or Harriet does.
(3)   Either Harriet lives in Seneca Falls, or Jane's sister does.

This observation might lead us to conclude that a disjunction simply inherits the elementary presupposition of its disjuncts. However, this is not always the case. (4) and (5) also have as an elementary presupposition the proposition that Jane has a sister, but in these cases, the presupposition is not inherited by the disjunction as a whole.

(4)   Either Jane has no sister, or her sister lives in Seneca Falls.
(5)   Either Jane's sister lives in Seneca Falls, or she has no sister.

The question with which this chapter will be concerned is just when a disjunction inherits the elementary presuppositions of its disjuncts, when it does not, and why.

3.1.2. The Theoretical Issues

As I discussed in Chapter One (section 1.2.), Stalnaker (1973) offered a simple account of the pattern of presupposition projection in conjunctions, using his own model of presupposition and assertion. This account then served as the basis for a general account of presupposition projection proposed by Heim (1983), and developed in particular by Beaver (1995a). Heim's proposal is that patterns of presupposition projection and non-projection in complex sentences are a consequence of the particular context update procedure required by the complex sentence. The account thus relies on stating an update procedure, or context change potential (CCP), for sentences of arbitrary complexity. (See Chapter One, section 1.3.2.3., for presentation of the notion of CCP.)

I begin the theoretical discussion in this chapter by discussing these CCP-based accounts in detail (section 3.3). I focus on two definitions for the CCP of disjunction that have been made in the literature, and show that neither of them suffices to account for the projection data. I will argue, in fact, that the presupposition properties of disjunction cannot be accounted for in parallel fashion to those of conjunction. This argument supports a claim originally put forward by Soames (1989).

The question then remains whether one can account for the projection properties of disjunction within a Stalnakerian framework in a way which meets the desiderata Stalnaker proposed, these being that the account be given "in terms of general maxims of rational communication rather than in terms of complicated and *ad hoc* hypotheses about the semantics of particular words and particular kinds of constructions" (1974: 198). I will argue that such an account can be given. Indeed, an account of this kind has already been proposed, by Van der Sandt (1992). The account I will defend is a "translation" into the Stalnakerian framework of the Van der Sandtian account.

In section 3.4. I set out the various component pieces of the account. The first piece is the idea that the projection of elementary presuppositions is to some extent determined by general conversational principles. This idea was first incorporated into an account of presupposition projection by Gazdar (1979), who developed a "cancellation" theory of presupposition projection, according to which elementary presuppositions are canceled if they conflict with a conversational implicature. I begin section 3.4. with a review of Gazdar's theory.

The second component of the account is an extension of the original notion of accommodation. Originally, accommodation was conceived as a modification of the context to which the content of an assertion is to be added. Heim (1983b) dubs this procedure *global accommodation*. But as Heim points out, once context update is understood as an incremental procedure, the possibility arises of modifying just the immediate context to which a constituent of a complex clause is added, a process which she calls *local accommodation*. Van der Sandt shows how the kinds of principles which, in Gazdar's theory, lead to presupposition cancellation, can be seen as constraining accommodation, sometimes forcing accommodation to be local. This will be a crucial element of the proposal I will defend.

The first step, though, is to describe in more detail the facts which are to be accounted for.

3.2. THE DATA

To talk about presupposition projection, we must first identify a set of presupposition triggers, and the presuppositions to which they give rise. Here, I will adopt some standard assumptions. In (PT), I list the presupposition triggers which I will use in my examples, illustrating the kinds of presupposition I assume they give rise to.

(PT)   Presupposition Triggers

Definite descriptions
(6)   My cat has got out.
       Presupposes: speaker has a cat

Factive verbs
(7)   I know that it is raining
       Presupposes: it is raining.

Clefts
(8)   It was a cat that got out.
       Presupposes: something got out

In my examples, I will also often use proper names. These, perhaps, carry a presupposition that there is an individual who bears that name, but I shall ignore this presupposition.

I have already illustrated the basic pattern of presupposition projection in disjunctions. In the basic case, a clausal disjunction inherits the elementary presuppositions of all of its disjuncts. For example, (9) and (10) each inherit the elementary presupposition of the clause *Jane's sister lives in Seneca Falls*, and (11) inherits the elementary presuppositions of both of its disjuncts.

(9)   Either Jane's sister lives in Seneca Falls, or Harriet does.
(10)   Either Harriet lives in Seneca Falls, or Jane's sister does.
       Presuppose: Jane has a sister

(11)   Either Maud's cat has got out, or she is hiding from Henry's dog.
       Presupposes: Maud has a cat and Henry has a dog.

However, as we've seen, elementary presuppositions do not always project. If an elementary presupposition of some disjunct is incompatible with the content of another disjunct, that elementary presupposition does not project. For example, the second disjunct of (12) presupposes that Jane has siblings. This proposition, though, is incompatible with the content of the first disjunct, the proposition that Jane is an only child. In this case, the presupposition does not project, that is, (12) as whole does not presuppose that Jane has siblings. The same is true of (13), which is identical to (12) except that the order of the disjuncts is reversed. (14-15) illustrate the same point, with a different presupposition.

(12)   Either Jane is an only child, or she dislikes her siblings.
(13)   Either Jane dislikes her siblings, or she is an only child.
       No presuppositions

(14)   Either no one understood that paper, or it was George who did.
(15)   Either it was George who understood that paper, or no one did.
       No presuppositions

There is a second case in which the elementary presuppositions of disjunctions fail to project. This is when the presuppositions themselves are incompatible, as illustrated in (16)[1]:

(16)   Either George regrets telling the truth, or he has discovered that he inadvertently lied.

The first disjunct of (16) presupposes that George told the truth, and the second that he lied. Neither presupposition projects.

There has been some debate as to whether the presupposition does or does not project in examples like (13) and (15), where the "incompatible" disjunct follows the presupposing disjunct. Karttunen (1973a) rejected such examples as ungrammatical, and the projection rules which he formulated for disjunction in that paper were asymmetric, predicting felicitous non-projection only when the second disjunct is presupposing.

Soames (1979) countered this claim, and since then, it has been generally assumed in the literature (including by Karttunen himself, in later work) that the projection properties of disjunction are symmetric: whether it is the first or the second disjunct which bears the presupposition, the presupposition will not project if it is incompatible with the content of the other disjunct.

The symmetry of disjunction contrasts with the asymmetry of the projection behavior of other connectives. Consider, for instance, conjunction. In a conjunction [A and B], any presupposition of B which is entailed by A will fail to project, as illustrated by (17):

(17) Jane visited George, but he has forgotten that she visited.

If the order is reversed, and the second conjunct entails a presupposition of the first, the result is infelicitous[2]:

(18) #George has forgotten that Jane visited him, but she visited him.

Sentence concatenation works in the same way. If we concatenate the clauses in (17) and (18), leaving out the connective, the "forwards" case is fine, with no presupposition projection, but the "backwards" case is infelicitous. There is thus a clear contrast between the asymmetric projection behavior of conjunction and sentence concatenation, and the symmetric behavior of disjunction.

The observation that order is irrelevant to the projection facts applies also to disjunctions of more than two clauses. Neither (19) nor (20) inherit the presupposition that Jane has a car:

(19) Either Jane doesn't have a car any more, or her car is in the shop, or she lent her car to her mother this weekend.
(20) Either Jane has lent her car to her mother this weekend, or her car is in the shop, or she doesn't actually have a car any more.

There is, though, one class of examples where the order of the disjuncts seems to make a difference. These are examples involving the presupposition triggers which Kripke (ms) has argued to be anaphoric: *too* and *again*. For instance, many speakers find (22) somewhat odd as compared with (21):

(21) Either we won't invite Henry, or we'll invite George too.
(22) ?Either we'll invite George too, or we won't invite Henry.

Standardly, the sentence *we'll invite George too* would be taken to presuppose that we are going to invite someone (from some salient domain) other than George. Kripke suggests (simplifying somewhat) that the presupposition of this sentence is correctly characterized as "George is distinct from a," where a is some previously mentioned individual. *Too* is thus anaphoric in that it requires an antecedent expression to provide a value for a.

If this were so, we would expect to find a parallel between this case and the standard case of pronominal anaphora across disjunction. This is indeed the case. A pronoun in one disjunct can easily be co-referential with a proper name in a preceding disjunct, but co-reference is harder when the order of pronoun and antecedent is switched. This is illustrated in (23)-(24).

(23) Either George dislikes Cleo or he is afraid of her.
(24) ?Either he dislikes her, or George is afraid of Cleo.

(24) would be fine if George and Cleo were already under discussion, but somewhat hard to process if this were the first mention of them in the discourse. The same is true of (22).

Given that "backwards" anaphora is quite highly constrained, it is not surprising that (24) is somewhat infelicitous. Similarly, if *too* has anaphoric properties, as Kripke suggests, then it is not surprising that it prefers to occur following its antecedent. But the behavior of *too* should not obscure the observation that presupposition projection in disjunction is, in general, symmetric, and contrasts sharply with the behavior of conjunction. So, following the earlier literature on presupposition projection (Gazdar (1979), Karttunen and Peters (1979), Soames (1979, 1982)), I hold that an adequate treatment of the projection properties of disjunction must predict that order is irrelevant.

3.3. THE SATISFACTION ACCOUNT OF PRESUPPOSITION PROJECTION

3.3.1. Basics of the Satisfaction Account.

Recall from Chapter One, section 1.2, the explanation that Stalnaker (1973) offers for the projection properties of conjunction. Suppose that a speaker asserts (25).

(25)   Jane visited George but he forgot that she visited him.

To update a context with (25), hearers will first update the context with the content of the first conjunct, *Jane visited George*, and only then incorporate the content of the second. Now ordinarily, a hearer who encountered the sentence *George forgot that Jane visited him* out of the blue would take the speaker to presuppose that Jane visited George, that is, to take this proposition to be in the context. But in this case, the speaker has gone to the trouble to introduce the proposition into the context, by making it the first conjunct. Therefore, there is reason to believe that the speaker did not take the proposition to be in the starting context.

In Heim's CCP framework, this kind of account is formalized and extended to all standard cases of non-projection. In this framework, as we have seen, sentences are assigned a context change potential, or CCP. The CCP is a function from contexts to contexts, defined recursively for complex sentences on the basis of the CCPs of the constituent clauses. Presuppositional requirements are captured by treating presuppositions as definedness conditions on update functions, which constrain the contexts to which the CCP of a presupposing sentence can successfully be applied. For any sentence S and context c, c+S (the result of updating c with S) is defined only if any presuppositions of S are true at every world in c. In other words, c must always entail the presuppositions of S. I will say, in this case, that c *satisfies* the presuppositions of S.

Because the CCPs of complex expressions are defined recursively, the definedness of the overall update operation will depend on the definedness of each of the intermediate updates. (It is assumed that undefinedness of any intermediate update results in undefinedness of the operation as a whole. This is reminiscent of the treatment of undefinedness in the weak Kleene logic, where, if any constituent of a complex sentence is undefined, so is the complex sentence itself, regardless of the truth values of other constituents.) These recursive definitions also have the effect that the presuppositional conditions of a constituent clause may be satisfied in its *local context* without being satisfied in the starting context to which the complex sentence as a whole is added. It is when this happens that elementary presuppositions fail to project.

As illustration of the framework, let's see how Stalnaker's informal explanation of the projection properties of conjunction is expressed in the CCP framework. The CCP schema for conjunctive sentences is given in (26):

(26)   c+[A and B] = [c+A]+B

What (26) says is that in order to update a context c with a sentence of the form *A and B*, first apply the CCP of A to c, and then apply the CCP of B to the result of the first operation. Now, because the CCP of A, the first conjunct, applies to c, c must satisfy A's presuppositional requirements, that is, it must entail any presuppositions of A. But the CCP of B applies to [c+A]. So it is not c, but [c+A], which is required to entail the presuppositions of the second conjunct, B.

Now, consider example (27). Intuitively, the conjunction as a whole inherits the presupposition of the second conjunct, that Jane has siblings.

(27)   Jane gets along with her parents, but she dislikes her siblings.

Letting A be the first disjunct, and B the second, [c+A] will be defined only if c entails that Jane has parents. [c+A]+B will be defined only if [c+A] entails that Jane has siblings. As the content of A says nothing about whether or not Jane has siblings, this condition will be satisfied only if c itself entails that Jane has siblings. So the definedness conditions of B (indirectly) impose a condition on c.

Now, compare (27) with (28), which intuitively does not inherit the presupposition of the second conjunct.

(28)   Jane has a brother and a sister, but she dislikes her siblings.

The first conjunct of (28) has no presuppositions, so its CCP imposes no presuppositional requirements on c. [c+A]+B is again defined only if [c+A] entails that Jane has siblings. But given that A itself entails that Jane has siblings, this condition will be satisfied for any c. So in this case, B imposes no condition on c. Its presuppositional requirements are satisfied in the local context to which its CCP applies by virtue of the content of the first conjunct.

Presupposition projection is thus understood as the case in which an update operation is defined relative to c only if c itself satisfies the presuppositional requirement. Non-projection is understood to occur when the presuppositional requirement is met locally without being met globally. In conjunctions, this situation comes about when the first conjunct contextually entails the presupposition of the next, and is due to the interaction of the recursive CCP and the content of the first conjunct. If it is assumed that this mechanism of local satisfaction is what is generally responsible for projection failure, then CCPs must be constructed in such a way as to ensure that in just those cases in which a presupposition fails to project, it is locally satisfied by virtue of the recursive definition. This is the strategy used in the two accounts I discuss in the next section.

3.3.2. CCPs for disjunction

The basic intuition underlying the CCPs for disjunction is that sentences like (29) are interpreted as in (30):

(29)   Either Jane isn't here, or George knows that she is.
(30)   Either Jane isn't here, or she is here and George knows that she is.

(29) has the form *A or B*. (30) has the form *A or [¬A and B]*. The two are truth-conditionally equivalent. But whereas the second disjunct of (29) bears a presupposition, the second disjunct of (30) does not. For the second disjunct of (30) is a conjunction whose first conjunct entails the presupposition of the second and so, by virtue of the projection properties of conjunction, the disjunct as a whole bears no presupposition.

This intuition is spelled out formally in several different proposals. Abstracting away from details of the various frameworks, these proposals can be translated into the terms of the basic CCP framework as follows:

(31)   c + [A or B] = [c + A] ∪ [c + ¬A] + B

(32)   c + [A or B] = c + ¬[¬A & ¬B]

(31) is a "translation" of proposals due to Roberts (1989) and Kamp and Reyle (1993). Both of these proposals were originally made to account for anaphora across disjunction, and not for presupposition projection. Nonetheless, the claims which are made point towards a satisfaction account of presupposition projection, so it is worth seeing how well the proposals fare in this respect. I will reconsider them with respect to the anaphora data in Chapter Four.

(32) is used in Beaver (1995a and elsewhere) as part of an explicit satisfaction account of presupposition projection in a CCP framework. It is also proposed by Groenendijk and Stokhof (1990) as one of three definitions for the semantics of disjunction in Dynamic Montague Grammar.

It will be useful to have names for each of the CCPs, for later ease of reference. In the CCP in (31), the second disjunct is supplemented with the negation of the first, so I will call this the *supplemented disjunct* proposal. The CCP in (32) capitalizes on the logical equivalence between [A∨B] and ¬[¬A&¬B], so I will call it the *logical equivalence* proposal.

Both of these proposals define the update procedure for disjunction in terms of the update procedures for conjunction and negation, so we need first to know what these procedures are. The CCP for conjunction, which I introduced above, is repeated in (33), and the CCP for negation is given in (34):

(33)   c + [A and B] = [c+A]+B
(34)   c + ¬S = c-[c+S]

(34) says that to update a context with a negated sentence ¬S, calculate c+S (i.e. c∩S) and then remove (subtract) all of the worlds in this set from c.

We can now use (33) and (34) to spell out the definitions in (31) and (32). In the final step of each calculation, look for the formula in bold print which immediately precedes "+A" and "+B". This will show you which context is the local context for each disjunct, and thus which context is required to satisfy the presuppositions of each disjunct.

(31') c + [A or B] = [c + A] ∪ [c + ¬A] + B
     = [c + A] ∪ [**[c-[c+A]]** + B]

(32') c + [A or B] = c + ¬[¬A & ¬B]
     = c - [c+[¬A & ¬B]]
     = c - [[c+¬A]+¬B]
     = c - [[c-[c+A]]+¬B]
     = c - [[c-[c+A]] - [**[c-[c+A]]**+B]]

In both cases, the local context for A, the first disjunct, is just c itself. The local context for B is, in both cases, [c-[c+A]], which is the result of eliminating from c any worlds at which A is true: more simply, the result of updating c with the negation of A. Both CCPs thus make the same predictions: that any presuppositions in A will always impose constraints on the global context, and so will project, but the presuppositions of B impose constraints on [c+¬A]. So if ¬A entails any presupposition of B, that presupposition will place no constraints on c itself, and the presupposition will not project.

It will be immediately obvious that there is a discrepancy between these predictions and the claims I made in the data section. There, I argued that the projection properties of disjunction are symmetric. These CCPs, though, are asymmetric. There are various other empirical difficulties too. I'll address these in the following sections. Throughout these discussions, we will also want to keep in mind the question of what it means to assign these CCPs to disjunctive sentences. I will turn to this question at the end of the section.

3.3.3. Critique
3.3.3.1. Symmetry

Both the supplemented disjunct and the logical equivalence proposals are inherently asymmetric. Both construct a local context for the second disjunct which includes the negation of the first, but not vice versa. Note that the conjunction which appears in the logical equivalence proposal is treated dynamically, and so is not commutative. Given the assumption that presuppositions fail to project just in case they are satisfied in their local context, these analyses predict that in a two disjunct disjunction, any presupposition of the second disjunct will fail to project if it is entailed by the negation of the first disjunct. But they predict that any presuppositions of the first disjunct must always be satisfied by the starting context, and therefore will always project. The prediction is thus that the projection properties of disjunction are asymmetric, or unidirectional, in contrast to what is actually observed.

Is there some way to modify these CCPs to make them symmetric? We could modify the supplemented disjunct CCP by conjoining the negation of the second disjunct with the content of the first, as follows:

(35) *Symmetric supplemented disjunct CCP*
c + [A or B] = [[c+¬B]+A] ∪ [[c+¬A]+B]
= [[c-[**c**+B]]+ A] ∪ [[c-[**c**+A]] + B]

But notice that now c constitutes the local context for each disjunct at some point in the derivation. (Note where c appears in boldface.) This CCP would thus predict, incorrectly, that the starting context must always satisfy the presuppositions of both disjuncts. This definition is symmetric, but it does not make the correct predictions.

The obvious way to make the logical equivalence CCP symmetric is as follows:

(36) *Symmetric Logical Equivalence CCP*
c + [A or B] = c + ¬[¬A & ¬B] ∪ c + ¬[¬B & ¬A]
= c-[[c-[**c**+A]]-[[c-[**c**+A]]+B]] ∪ c-[[c-[**c**+B]]-[[c-[**c**+B]]+A]]

But this suffers from just the same problem as the symmetric supplemented disjunct CCP: both A and B are, at some point, added directly to c. The reason we keep encountering this problem is simple. The basic idea is that each disjunct is added to a context which includes the negation of the other. But given the CCP for negation, calculating this requires calculating the result of adding that other disjunct to the starting context. If we do this with both disjuncts, we end up requiring that each disjunct be added to the starting context at some point. The only way around this would be to change the update procedure for negation. But the CCP given here for negation is not arbitrary. It captures the projection properties of negated sentences, which standardly inherit the elementary presuppositions of the clause embedded under the negation. And it is precisely this property of negated sentences which leads us into the difficulty observed with the CCPs for disjunction[3].

An alternative solution to the symmetry problem would be to assume that different mechanisms are at work in the "forwards" and "backwards" cases. But to invoke an additional mechanism would be to undermine the motivation for these CCPs. The CCPs are constructed, supposedly, to ensure that all standard cases of projection failure are cases of local satisfaction. But they do not, in fact, achieve this and, as Soames (1989) points out, there seems to be no way to construct a CCP for disjunction which would do so.

3.3.3.2. Conflicting Presuppositions

We saw in the data section that when disjunctions contain disjuncts with incompatible elementary presuppositions, the disjunction may be felicitous, but the presuppositions do not project. This kind of case has proved particularly problematic in the attempt to account for the projection properties of disjunction, and it is problematic for the two CCP-based proposals being considered here.

Examples (37-38) illustrate the phenomenon. (Example 37 is from Soames (1982)):

(37) Either George has just started smoking, or he's just stopped.

(38) [After seeing Henry give testimony in court, and noticing that he is unhappy]
Either he regrets that he told the truth, or he has realized that he inadvertently told a lie.

The first disjunct of (38) presupposes that Henry told the truth; the second, that Henry told a lie. Clearly, these presuppositions conflict: the speaker cannot simultaneously take for granted that Henry both told the truth and lied. The sentence as a whole is perfectly felicitous, however. It simply does not inherit the presupposition of either disjunct.

Both the supplemented disjunct proposal and the logical equivalence proposal make incorrect predictions with respect to such examples. Moreover, both CCPs give rise to the incorrect prediction for the same reason. Let's look first at the supplemented disjunct CCP. (39) spells out the calculation that would be required to update a context with (38) on this proposal:

(39)
(i)   c + Either he regrets that he told the truth, or he has realized that he inadvertently told a lie   =
(ii) c + he regrets that he told the truth ∪
      c + ¬(he regrets that he told the truth) + he has realized that he inadvertently told a lie

(39ii) shows that in the course of the context update, the starting context must be updated with the negation of the first disjunct, *he regrets that he told the truth*. Now, in order for this intermediate update to be defined, c must entail that Henry told the truth. Let's suppose that it does, and that this intermediate update goes through. The resulting context, [c+ ¬(he regrets that he told the truth)] will itself entail that Henry told the truth. This context then serves as the local context for the second disjunct, *he has realized that he inadvertently told a lie*. But in order for update with this disjunct to be defined, its local context must entail that Henry told a lie. Clearly, it does not. Moreover, if we attempt to accommodate this presupposition into [c+ ¬(he regrets that he told the truth)], we will derive a contradiction, the empty context. The CCP does not provide a way for the elementary presuppositions of both disjuncts to be satisfied, and therefore predicts that sentences such as these should be highly infelicitous. As we have seen, this is not the case.

The logical equivalence CCP faces exactly the same difficulty, as the last clause of (40) shows:

(40)
(i)   c + Either he regrets that he told the truth, or he has realized that he inadvertently told a lie   =
(ii)   c - ([c+ ¬(he regrets that he told the truth)] + ¬(he has realized that he inadvertently told a lie)

Here, we are required to calculate [c+ ¬(he regrets that he told the truth)], which requires that c entail that he told the truth. The result of the calculation will itself, in turn, entail that he told the truth. But this result is to serve as the local context for *he has realized that he inadvertently told a lie*, the local context for which must entail that he lied. This CCP, too, predicts that a single context will be required to meet contradictory requirements. Neither of these proposals, then, can account for disjunctions with conflicting presuppositions.

3.3.3.3. The correct generalization

Karttunen's original formulation of the projection properties of disjunction says that presuppositions of disjuncts project except where the presupposition of the second is entailed by the negation of the first. (Set aside for now the issue of symmetry, which is not relevant here.) I have used a somewhat different formulation of the generalization, due to Chierchia and McConnell-Ginet (1990), saying that presuppositions fail to project if they are contextually incompatible with the content of some disjunct. What I want to show here is that these two formulations are not equivalent, and that it is the latter which is empirically correct. The CCP proposals being considered here, however, aim to capture the first generalization, and so naturally make incorrect predictions with respect to examples which it does not cover.

(41-42) are typical of the examples on which Karttunen's generalization is based.

(41)   Either Jane is an only child, or she dislikes her siblings.
(42)   Either no one understood this paper, or it was George who did.

In these examples, Karttunen's formulation and the Chierchia and McConnell-Ginet formulation are interchangeable: the negation of the first disjunct entails the presupposition of the second, but also the presupposition entails the negation of the first disjunct (i.e. is incompatible with it). However, there are examples in which the two are not equivalent. (43) is one such[4]:

(43)   Either George has no grandchildren, or he has a poor relationship with his children.

The negation of the first disjunct is the proposition that George has grandchildren. In conjunction with the usual assumptions about how people come to have grandchildren, this entails that George has children, meeting the conditions of the Karttunen-style generalization. However, as it is quite possible for someone to have children but no grandchildren, it is not the case that the presupposition of the second disjunct is contextually incompatible with the content of the first.

Because the negation of the first disjunct entails the presupposition of the second, both the supplemented disjunct proposal and the logical equivalence proposal predict that the presupposition will be satisfied locally and thus will not project to the disjunction as a whole. However, I think it is very hard to read the sentence as failing to presuppose that George has children. As illustration, consider how odd it would be for the speaker of (43) to precede it by asserting that she doesn't know whether George has children or not.

Example (44) illustrates the same point.

(44)   [As soon as Jane gets to London, George will hear that she is in the country. So] Either Jane isn't yet in London, or George knows that she is in England.

Again, the negation of the first disjunct entails the presupposition of the second, but this presupposition projects.

These examples show that it is not the case that entailment by the negation of a disjunct guarantees non-projection of an elementary presupposition. This undermines the basic premiss of the CCP-based satisfaction accounts.

We can also construct examples in which the incompatibility condition holds, but the entailment condition doesn't. Here is one such:

(45) [Upon seeing George in what appears to be a state of undress] Either George is naked, or the skin-colored body suit he's wearing is a very good fit.

The negation of the first disjunct does not entail that there is a skin-colored body suit that George is wearing, even in the imagined context. He might, for instance, be wearing a see-through body suit. However, the elementary presupposition of the second disjunct, that there is a skin-colored body suit that George is wearing, is incompatible with the proposition that George is naked, which is the content of the first. The elementary presupposition does not project to the disjunction as a whole, validating the predictions of the incompatibility generalization. We therefore have reason to believe that it is the predictions of this generalization which our theoretical account should explain.

As an interesting aside, note that it is actually quite hard to construct examples of the sort in (45) which distinguish the two generalizations. Here is the problem. Consider example (46), a variant of an example in Heim (1983b), which Heim attributes to Stanley Peters:

(46) Either George has no children, or his sons are noisy.

This straightforwardly meets the incompatibility condition: George cannot simultaneously have sons (as presupposed by the second disjunct) and have no children. It apparently does not meet the entailment condition: the negation of the first disjunct does not entail that George has sons. However, the only way to make sense of the disjunction as a whole is to assume a background assumption that if George does have children, he has sons. But in conjunction with this background assumption, the negation of the first disjunct in fact does entail the presupposition of the second.

The question is why (46) should give rise to the observed implication. According to Karttunen and Peters (1979) and Soames (1982), this proposition is not merely an implication but a presupposition. Both accounts would generate the logically equivalent "either George has no children or he has sons" as a presupposition of the sentence. However, if it is a presupposition, it is not strictly a *linguistic* presupposition, for it is not triggered by any lexical item or syntactic construction. Rather, it arises from our attempts to construct a context in which the sentence would satisfy the felicity conditions of disjunction. Presented with this sentence "out of the blue," hearers attempt to construct a context containing a question to which each disjunct would provide a possible answer. One that springs to mind for example (46) is as follows. Let's suppose that we assume that boys are noisy and that girls are not. We've noticed that it's always quiet around George's house. Then we can conclude (46) – but only if we assume that if George does have children, then they are sons. Because the other possible explanation for George's quiet house is that he has only daughters.

It should be possible to eliminate the need for this assumption by constructing a situation in which George's having daughters would be irrelevant to the question under discussion. So far, any such situation has eluded me. However, it does not seem necessary for us to construct an account of the presupposition projection properties of disjunction which generates this proposition as a presupposition of the sentence. The implication arises by virtue of hearers' assumptions that the disjunction meets the necessary felicity conditions.

3.3.3.4. What is a CCP?

In the previous sections, I have shown a number of empirical shortcomings of the two CCP-based proposals I introduced. But there is also a more fundamental question to consider, which is whether there is independent justification for assuming that disjunctions give rise to the kind of complex context change operations which these CCPs assign to them.

As I have said a number of times by now, the CCP-based satisfaction accounts have their origins in Stalnaker's informal proposal as to how to account for the projection properties of conjunction. The original proposal relied on the assumption that the context update procedure for conjunction is incremental, with each conjunct added in turn to the context. This assumption, which is embodied in the CCP for conjunction, is founded on a very solid intuition that conjunctions are indeed understood incrementally. It is often the case that one conjunct provides the informational background against which to interpret other conjuncts. This, in turn, may give rise to temporal or causal implications, as in (47), which would naturally be understood to imply that Jane got her degree and *then* got an interesting job, and perhaps also as saying that she got a good job *because* she got her degree:

(47)   Jane got a degree in physics and she got a very interesting job.

It is possible to understand conjunctions in this way because in asserting a conjunction a speaker inevitably commits herself to the truth of all conjuncts. There is thus no obstacle to immediate assimilation of the content of each conjunct to the hearer's set of assumptions.

This, then, is the intuition that underlies the CCP for conjunction. What intuition underlies the proposed CCPs for disjunction? Let's look again at what I have been calling the supplemented disjunct CCP:

(48)   c+[A or B] = [c+A] ∪ [[c+¬A]+B]

Both Roberts (1989) and Kamp and Reyle (1993) motivate this CCP by observing that disjunctions tend to be interpreted as alternatives. This means, they suggest, that one disjunct is interpreted relative to the negation of the other. However, to the extent that this is true, it applies equally to all disjuncts, so the asymmetric supplemented disjunct CCP does not really capture this intuition. Moreover, as I have shown in Chapter Two, the tendency to interpret disjuncts as exclusive alternatives follows from general principles. There is no need for it to be incorporated explicitly into the update procedure. By doing so, we render the update procedure non-compositional, in that it includes material which is not present in the syntactic representation being interpreted.

The logical equivalence CCP, which I repeat here, is similarly problematic.

(49)   c+[A or B] = c+ ¬[¬A & ¬B] = c-([c+¬A]+¬B)

To begin with, it is odd to rely on logical equivalences in proposing a dynamic semantics for an expression, for one of the fundamental observations of dynamic semantic theories is that logically equivalent expressions are not necessarily dynamically equivalent. In other words, logically equivalent expressions do not necessarily have the same presupposition projection properties or license anaphoric relations in the same way. Conjunction, again, is the classic illustration of this. Although it is logically commutative, it is not dynamically commutative. Indefinites in the first conjunct can serve as antecedents to pronouns in later conjuncts, but not vice versa. And as we have seen, the projection properties of conjunction are not symmetric.

The logical equivalence CCP for disjunction seems to entail that the dynamic properties of disjunction are identical to those of sentences of the form ¬[¬A & ¬B]. Data of a somewhat different kind suggest that this is not the case. As I discuss in detail in Chapter Five, disjunctions of NPs can serve as antecedents to a pronoun in a following sentence (what Groenendijk and Stokhof (1990) call *external anaphora*). This is illustrated in (50).

(50)   Either a soprano or an alto will sing. She will perform Mozart.

The pronoun *she* is not dependent on either of the NP disjuncts, but means something like "whoever sings." No such reading is available for the pronouns in any of (52-54), the first sentences of which are natural language renderings of (51). (51), of course, is truth conditionally equivalent to the disjunction in (50).

(51)   ¬ [¬ [a soprano will sing] & ¬ [an alto will sing]]

(52)   #It's not the case that a soprano won't sing and an alto won't sing. She will perform Mozart.
(53)   #It's not the case that no soprano will sing and no alto will sing. She will perform Mozart.
(54)   #It's not the case that neither a soprano nor an alto will sing. She will perform Mozart.

In the dynamic frameworks currently under consideration, it is assumed that the CCP governs the possibilities for anaphora. So if a sentence of the form [φ or ψ] has the same CCP as ¬[¬φ and ¬ψ], the two should have identical anaphora properties. This is not the case.

Nonetheless, we still might ask whether the logical equivalence proposal expresses some intuition about how contexts are updated with disjunctions. One way to understand this CCP informally is that it defines a procedure for finding and eliminating the worlds in the context at which neither disjunct is true. In other words, given an assertion of a disjunction, we look for those worlds at which the disjunction is false, and eliminate them from the context. But this contrasts with the usual idea that update is a "positive" procedure, involving intersection of the context with the worlds at which the proposition expressed is true. This idea itself perhaps derives from the notion that to determine that a proposition is false is to determine that it is not true, i.e. the notion that truth is basic. This is what is reflected in the update procedure for negated sentences, in which the context is first intersected with the worlds at which the *non*-negated sentence is *true*. This set of worlds is then eliminated from the context. So it is hard to see why in the case of disjunction we should want to do things the other way around.

The logical equivalence CCP is also strongly non-compositional. There is no operation corresponding to disjunction, but there are operations corresponding to logical operators which are not present in the syntactic structure. But perhaps the most straightforward objection to the logical equivalence CCP is the complexity of the procedure that it postulates. It is clear what the final result of updating a context with a disjunction must be: we must be left with the set of worlds at which some disjunct is true. Considerations of simplicity would require that we maintain as simple a procedure as possible for attaining this result.

3.4. TOWARDS A NEW ACCOUNT

The CCP-based satisfaction accounts constitute one attempt to give a general account of presupposition projection within the Stalnakerian framework. I have shown that these accounts are unsatisfactory with respect to disjunction. In the remainder of this chapter, I will show that the disjunction data can, nonetheless, be accounted for within the Stalnakerian framework. However, we must give up the idea that presupposition projection is governed primarily by update procedures, and allow that it is also affected by general conversational principles. Given the pragmatic approach to presupposition, this is to be expected. Presupposition projection involves inferences made by a hearer about the assumptions of a speaker, and such inferences may sometimes be defeated by other conversational clues. This point goes back to a discussion in Stalnaker (1974:207-210).

The basic idea of the account is this. We have already seen that it is infelicitous to utter a disjunction one disjunct of which is incompatible with the context. To do so is to violate the Simplicity condition. Moreover, as we know from Grice, hearers tend to look for ways to give a felicitous interpretation to an utterance made. Thus, when one disjunct bears an elementary presupposition incompatible with the content of another disjunct, the hearer does not take the speaker to assume that proposition to be part of the context. Rather, she assumes it to be part of the possibility expressed by the relevant disjunct. So, she accommodates the presupposition into the *local context* to which the disjunct is added. The effect of this is that the presupposition does not project.

The most developed theory of how conversational principles affect presupposition projection is that of Gazdar (1979) so, as background, I begin this section with a review of his theory. In 3.4.2., we will see how Van der Sandt incorporates elements of a Gazdar type explanation into a DRT account. This DRT account provides the basis for the proposal I will make. Section 3.4.3 deals with some issues relating to the "translation" of the account from DRT to the Stalnakerian framework.

3.4.1. Gazdar's cancellation theory

Gazdar's theory is itself a kind of context change theory. For him, a context is a set of consistent propositions which is updated by the information contained in utterances. Gazdar is primarily interested in representing the information that discourse participants have about each other's knowledge, so the context is assumed to contain propositions of the form "*a* knows that p." Likewise, utterances are assumed to convey information about what the speaker knows, and only by extension about what the world is like. Utterances convey information about their speakers' knowledge in three different ways: through propositional content; through implicatures; and through presuppositions. Each type of information is added in a separate step, following the order just indicated. Each addition, moreover, is required to maintain consistency. Consequently, an elementary presupposition which is inconsistent with a proposition already in the context, with an implicature, or with any other elementary presupposition cannot be added, and so is "filtered" or "canceled." Presuppositions which survive this selection process are projected.

The consistency requirement is expressed in the notion of *satisfiable incrementation*. The satisfiable incrementation of a context X with a set Y of propositions is just the original context plus all those propositions in Y which cannot introduce inconsistency. A proposition y cannot introduce inconsistency just in case all consistent subsets of X∪Y are still consistent after addition of y. The formal definition is as follows[5]:

(55) *Definition of Consistency and of Satisfiable Incrementation*
 (i) cons(X) (i.e. X is consistent) iff X ⊬ ⊥
 (ii) X∪!Y (the satisfiable incrementation of X with Y) =
  X ∪ { y∈Y : ∀Z ⊆ (X∪Y) (cons(Z) → cons(Z ∪ {y})) }

In calculating the update of a context with the information contained in an utterance, we reach a point at which the propositional content and all mutually consistent conversational implicatures have been added. The final step is to calculate the satisfiable incrementation of the updated context with the set of all elementary presuppositions of the utterance (what Gazdar calls its *potential presuppositions*). As the updated context already contains all of the implicatures of the utterance, any presuppositions which conflict with an implicature cannot be added. Moreover, the definition of satisfiable incrementation entails that any potential presuppositions which are mutually inconsistent also cannot be added.

Let's see now how this works in the case of disjunction. Consider for example:

(56) Either Jane is an only child or she dislikes her siblings.

The clausal implicatures of (56) are listed in (57), and its elementary presupposition in (58)[6]. Note that Gazdar takes presuppositions, too, to be propositions about the knowledge of the speaker, of the form "speaker knows that p," and that is how I have represented the presuppositions here.

(57) ¬K_s(Jane is an only child)
 ¬K_s¬(Jane is an only child)
 ¬K_s(Jane dislikes her siblings)
 ¬K_s¬(Jane dislikes her siblings)

(58) K_s(Jane has siblings)

The presupposition is inconsistent with the first two clausal implicatures[7]. As the implicatures are added first, addition of the presupposition would lead to inconsistency. Hence, the presupposition is not added to the context, and does not project.

Note that the order of the disjuncts is irrelevant in this explanation, so the symmetry of presupposition projection is straightforwardly accounted for. So too is the non-projection of conflicting presuppositions, as in (59)[8]:

(59)　Either Fred knows that he's won or he's upset that he hasn't.

The elementary presuppositions of (59) are:

(60)　K_S(Fred has won)
　　　K_S(Fred hasn't won)

As these are mutually inconsistent, the rule for satisfiable incrementation rules out adding either of them to the context.

The basic intuition here is that presuppositions are defeasible inferences, an idea that is compatible with (although not required by) the Stalnakerian treatment of presupposition. But Gazdar's particular proposal raises a question: Why is it that implicatures always cancel presuppositions, and not vice versa? It would, after all, be natural to expect things to be the other way around. Presuppositions, intuitively, are propositions which constitute the necessary background of an utterance. Implicatures are inferences which arise from the utterance of a given sentence in a particular context. Presuppositions thus seem to be antecedent to implicatures, and it would be natural to expect presuppositional inferences to take precedence.

Van der Sandt's account offers a solution to this problem by formulating the principles which result in non-projection somewhat differently.

3.4.2. The accommodation view: Van der Sandt (1992)

Van der Sandt (1992) argues that presupposition is a species of anaphora. Presuppositions, on this view, give rise to pieces of a DRS which require antecedents. For example, the sentence *It was Jane who won* gives rise to the presupposition that someone won, which is represented by the DRS condition $won(x_i)$. The presuppositional condition requires an antecedent, that is, a condition of the form $won(x_j)$, which must occur in a position in the DRS accessible from the insertion site of the presuppositional condition. Thus, if the presupposition occurs in an *if*-clause, its antecedent will need to be in that same clause, or in the global DRS. An antecedent in the *then*-clause will not do, as this position is not accessible from the *if*-clause. If an accessible antecedent is found, the presupposition is said to be *bound*.

This notion of presupposition binding corresponds to satisfaction in the satisfaction theory. In the satisfaction theory, a presupposition which is satisfied by virtue of the content of the sentence in which it occurs does not project. In the DRT theory, a presupposition which is bound inside the sentence in which it occurs does not project. A presupposition projects to a sentence S, or is inherited by S, when the presupposition is bound outside of S.

The interesting case for our purposes is the case where the DRS does not contain an antecedent for a presupposition. In this case, Van der Sandt says, a hearer must *accommodate* the presupposition. We have so far encountered accommodation as a process whereby a hearer, recognizing that a speaker's assertion presupposes something which is not in fact in the context, modifies the context to render the assertion appropriate. The notion of accommodation is here essentially the same, but now accommodation is taken to be an operation on DRSs, not on contexts. If an antecedent condition cannot be found, the hearer can simply insert one, making it possible to fully process the presupposing sentence. But due to the hierarchical nature of DRSs, there are generally multiple possible accommodation sites. Consider, for instance, what would be required to update a DRS with:

(61)   If Jane visits, she will bring her dog.

Suppose that this is the first assertion made in the discourse, so the DRS looks as in (62). The conditions in the double-lined box represent the presupposition.

(62)

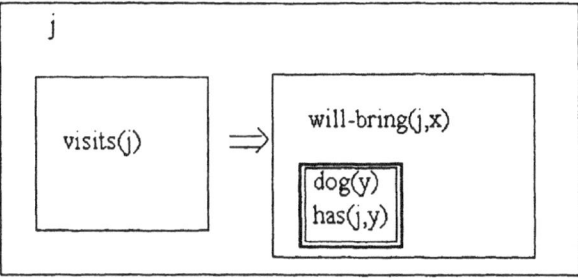

Accommodation of the presupposition requires inserting the pair of conditions *dog(x), has(j,x)* into a position accessible from the consequent of the conditional. There are three such positions: the consequent itself, the antecedent, and the main DRS. Now, accommodation into either the consequent or the antecedent would have the same effect as local binding. The presupposition "finds" its antecedent inside the sentence in which it occurs, giving rise to a reading of the sentence in which the presupposition does not project. But accommodation into the global context would be the same as first asserting that Jane has a dog, and then asserting the conditional. This corresponds to what we describe as presupposition projection.

The question which now arises is what governs the choice of accommodation site in particular instances. This is where we come back to the Gazdarian idea that presupposition projection is constrained by the requirement to preserve the coherence of the discourse. In earlier work, Van der Sandt (1988) cashed this out as a requirement that each clause be consistent and informative with respect to the context. Van der Sandt (1992) recasts this requirement as conditions on DRSs, but the idea is fundamentally the same. The conditions are as follows[9]:

(63)   *Admissibility conditions on DRSs*
Let K_0 be a DRS, and let K_1 be the result of updating K_0 with information from a new sentence. The update of K_0 to K_1 is admissible only if it meets the following conditions:

(i) K_1 is informative with respect to K_0, that is, K_0 does not entail K_1.
(ii) Updating K_0 to K_1 maintains consistency.
(iii) Updating K_0 to K_1 does not give rise to a structure in which for some subordinate DRS K_i either:
   (a) K_i is entailed by the DRSs which are superordinate to it OR
   (b) $\neg K_i$ is entailed by the DRSs which are superordinate to it

Van der Sandt notes that conditions (i) and (ii) encapsulate Stalnaker's (1979) conditions on felicitous assertion, namely, that each assertion be informative and consistent with respect to the context in which it is uttered. These conditions, of course, derive ultimately from Gricean considerations. (Recall that the requirement for consistency ignores the possibility of belief revision, which complicates the issue.) Condition (iii) is required (minimally) for an assertion to meet the Simplicity condition which I invoked in Chapter Two, which is itself a formalization of the Gricean Maxim of Manner. Van der Sandt makes clear that his condition, too, is motivated by the same considerations:

> A local violation of consistency or informativeness [i.e. a violation of condition (iii)] need not give rise to uninformativeness of the whole utterance processed. It often signals that the information carried by the utterance is conveyed in an unnecessarily redundant and complex way [and that]...the same information could have been conveyed in a shorter and thus more efficient way (p. 375, fn.32).

This makes it clear that Van der Sandt wants to rule out as infelicitous utterances which convey a proposition in a more complex manner than necessary. Note, however, that Van der Sandt's condition is not equivalent to the Simplicity condition. A disjunction in which one disjunct entails another may satisfy his condition (iii), as each disjunct may be consistent and informative with respect to the DRS so far constructed. However, such disjunctions still violate Simplicity as I have formulated it, for the disjunction as a whole has the same degree of

Presupposition Projection

informativity as one of its disjuncts. Thus, all violations of condition (iii) are violations of Simplicity; but not all violations of Simplicity are violations of condition (iii).

It will turn out that global accommodation sometimes gives rise to a violation of one of the admissibility conditions. When this happens, local accommodation is forced, resulting in non-projection of the presupposition. Let me go straight to the case of disjunction to illustrate this, and then come back afterwards to some further discussion.

Van der Sandt adopts the standard DRT assumptions about the representation of clausal disjunctions which I introduced in Chapter One: each disjunct introduces a sub-DRS, and no sub-DRS is accessible from any other. So the sentence in (64) gets the representation in (65). The "X" in the DRS is to be understood as a plural discourse referent.

(64)   Either Jane is an only child or she dislikes her siblings.

(65)

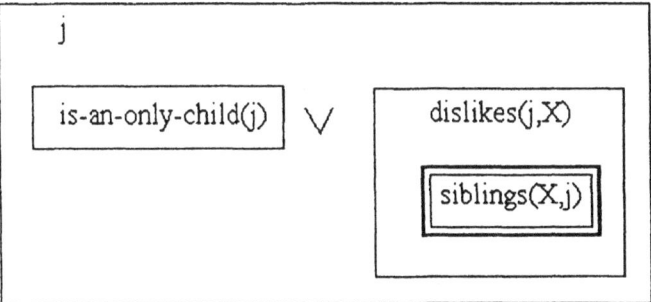

There are two possible accommodation sites in this case: the global DRS, and the DRS representing the second, presupposing disjunct. The first DRS is not a possible accommodation site, as information inside a disjunct is inaccessible to antecedent-seeking expressions in any other. Suppose, then, that we accommodate the presupposition into the global DRS. As a result, the global DRS will entail that Jane has siblings. But then the sub-DRS representing the first disjunct will be in violation of condition (iii.b) i.e. it will be inconsistent with the DRS in which it is embedded. Another way to put this is that the result of global accommodation is identical to the DRS that would be produced by the following string:

(66)   Jane has siblings. Either Jane is an only child or she dislikes her siblings.

Global accommodation, or projection, of the elementary presupposition of (64) is infelicitous for just the same reason that this sentence sequence is. Utterance of the disjunction in the local context violates a general discourse principle.

As global accommodation does not lead to an acceptable DRS update, we must resort to local accommodation. The only remaining accommodation site is the presupposing disjunct itself. Just like local binding, local accommodation has the effect of non-projection of the presupposition. The presupposition has not had to "go looking" for an antecedent outside of the sentence in which it occurs. Because local accommodation is the only option for sentence (64), the elementary presupposition never projects.

Before moving on, let's look at a case in which the elementary presupposition intuitively is inherited by the disjunction as a whole:

(67)   Either Jane has no interesting family stories or she dislikes her siblings.

Assume once again that this is the first utterance in a discourse, and so the first information to be entered in the DRS. The DRS that results will be just like that in (65), except for the content of the first disjunct. As there is no antecedent for the presupposition, it must be accommodated. Once again, there are two available sites. This time, though, accommodation in the global DRS will not lead to any infelicity, as the presupposition that Jane has siblings neither entails nor contradicts the content of either disjunct. In other words, there is nothing infelicitous about the following discourse:

(68)   Jane has siblings. Either she has no interesting family stories or she dislikes her siblings.

However, it's also the case that local accommodation would be felicitous here too, giving rise to a DRS equivalent to:

(69)   Either Jane has no interesting family stories or she has siblings and she dislikes her siblings.

Local accommodation corresponds to an interpretation of the sentence on which the presupposition does not project. There is no obvious obstacle to local accommodation, so the account would seem to predict that (67) could be read as either presupposing or not presupposing, depending on where we choose to accommodate. However, (67) in fact has only a presupposing reading. To account for this, Van der Sandt must adopt a further constraint on DRS construction: always accommodate to the highest position possible[10]. More precisely:

(70)   *Accommodation Preference Rule*
Given a choice between two accommodation sites K_1 and K_2 s.t. K_1 subordinates K_2, accommodate to K_1.

Obviously, such a stipulation is undesirable, and this is something I will come back to later.

We have now seen how Van der Sandt's account incorporates aspects of the satisfaction theory and of Gazdar's theory. Non-projection is always accounted for by saying that the presupposition "finds" its antecedent inside the sentence in which it occurs. In this respect, the theory is like satisfaction theories[11]. In some cases, the antecedent occurs locally by virtue of the content of some clause of the complex sentence. In other cases, it is there because it has been accommodated into that position. But this local accommodation occurs only when global accommodation is blocked by the need to preserve discourse coherence. In the absence of a local antecedent, then, presuppositions are predicted to project unless the result of projection would be an infelicitous discourse.

Van der Sandt adopts the standard DRT assumption that disjuncts are hierarchically independent of one another, or inaccessible to one another.

Hence, a presupposition in one disjunct can never be bound by a condition in another disjunct. Contra the CCP-based satisfaction theories, non-projection in disjunctions is not attributable to the binding (satisfaction) of the presupposition of one disjunct by the content of another. Non-projection can only arise through local *accommodation*. And as we've seen, the standard cases of non-projection in disjunctions are those in which the presupposition is incompatible with the content of some disjunct, in which case global accommodation would lead to violation of the Simplicity condition.

The general constraints on DRS acceptability that Van der Sandt assumes are structural counterparts of basically Gricean constraints on Stalnakerian context change. If we can "translate" Van der Sandt's proposal into the Stalnakerian framework, we will have a way of accounting for the projection properties of disjunction in terms of general constraints on context update, without stipulating the kind of complex update procedures discussed earlier. However, there are two things that we need. Van der Sandt's account requires that each disjunct be checked against the context for consistency and informativity, so we need to give an update procedure for disjunction which will allow this. We also need a notion of local accommodation within a Stalnakerian framework. I turn to these two issues in turn in the next section.

3.4.3. Translating DRSs into Stalnakerian contexts
3.4.3.1. A simple context update procedure for disjunction

To implement Van der Sandt's account in a Stalnakerian framework, we will need to assume that contexts are updated with disjunctions according to the schema in (71)[12]. (I return here to Heim's "+" notation to denote the update function.)

(71) $c + [\,S_1 \text{ or } S_2 \text{ or } \ldots \text{ or } S_n\,] = [c+S_1] \cup [c+S_2] \cup \ldots \cup [c+S_n]$

According to (71), updating a context with a disjunction involves first updating it with each disjunct in turn, and then combining the results of each of these operations by set union. Earlier in the chapter, I argued against the CCP-based satisfaction accounts both on the grounds that they are empirically unsatisfactory, and also on the grounds that the CCPs which they postulate are unmotivated. Is the update procedure in (71) any better motivated?

If we accept that context update should basically be represented as intersection, and also that context update should be a compositional operation, then (71) is motivated as the simplest way to get to the result dictated by the truth conditions of disjunction. We have to end up, one way or another, with the set of worlds from the starting context at which at least one disjunct is true. (71) does this with no assumptions other than the standard treatment of disjunction as set theoretic union (Boolean join). Unlike the supplemented disjunct CCP, it posits no "invisible content" for any disjunct. Nor, like the logical-equivalence CCP, does it involve embedding the disjuncts under logical operators which are not realized in the surface string.

Finally, there is the fact that assuming the update procedure in (71) will allow us to give a satisfactory account of the projection properties of disjunction, and this in itself must be taken as providing some evidence in its favor.

3.4.3.2. Local accommodation in the Stalnakerian framework

As noted earlier, the idea of local accommodation originates with Heim (1983). She points out that the recursive definition of the CCPs of complex sentences allows for accommodation at different levels. The kind of accommodation originally discussed by Lewis and Stalnaker is accommodation of a proposition into the starting or global context. But it is also possible to accommodate presuppositions into the local context to which a constituent of a complex sentence is added, doing a kind of running repair. Global accommodation of a proposition p, Heim says, is like "pretending that c&p obtained all along" (1983:120) or, to use Van der Sandt's terms, is like pretending that the utterance of the presupposing sentence was preceded by an assertion of the presupposed proposition. Local accommodation involves adjusting the context only for the purposes of evaluating a single constituent clause. In the case of disjunction, the distinction between global and local accommodation comes to this: Suppose that we are calculating c+[A or B]. This requires calculating $[c+A] \cup [c+B]$. If we globally accommodate some presupposition p, we begin by updating c with p, and then calculate the result of updating with the disjunction. The calculation we actually perform is thus:

(72)　　[c+p]+[A or B] = [[c+p]+A] ∪ [[c+p]+B]

If, on the other hand, we locally accommodate p to the local context of A, we calculate as follows:

(73)　　[[c+p]+A] ∪ [c+B]

As will become clear in what follows, a presupposition which is locally accommodated will not necessarily be entailed by the resulting context. This corresponds to the intuition that the presupposition does not project.

The possibility of local accommodation introduces the same problem for Heim as it does for Van der Sandt. If local accommodation is possible, why do presuppositions ever project? Heim, like Van der Sandt, suggests that global accommodation is strongly preferred. Local accommodation is to be used only when "we are for some reason discouraged from assuming" the elementary presupposition to hold (1983: 120). She goes on to say that "by stipulating a ceteris paribus preference for global over local accommodation, we recapture the effect of Gazdar's assumption that presupposition cancellation occurs only under the threat of inconsistency" (120). As Beaver (1997) observes, this allows us to reframe the preference for global accommodation as a preference for projection over cancellation, as a preference for drawing an inference from a presupposition trigger over cancellation of the inference. To say that global accommodation is preferred is to say that hearers prefer to interpret a presupposition trigger as an indication of what the speaker presupposes, and will give up on this only if to do so would be to ascribe an infelicitous utterance to the speaker.

3.5. THE ACCOUNT IN ACTION

3.5.1. Basic cases

The idea now is quite simple. Assume that the process of updating a context with a disjunction involves adding each disjunct independently to the starting context, and then combining the results with set union. Assume further that the preference is to maintain the same starting context for each disjunct, unless this would lead to infelicity. This is just to say that we prefer global accommodation to local. Then we look at each disjunct in turn and ask whether its assertion in the context indicates that the speaker presupposes some proposition p, i.e., that she assumes p to be in the context. If it does, but p is not currently in the context, accommodate p into the starting context, and calculate the result of updating this revised context with each disjunct in turn. But if this leads to an infelicitous discourse, revert to local accommodation, i.e., add p to the context only for the purposes of calculating the update of the presupposing disjunct.

Here is an example of a disjunction which inherits an elementary presupposition:

(74)   Either Jane is too tired to work today, or she realizes that the problem's been solved.

First update the context with *Jane is too tired to work today*. This is straightforward, as the sentence has no elementary presuppositions. Next update the context with *Jane realizes that the problem's been solved*. This clause bears the elementary presuppositions that there is a problem, and that the problem has been solved. If the hearer has not so far presupposed these propositions, she will accommodate them globally, revising her starting context. The hearer now begins the calculation over again, with the revised context as the starting context. Each disjunct is added to this, and the results combined with set union. The result is the set of worlds from the starting context in which there is a problem, the problem has been solved, and either Jane is too tired to work or she realizes that the problem has been solved. The new context entails that there is a problem and that it has been solved, corresponding to the intuition that these presuppositions project. As Van der Sandt puts it, the result of projection is equivalent to preceding utterance of the presupposing sentence by an assertion of the proposition presupposed.

Now, compare with a non-projection case.

(75)   Either the problem hasn't been solved, or Jane realizes that it has been.

Let's assume, first, that the context does entail that there is a problem to be solved, so the first disjunct is appropriate in the context of utterance.

Updating the context with this disjunct is thus straightforward, resulting in the set of worlds in which the problem hasn't been solved. Now, we attempt to update the context with the second disjunct. This disjunct bears the elementary presupposition that the problem has been solved. Suppose then that the hearer accommodates this to the global context, and begins the calculation again. Now, she must update a starting context which entails that the problem has been solved with the proposition that it hasn't been solved. But this is contradictory. If the speaker indeed presupposes that the problem has been solved, then her utterance of the disjunction would be infelicitous. Assuming that the speaker intends to speak felicitously, the hearer must conclude that she does not presuppose that the problem has been solved. Her use of the presupposition trigger must indicate, rather, that she wants the second disjunct to be evaluated in a context which entails that the problem has been solved. The hearer must thus revert to local accommodation, calculating as follows:

(76) i. $c \cap \{w: \text{the problem hasn't been solved in w}\} = c'$
ii. $c \cap \{w: \text{the problem has been solved and Jane realizes it in w}\} = c''$
iii. $c' \cup c'' = \{w \in c: \text{the problem hasn't been solved in w or the problem has been solved and Jane realizes it in w}\}$

The final result does not entail that the problem has been solved, corresponding to the intuition that the presupposition does not project.

Notice that failure of projection does not correspond to cancellation of the presupposition, as in Gazdar's theory, but only to local accommodation. The requirement that the presupposition be entailed by the local context remains in force, and the presupposition trigger still provides the hearer with information. The information, though, is about the local context in which the presupposing disjunct is to be evaluated, rather than information about the global context. In contrast to the Gazdarian theory, on this approach we are not required to say what it would mean for a presupposition to be canceled.

The case of conflicting presuppositions is explained in similar fashion to the previous example, although the reasoning is a little more complicated. Consider:

(77) Either George knows he's won, or he's upset that he hasn't.

Assume that the starting context entails neither that George won nor that George has not won. Suppose that the hearer takes the presupposition trigger in each disjunct as an indication of presuppositions held by the speaker, and attempts to globally accommodate both of the propositions. Then she must add to the starting context both the proposition that George has won, and the proposition that he hasn't. As these are contradictory, she must conclude that the speaker does not, in fact, simultaneously presuppose both.

The hearer also has the option of globally accommodating one of the presuppositions, and locally accommodating the other. This, too, will lead to an infelicity. Suppose that she globally accommodates the proposition that George has won, and accommodates the proposition that George hasn't won to the local context of the second disjunct. This is equivalent to taking the speaker to have said (78) in a context which entails that George has won.

(78)   Either George knows that he has won, or he hasn't won and he's upset that he hasn't.

But then the second disjunct would be incompatible with the global context, in violation of Simplicity.

Global accommodation of the proposition that George hasn't won and local accommodation of the proposition that he has will have the same effect. The result would be equivalent to taking the speaker to have said (79) in a context which entails that George hasn't won.

(79)   Either George has won and he knows that he's won, or he's upset that he hasn't.

Now the first disjunct is incompatible with the assumed global context.

There is only one option remaining for a hearer who wishes to take the speaker to hold consistent beliefs and to be speaking felicitously, and this is to accommodate both presuppositions locally. Each presupposition trigger is understood as an indication of the context in which the presupposing disjunct is evaluated, not as an indication of the context actually assumed by the speaker. Local accommodation of each presupposition is equivalent to updating with:

(80) Either George has won and he knows that he's won, or he hasn't won and he's upset that he hasn't won.

This, of course, is felicitous, but does not entail either that George won or that he didn't, corresponding to the intuition that neither presupposition projects.

Notice that on this Van der Sandtian account, exactly the same kind of explanation is given for non-projection due to conflict with another presupposition as is given for non-projection due to conflict with another disjunct. In contrast, the satisfaction accounts discussed earlier in the chapter would have to treat the two cases as instantiating different phenomena, for they explain the latter cases in terms of the CCP of the expression and its *content*. Of course, one could maintain different accounts for the two cases, but considerations of simplicity would seem to tell against it.

The account also motivates rather nicely one of the stipulative aspects of Gazdar's theory. Gazdar's definition of satisfiable incrementation says that the satisfiable incrementation of a set X with a set Y cannot contain any members of Y which are mutually inconsistent. Suppose that X is the result of incrementing a context with the entailments and implicatures of an utterance U, and Y is the set of potential presuppositions of U. The definition tells us that if Y contains both p and ¬p, neither can be added to X, even if one of them alone could be added without rendering X inconsistent. But it is not really obvious why this should be so. After all, the point is only to maintain the consistency of the context. If we can add either p or ¬p without causing inconsistency, why not do so? If we add at least one, we would after all be making use of more of the potential information offered by the utterance.

On the Van der Sandtian account, it is clear why neither conflicting presupposition can be added to the global context. It is because presuppositions, even if accommodated "after the fact," are understood as providing the background against which an utterance is made, and this background then affects the felicity of the utterance made. If two disjuncts have conflicting elementary presuppositions, then projection of the presupposition of one will render inclusion of the other disjunct infelicitous. On the Van der Sandtian account, it is not just considerations of consistency which affect presupposition projection.

3.5.2. Entailing disjunctions again

The interaction of presupposition projection with general felicity requirements is further apparent in examples like the following:

(81)   #Either the problem has been solved, or Jane doesn't realize that the problem has been solved.

The infelicity of (81) is reminiscent of the entailing disjunctions discussed in Chapter Two. It is easy to see why. The second disjunct bears the elementary presupposition that the problem has been solved. Suppose that this proposition is included in, or is accommodated into, the global context in which the sentence is uttered. Then the first disjunct, and hence the disjunction as a whole, will be entailed by the context. The disjunction, being uninformative, will be infelicitous.

Suppose, then, that the presupposition is not in the context. As global accommodation leads to infelicity, we try local accommodation instead, and calculate as follows:

(82)   [c+the problem has been solved] ∪ [c+the problem has been solved+Jane realizes that the problem has been solved]

But observe that:

[c+the problem has been solved+Jane realizes that the problem has been solved] ⊆ [c+the problem has been solved]

Hence, the context update produced by the entire disjunction is just what would have been produced by the first disjunct alone, so the disjunction is again in violation of the Simplicity condition.

However we try to accommodate the elementary presupposition of (81), the result will violate Simplicity. Hence, there is no way for the sentence to be felicitously asserted in a context in which the usual felicity conditions apply.

3.5.3. Beaver's counterexample

Beaver (1995a: 111) gives some purported counterexamples to Van der Sandt's account of the projection properties of disjunction which warrant some discussion. The examples are as follows:

(83)   Either John didn't solve the problem, or Jane realizes that it has been solved.
(84)   Either Jane's autobiography hasn't been published yet, or else John must be very proud that Jane has had a book published.

Beaver observes that in neither of these examples does the elementary presupposition project. It is also the case that in both cases, the negation of the first disjunct entails the presupposition of the second, so both cases match the predictions of the satisfaction accounts we looked at. However, in neither case is the presupposition incompatible with the content of any disjunct so Van der Sandt's account appears to predict, incorrectly, that the presupposition should project.

First, let's note that these examples are structurally identical to those with which I argued that the generalization captured by the satisfaction account is incorrect. (See section 3.3.3.3. above.) In (85-86), the negation of the first disjunct entails the presupposition of the second, but the sentence is most naturally read with the presupposition projecting:

(85)   Either George has no grandchildren, or he has a bad relationship with his children.
(86)   Either Jane isn't yet in London, or George knows that she's in England.

So it's certainly not the case that this type of example generally constitutes a counterexample to the Van der Sandtian analysis. What, then, distinguishes Beaver's examples from (85-86)? The difference is that global accommodation still results in infelicity in Beaver's examples, even though the presupposition is not incompatible with the first disjunct.

Consider first the felicity of the following string:

(87)   (a)The problem has been solved. (b)John didn't solve the problem/it.

It is a little odd to follow (a) with (b). Far more natural would be "It wasn't John that solved it," or "John wasn't the one who solved it." If (87b) is used, it requires marked intonation, focusing *John*. Similarly, in the following string, *John* must be intonationally focused, but again, it would be more natural to use a cleft structure in the first disjunct:

(88)   The problem has been solved. Either John didn't solve it, or Jane realizes that it's been solved.

This is not surprising, for each disjunct will be evaluated in the starting context, so, in effect, each disjunct will be treated as a possible continuation of the discourse.

As Van der Sandt makes clear, projection of a presupposition is equivalent to preceding the presupposing utterance with assertion of the presupposed proposition. What (88) shows is that the felicity of this sequence requires a marked intonation pattern on the first disjunct. So presumably projection of the presupposition in (83) will also be felicitous only with that same intonation pattern. A hearer will generally prefer not to project the presupposition in (83), because the disjunction is a little odd in a context in which it is presupposed that someone solved the problem.

Beaver observes that some intonation patterns do result in a presupposing reading of (83). The ones that do, I would think, are the same ones which would render (88) fully felicitous. For these are the intonation patterns which a speaker who presupposed that someone solved the problem would use in uttering (83).

A more straightforward argument can be given for (84). The following string is quite odd:

(89)   Jane has had a book published. Either her autobiography has not been published yet, or else John must be very proud that Jane has had a book published.

If it is already given that Jane has had a book published, then John's being proud of her having a book published is not an alternative to her autobiography not yet being published. A speaker who presupposed that Jane had published a book could not felicitously assert (84). So a hearer who assumes the speaker of (84) to be speaking felicitously would not globally accommodate. Hence, we do not read the sentence as inheriting the presupposition.

These examples show the strength of the Van der Sandtian account. It does not rely on any single, mechanical procedure in determining presupposition projection, but allows general considerations of felicity to constrain the process. This is entirely in accord with the Stalnakerian view of presupposition as a pragmatic phenomenon. As such, it is only to be expected that it will interact in multiple ways with other conversational constraints.

3.6. CONCLUSION

I have argued in this chapter that the Stalnakerian framework allows for a natural account of the presupposition projection properties of disjunction. The account defended here takes seriously the idea that presuppositional expressions provide clues as to the speaker's epistemic state, but that there are other clues which may bear greater weight. A hearer's over-riding consideration is to provide a felicitous interpretation for the speaker's utterance.

In some early accounts such as Gazdar's, it was assumed that presuppositions which conflict with the conversational background are canceled. This assumption is displaced in the current account by allowing for the possibility of local accommodation. Thus, even when presuppositions do not project, they still act as interpretative clues. In the non-projection case, they indicate the speaker's intention as to the local context in which a given disjunct is to be evaluated, rather than as to the global context which the speaker assumes.

The account I have given does not rely on a complex context change procedure for disjunction. The projection properties are explained on the basis of a procedure which mirrors the Boolean treatment of inclusive disjunction: Boolean join. No further semantic assumptions were necessary.

NOTES

1. According to Beaver (1997:961), examples of this type were first discussed by Hausser (1976).
2. If the second disjunct contains an emphatic *do*, as in (i), the sentence is improved. With VP ellipsis, and focal stress on *did*, as in (ii) the sentence is further improved.
(i) George has forgotten that Jane visited him, but she DID visit him.
(ii) George has forgotten that Jane visited him, but she DID.
These sentences seem to require a situation in which some speaker is attempting to deny that Jane visited George. (i) or (more likely) (ii) might be used to insist that the presupposition be maintained. How exactly the focal stress works here remains to be investigated.
3. One might argue that the negation introduced in the CCP for disjunction, which is not a translation of any linguistic element in the surface string, need not reflect the presupposition projection properties of sentential negation. I will not pursue here how this might be worked out.
4. This example is adapted from Van der Sandt (1992: 351, ex32). The original example is a conditional sentence, with which Van der Sandt illustrates the insufficiency of the standard formulation of the projection properties of conditionals. Soames (1989: 600, exs. 66-67) discusses examples parallel to (43), but claims, I believe incorrectly, that the presupposition does not project.
5. This definition is from Beaver (1997), and is an equivalent but slightly modified version of Gazdar's own definition.
6. I discussed Gazdar's definition of clausal implicatures in Chapter Two, section 5.2. The basic idea is as follows: Suppose a complex sentence S has a constituent φ, and S entails neither φ nor $\neg\varphi$. Then utterance of S clausally implicates that the speaker does not know that φ is true and does not know that φ is false.
7. The presupposition is incompatible with the first clausal implicature listed here where $\neg K_s(P)$ is understood as "Speaker is ignorant of the truth value of P."
8. Example from Beaver (1997: 961).
9. Van der Sandt's conditions make use of a notion of entailment between sub-DRS's which, as Beaver (1997: 32, fn.43) points out, is not given a formal definition. Beaver offers a restatement of the conditions in terms of the standard notion of DRS embedding, which clearly captures the original intent. I have given Van der Sandt's original statement of the

conditions simply for ease of exposition.

10. In earlier versions of the theory (see Van der Sandt and Geurts 1991), the preference for global accommodation fell out from the general procedure for interpreting presuppositions, which was roughly as follows: Starting from the insertion site of the presupposition, check each successive DRS along the accessibility path of the presupposition for a possible antecedent. Bind the presupposition to the first antecedent you find. If, when you reach the global DRS, no antecedent has been found, go back down the path, attempting to accommodate at each DRS. Accommodate in the first allowable site. From this procedure, it follows that you will always bind to the antecedent closest to the trigger, and accommodate in the site closest to the global DRS. But in Van der Sandt (1992), this procedure is abandoned, and the preference for global accommodation is simply stipulated.

11. Although the DRT treatment of conditionals and conjunctions is very similar to the satisfaction theory, there are important differences which result in the two making different predictions, in particular with respect to the generation of conditional presuppositions. Further discussion of these differences is tangential to my interests here, but see Beaver (1995a) and Geurts (1994) for discussion.

12. I continue to assume that what is being updated is a Discourse Context, as presented in Chapter Two. However, as update of QUD is irrelevant to this discussion, I will go back to talking only about the Stalnakerian context.

CHAPTER FOUR
Internal Anaphora

4.1. INTRODUCTION

In this chapter, I turn to some data which are closely related to the presupposition projection data discussed in Chapter Three. The data involve anaphora between a quantificational antecedent in one disjunct and a pronoun in another. Following Groenendijk and Stokhof (1990), I call this *internal anaphora*.

The basic data are illustrated in (1-2). Here and throughout, subscripts indicate intended anaphoric relations.

(1) Either Jane doesn't have a car$_i$, or it$_i$'s in the shop.
(2) #Either Jane has a car$_i$, or it$_i$'s in the shop.

These examples are parallel to examples containing presupposition triggers:

(3) Either Jane doesn't have a car, or her car is in the shop.
(4) #Either Jane has a car, or her car is in the shop.

When the antecedent of the pronoun or the (apparent) satisfier of the presupposition appears in another disjunct embedded under negation, the resulting sentence is acceptable. When the antecedent/satisfier appears in another disjunct without negation, the resulting sentence is unacceptable. In Chapter Three, I argued that general felicity conditions on disjunction govern the interpretation of examples like (3) (as not inheriting the

125

elementary presupposition) and the unacceptability of examples like (4). In this chapter, I will show that the difference of acceptability between (1) and (2) is also due to these general conditions.

In the dynamic literature, the contrast between (1) and (2) has been characterized as a difference in anaphoric possibilities. It is claimed that anaphora between the indefinite and the pronoun is possible in (1) and impossible in (2). This characterization of the difference leads to what I will call *anaphora-based accounts*. The question these accounts try to answer is: Why is anaphora possible in (1) and impossible in (2)? I will argue that this is the wrong question to ask. The right question is: Why is the disjunction in (1) acceptable, and the disjunction in (2) not? In effect, we already have the answer to this question: (1) meets all of the felicity conditions on disjunction, but (2), as we will see once we give an interpretation for the pronoun, is an entailing disjunction, and hence is infelicitous in any context.

Anaphora based accounts of the internal anaphora data face just the same problem as satisfaction accounts of presupposition projection: how to get the antecedent, which is in a different disjunct and embedded under negation, into the context in which the pronoun is interpreted. In DRT terms, the problem is how to get the discourse referent introduced by the indefinite into a position from which it is accessible to the pronoun. We will thus need to revisit the supplemented disjunct proposal and the logical equivalence proposal, and see how they are applied to the internal anaphora data. In this chapter, I will discuss the former proposal in its DRT guise, and the latter in its DMG (Dynamic Montague Grammar) guise, as these are the frameworks in which the proposals have been applied to the internal anaphora data. I will also discuss an additional DRT account, due to Krahmer and Muskens (1994). All of these accounts will be rejected as having empirical shortcomings and also as failing to provide a real explanation of the internal anaphora puzzle.

Having discussed existing accounts (section 4.2.), I will turn to my own proposal (4.3.). The fundamental idea is that anaphora is possible across disjunction whether or not the antecedent is embedded under negation. However, when the antecedent is not embedded under negation, the disjunct containing the pronoun will entail the disjunct containing the antecedent, producing an infelicitous disjunction.

The proposal, of course, requires some account of how the pronouns in examples like (1) and (2) are interpreted. The account I will give is a

Internal anaphora *127*

version of the E-type approach to anaphora, originally due to Evans (1977, 1980). On the E-type approach I will adopt, pronouns are interpreted as definite descriptions constructed on the basis of the content of the pronoun's antecedent clause. This theory will be elaborated in section 4.3.2.

Once the treatment of anaphora has been worked out, I will go on to apply it to some more complex cases of internal anaphora which have not previously been discussed in the literature (section 4.4.). We will find additional contrasts, such as that between (5) and (6):

(5)   Either Jane doesn't have a car_i, or it_i's in the shop.
(6)   #Either someone doesn't have a car_i, or it_i's in the shop.

I will argue that these cases *do* require an anaphora based account, that is, that the infelicity of (6) is due to the impossibility of constructing an interpretation for the pronoun with *a car* understood as its antecedent. The infelicity of (6) thus has a quite different explanation from that of (2).

4.2. ANAPHORA-BASED ACCOUNTS IN DYNAMIC SEMANTIC THEORIES

Let me begin by elaborating on the problem that the basic internal anaphora data pose from the perspective of dynamic semantic theories in which anaphora always involves some form of variable-sharing, or dynamic binding. Their claim is that anaphora is possible in (1), but impossible in (2). (Examples are repeated from above.)

(1)   Either Jane doesn't have a car_i, or it_i's in the shop.
(2)   #Either Jane has a car_i, or it_i's in the shop.

(2) is taken to show that generally, anaphora is impossible across disjunction. Moreover, on the basis of examples like (7) and (8), it is assumed that anaphora is usually impossible across negation:

(7)   #Jane doesn't own a car_i. It_i's in the shop.
(8)   #If Jane doesn't own a car_i, it_i's in the shop.

The infelicity of (2) is explained simply by assuming that disjuncts are inaccessible to one another. But (1) is a puzzle, for here we seem to have anaphora across both disjunction and negation. What is to be explained is how this is possible.

4.2.1. DMG: Groenendijk and Stokhof (1990)

Groenendijk and Stokhof treat the data by pursuing an ambiguity approach. For them, the data show that some operators have more than one semantic representation, and that the representations may differ with respect to their dynamic properties. A full explication of the formal machinery involved would take me too far afield, so I have confined myself to a very informal presentation here. For those with some familiarity with the system, the relevant formal definitions are given in the notes.

Groenendijk and Stokhof assume a version of the logical equivalence proposal, but one which makes use of their notion of *dynamic conjunction*. Roughly, a dynamic operator is one which does not block anaphoric relations between quantifiers and pronouns. To be a little more precise, recall that in DMG, anaphora is always expressed as a binding relation. This is made possible by redefining the standard quantifiers in a way which allows them to bind variables which lie outside of their syntactic scope. To say that conjunction is dynamic is to say that it does not close off the binding-scope of dynamic quantifiers in its leftward argument. Hence, a sentence with the form of (9a) comes out equivalent to (9b). Dynamic operators are underlined. (This convention is adopted from Chierchia 1992, 1995).

(9) a. $\exists x A \underline{\&} B$
 b. $\exists x [A \& B]$

Groenendijk and Stokhof use dynamic conjunction in their translation of disjunction, shown in (10).

(10) $A \lor B = \neg(\neg A \underline{\&} \neg B)$

Internal anaphora

The cases of interest to us are those in which the first disjunct contains an indefinite. Applied to sentences of this form, Groenendijk and Stokhof's logical equivalence proposal gives us:

(11) $\exists x A \vee B = \neg(\neg \exists x A \,\underline{\&}\, \neg B)$

However, the dynamic conjunction in (11) still does not allow the dynamic existential quantifier in the leftmost disjunct (now conjunct) to bind pronouns in the right-hand disjunct. This is because the negation in whose scope it falls is a *static* operator, which closes the binding-scope of quantifiers embedded under it[1]. Negation is generally defined as a static operator to account for examples like (7) and (8) above, where anaphora indeed appears to be blocked by negation. So if disjunction is translated as in (10), anaphora between disjuncts will be ruled out by virtue of the static negation. Groenendijk and Stokhof thus use this translation for the disjunction in examples like (2), where anaphora gives rise to infelicity. Their translation of (2) is given in (12):

(2)   #Either Jane has a car_i, or it_i's in the shop.
(12) $\neg(\neg \exists x[car(x) \,\&\, has(j,x)] \,\underline{\&}\, \neg in\text{-}the\text{-}shop(x))$

Now, what about examples like (1), where anaphora is possible across disjunction and negation?

(1)   Either Jane doesn't have a car_i, or it_i's in the shop.

Applying the translation in (10) to sentences of this form gives us:

(13) $\neg \exists x A \vee B = \neg(\neg \neg \exists x A \,\underline{\&}\, \neg B)$

At first glance, we might think that because the existential quantifier in the first disjunct now falls under a double negation, which is equivalent to none at all, the negation does not close off the binding-scope of the dynamic existential quantifier. This is not the case, however. The definition of static negation ensures that formulas embedded under it are rendered static, even if the negation is doubled[2].

But it is possible to give a second definition for negation which allows dynamic quantifiers in its scope to bind through it[3]. So Groenendijk and Stokhof assume a second possible translation for disjunction, just like (10) but with *dynamic* negation, i.e.:

(14) *Dynamic disjunction*
      $A \vee B = \neg(\neg A \underline{\&} \neg B)$

Application of dynamic negation to a sentence containing a dynamic existential quantifier does not close off its binding scope. So when the translation in (14) is used for sentences of the form of (1), the existential quantifier in the first disjunct is able to bind the pronoun in the second, as indicated schematically in (15). Note, by the way, that both the negations introduced by the translation rule for disjunction and the negation which appears in the surface form of the first disjunct must be interpreted dynamically.

(15) $\neg \exists x A \vee B = \neg[\neg \neg \exists x A \underline{\&} \neg B]$
       $= \neg[\exists x A \underline{\&} \neg B]$ (by double neg. elim.)
       $= \neg \exists x[A \underline{\&} \neg B]$ (by def. of $\underline{\exists}$ and $\underline{\&}$)

This, then, is the translation which Groenendijk and Stokhof adopt for sentences like (1).

This ambiguity approach does not purport to provide an explanation of the dynamic variability of disjunction, nor, I think, do Groenendijk and Stokhof intend to propose that disjunction is actually ambiguous in the way described. If it were, it would be very puzzling that the dynamic reading appears only when there is a negation in the first disjunct. When there is no negation, as in (2), the disjunction can never be interpreted dynamically. But Groenendijk and Stokhof's attempt to use the logical equivalence proposal brings out another insufficiency to add to those discussed in Chapter Three. The logical equivalence proposal *alone* does not suffice to account for the internal anaphora data. It suffices only in combination with a treatment of negation as ambiguous.

4.2.2. DRT: Kamp and Reyle (1993)

Kamp and Reyle take cases like (2) to be the basic case, and to indicate that anaphora across a disjunction is not possible. In DRT terms, this means that disjuncts are inaccessible from one another.

(2)   #Either Jane has a car$_i$, or it$_i$'s in the shop.

They further take cases like (7), repeated from above, to constitute the basic case with respect to negation: negation, too, is taken to be an operator which blocks anaphora.

(7)   #Jane doesn't own a car$_i$. It$_i$'s in the shop.

Consequently, for them, (1) is the problematic case for which some special explanation is required.

(1)   Either Jane doesn't have a car$_i$, or it$_i$'s in the shop.

Kamp and Reyle advocate the supplemented disjunct approach as a solution. Let's now see how this approach is implemented within DRT, and how it addresses the anaphora puzzle.

Recall that on the supplemented disjunct approach, the negation of the first disjunct is incorporated into the representation of the second. Kamp and Reyle support this proposal by observing that "almost any disjunction of the form 'A or B' can be paraphrased as 'A or else B'" (p.189). *Else*, they suggest, along with *otherwise*, "refers to 'the other case,'" which in the case of disjunction is the case other than the one described by the first disjunct. They take the possibility of paraphrasing with *else* to show that the interpretation of the second disjunct involves postulating a representation for "the other case." This representation is then incorporated into the DRS which represents the second disjunct. They assume further that when the first disjunct is a non-negated sentence, the representation for "the other case" will be the negation of that sentence. So the representation of (2) will be as in (16):

(16)

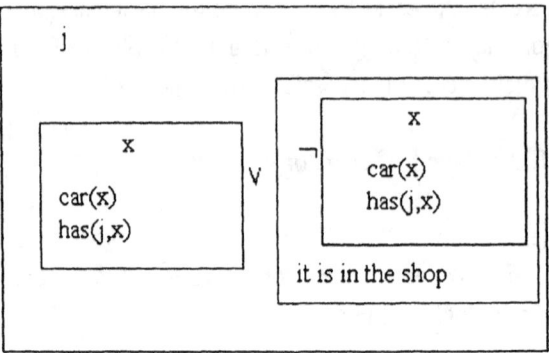

Now, if the pronoun *it* is to be anaphoric on *a car*, the discourse referent x must be accessible to it. But by the accessibility relations which Kamp and Reyle assume, no occurrence of x is accessible. x occurs once in the first disjunct, which is inaccessible. It occurs again in the second disjunct, but there is under the scope of negation, which again makes it inaccessible. Hence the impossibility of anaphora in (2).

But when the first disjunct is itself negated, Kamp and Reyle claim that "the other case" is given by the corresponding non-negated sentence. So (1) will come out as (17):

(17)

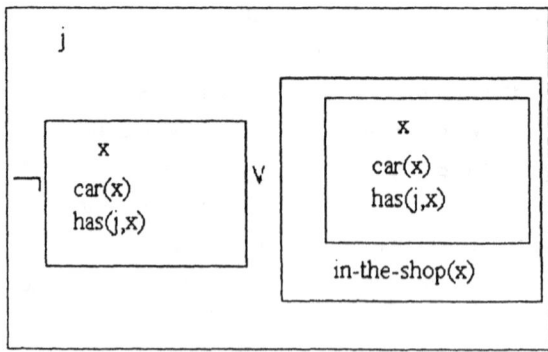

Internal anaphora

The occurrence of x in the first disjunct is still inaccessible to the pronoun *it* in the second; indeed, it is now doubly inaccessible, as it is embedded under negation. But the occurrence of x in the second disjunct is now accessible, so the anaphora can be resolved, as shown.

I discussed some objections to the supplemented disjunct proposal in Chapter Three. In addition, Krahmer and Muskens (1994) raise two further objections to Kamp and Reyle's implementation of this proposal in DRT. The first objection hinges on an asymmetry in the way in which material from the first disjunct is added to the second. If the first disjunct is non-negated, then what is added to the second disjunct is the explicit negation of the first. If the first disjunct is negated, then what is added is the content which appears *under* the negation. Krahmer and Muskens suggest that the rule could be regularized in the following way: whenever this interpretation strategy is applied, the second disjunct contains the negation of (the DRS representing) the first disjunct. But this, they point out, leads to a problem. Following this rule, the DRS which would be produced for (1) is not (17), but (18):

(1)   Either Jane doesn't have a car$_i$, or it$_i$'s in the shop.

(18)

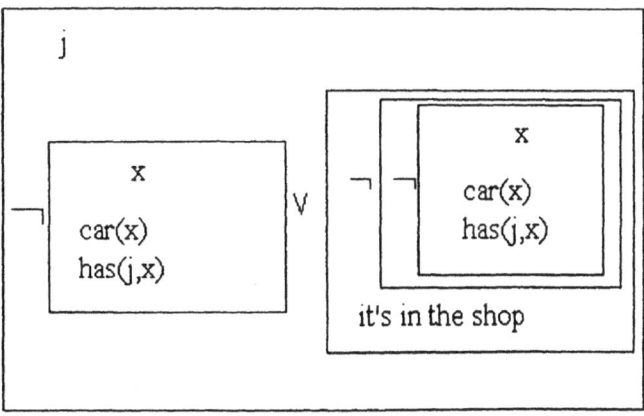

In (18), the occurrence of the discourse referent x in the second disjunct is doubly embedded under negation, and so is not, in fact, predicted to be accessible. The problem is that the formulation of DRT which Kamp and

Reyle themselves assume does not allow for the canceling of a double negation. (Their theory is just like Groenendijk and Stokhof's DMG in this respect.) Krahmer and Muskens argue, moreover, that simply adding a rule that erases double negation would be:

> very much ad hoc and would be quite unlike all other DRT construction rules. It would have the useful property of being able to make certain referents accessible to certain pronouns ... but this very property would also make it be theoretically suspicious for not being meaning preserving. If meanings determine context change potentials, as the dynamic perspective has it, then a rule to erase double negations that would change [(18)] into [(17)] cannot be meaning preserving since [(18)] gives a context which does not allow reference to [x] while [(17)] gives one which does.

The second objection which Krahmer and Muskens raise is that Kamp and Reyle's treatment of sentences like (1) does not predict correct truth conditions for them. Suppose that Jane has two cars, one of which is in the shop, and one of which is not. Krahmer and Muskens argue that (1) is false in this case: its truth requires that *any* car which Jane owns is in the shop. But the DRS in (17) will come out true: its second disjunct is verified if there is *some* car which Jane owns which is in the shop[4].

We now have two further arguments against the supplemented disjunct proposal, one empirical and one DRT-internal. In the next section, I will present Krahmer and Muskens's positive proposal, which aims to solve both of these problems.

4.2.3. A second DRT proposal: Krahmer and Muskens (1994)

Krahmer and Muskens's proposal is also an anaphora-based one. Their strategy is to reformulate the accessibility relations between disjuncts so as to allow a pronoun in one disjunct to access a discourse referent embedded under negation in another. The reformulation must still ensure that a discourse referent in another disjunct not embedded under negation will be inaccessible.

To do this, Krahmer and Muskens introduce what they call *passive discourse referents*. Essentially, passive discourse referents are discourse referents belonging to a DRS K which is negated. So, for instance, if the set of discourse referents of K is $\{x,y\}$, then the set of passive discourse

Internal anaphora

referents of ¬K (PDR(¬K)) is also {x,y}. It is only negated DRSs which have passive discourse referents. For DRSs of any other form, the set of passive discourse referents is empty.

Krahmer and Muskens use this notion to define the accessibility relations between disjuncts. They state the following rule for determining the set of discourse referents accessible to the sub-DRSs in a disjunctive condition:

(19) If $ACC(K_1 \vee K_2) = X$, then
      $ACC(K_1) = X$ and $ACC(K_2) = X \cup PDR(K_1)$

(19) says that no discourse referents – either active or passive – of the second disjunct are accessible to the first, but that any *passive* discourse referents of the first disjunct are accessible to the second. Consequently, whenever the first disjunct of a disjunction is negated, any discourse referents it contains will be accessible to the second disjunct.

Given these accessibility relations, we can produce the DRS in (20) for sentence (1):

(1) Either Jane doesn't have a car$_i$, or it$_i$'s in the shop.

(20)

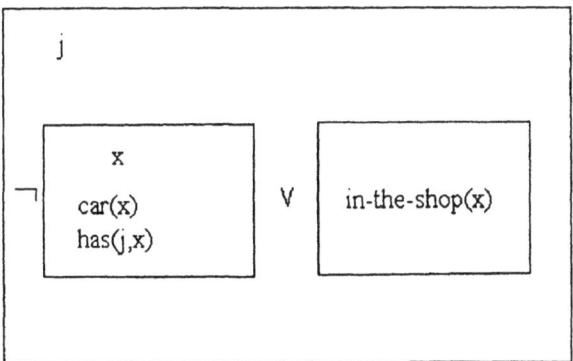

The innovation in (20) is that the discourse referent x introduced by *a car* in the first disjunct can be used to translate the pronoun *it* in the second. This has been licensed by the restatement of the accessibility relations.

Now, what are the truth conditions of (20)? Recall that a DRS is always evaluated with respect to an embedding function, and is true iff that embedding function verifies each of the conditions of the DRS. In standard DRT, the verification conditions for a disjunction are as follows:

(21)   *Standard verification condition for disjunction*
       f verifies a DRS condition $K_1 \vee K_2$ iff $\exists g$ s.t. g is an extension of f and either g verifies K_1 or g verifies K_2.[5]

(21) is simply a "translation" into DRT of the standard truth conditions for disjunction. It says, essentially, that a disjunctive condition is verified iff at least one of the disjuncts is.

If we use this verification condition to evaluate the DRS in (20), we find that it assigns the sentence much weaker truth conditions than it should. For an embedding function will verify the second disjunct of (20) just in case there is something in the domain which is in the shop. That something need not be a car belonging to Jane.

So Krahmer and Muskens must not only reformulate the accessibility relations between disjuncts, but also the semantics for disjunction. In doing this, they utilize the logical equivalence between disjunctions of the form [A or B] and conditionals of the form [if ¬A, B]. (Thus their proposal too is a kind of logical equivalence proposal.) In standard DRT, conditionals like (22) are represented as in (23), and have the verification conditions given in (24).

(22)   If Jane has a car, it's in the shop.

(23)

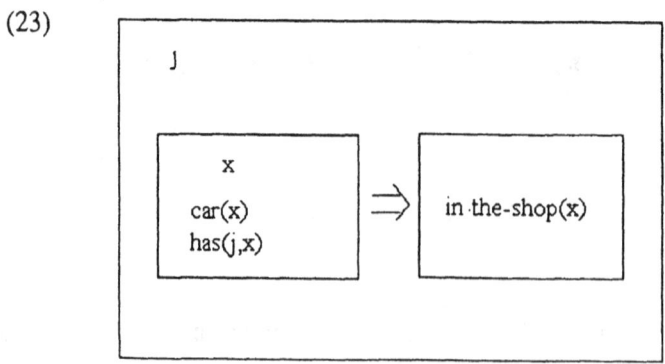

(24) *Verification condition for conditionals*
f verifies a DRS condition $K_1 \Rightarrow K_2$ iff, for every extension g of f which verifies K_1, there is an extension h of g s.t. h verifies K_2.

What (24) says, roughly, is that a conditional is verified just in case every true embedding of K_1 (the antecedent) into the model can be extended to a true embedding of K_2 (the consequent).

Krahmer and Muskens adopt a parallel condition for disjunction. What the disjunction condition says is that a disjunction *A or B* is true just in case every *false* embedding of the first disjunct into the model can be extended to a *true* embedding of the second. More formally:

(25) *Revised verification condition for disjunction*
f verifies a DRS condition $K_1 \vee K_2$ iff, for every extension g of f which verifies $\neg K_1$, there is an extension h of g s.t. h verifies K_2[6].

According to this new verification condition, (20) is verified just in case every embedding function which maps x to a car Jane owns also maps x to something which is in the shop. So the disjunction will be verified iff either Jane has no car or every car she owns is in the shop. (Notice that now the universality/uniqueness condition is built in to the truth conditions.)

Krahmer and Muskens's proposal is formally elegant, but provides no real insight into the internal anaphora puzzle. It provides no account of why disjunctions show these oddly reversed accessibility relations. Moreover, as the dynamic semantic rule for disjunction is now modeled after that for conditionals, certain differences between disjunctions and conditionals become puzzling. In particular, if the dynamic semantic properties of the two constructions are the same, why is it so hard to iterate conditionals, and so easy to iterate disjunctions?

The discussion of this proposal brings out an important point. If, as I shall argue, anaphora between disjuncts is possible, then the natural way to represent this in DRT is to allow disjuncts to be accessible to one another, and to allow sharing of discourse referents across disjuncts. This is what Krahmer and Muskens try to do. And this forces them to abandon the standard semantics for disjunction[7]. The DRT theorist is thus in a double bind. To maintain a simple treatment of anaphora, one must give up on the simple semantics for disjunction; to keep the semantics simple, one must opt for a non-standard explanation of the anaphora.

4.2.4. Van der Sandt (1992) revisited

The account of presupposition projection developed in Chapter Three was based in part on Van der Sandt's (1992) DRT account of presupposition and anaphora. In particular, the account builds on the idea that presupposition accommodation is constrained by general conversational principles. I do not, however, adopt Van der Sandt's view that presupposition accommodation is a process analogous to anaphora resolution, or that presuppositional expressions are a kind of anaphor.

Van der Sandt argues that by treating presupposition as a species of anaphora, an account is provided of the parallelism between anaphora resolution and presupposition projection illustrated in examples such as these:

(26) a. Either Jane doesn't have a husband, or he lives elsewhere.
 b. Either Jane isn't married, or her husband lives elsewhere.
(27) a. #Either Jane has a husband, or he lives elsewhere.
 b. #Either Jane is married, or her husband lives elsewhere.

Disjunction, interestingly, constitutes a problem for this account, because Van der Sandt's treatment of the presupposition projection properties of disjunction does not carry over to the anaphora case.

Recall that Van der Sandt's treatment of presupposition projection in disjunction relies on accommodation. Presuppositional conditions in one disjunct are never bound by conditions in another, as disjuncts are assumed to be inaccessible from one another. If a disjunct contains a presuppositional condition which cannot be bound by any condition in the main DRS (the starting context), the presupposition must be accommodated. Where accommodation to the main DRS produces infelicity, the presupposition is accommodated locally, and non-projection results.

But another tenet of Van der Sandt's proposal is that pronouns, unlike presuppositions, cannot be accommodated. When no antecedent occurs in an accessible position, it is not possible to simply introduce one, and uninterpretability is predicted to result. Consequently, Van der Sandt lacks an account for the acceptability of examples like (26a) above. The pronoun in the second disjunct lacks an accessible antecedent and, given Van der Sandt's assumptions, none can be introduced (accommodated) for it. Further, although he would predict both (27a) and (27b) to be unacceptable, the unacceptability of each involves quite different mechanisms.

Geurts (1994) points out the difficulty which internal anaphora poses for Van der Sandt's account, observing that it carries over to his own theory, which develops and extends Van der Sandt's approach. Geurts sketches a possible treatment for anaphora across disjunction, but his solution introduces new mechanisms for anaphora resolution which are not utilized elsewhere. What he proposes can be construed as a DRT version of a pragmatic E-type account (see below).

The disjunction case offers a challenge to Van der Sandt's explanation of the anaphora/presupposition parallelism. He explains the parallelism by arguing that anaphora and presupposition are subcases of the same phenomenon, and that the same mechanisms are at work in the interpretation of each. However, on his view, and on Geurts's view, different mechanisms must account for the interpretations of pronouns and of presuppositional expressions in the case of disjunction. Nonetheless, the intuitive similarities between the phenomena are as clear in the case of disjunction as in the case of all other operators.

The view which will emerge from my account is that the anaphora/presupposition parallelism is a reflection of the fact that the interpretation of both kinds of expression is constrained by the same general felicity conditions. Whether a disjunction contains a presupposition trigger or an anaphoric pronoun, it is required to meet the conditions of Relevant Informativity and Simplicity. We have already seen how these conditions affect the interpretation of presupposition triggers. In the next section, I will show how the same factors affect the interpretations of pronouns in disjunctions.

4.3. A FELICITY-BASED APPROACH

4.3.1. Introduction to the account

The internal anaphora puzzle comes down to three observations, which, on DRT-type assumptions, seem incompatible:

(A)   *In sentences of the form [¬A and B], anaphora between conjuncts produces infelicity. The same holds of anaphora between sentences in sequences of the form [¬A;B].*

(28)   #Jane didn't bring an umbrella. It was blue.

(B)   *In sentences of the form [A or B], anaphora between the clauses produces infelicity.*

(29)   #Either Jane brought an umbrella, or it was blue.

(C)   *In sentences of the form [¬A or B], anaphora between the clauses is allowed.*

(30)   Either Jane didn't bring an umbrella, or it was blue.

But note now that the same pattern of felicity and infelicity emerges in the absence of anaphora. The sentences in (31) below show pattern (A), and exhibit the same infelicity as (28).

(31)   a.   #Jane didn't bring an umbrella. The umbrella she brought was blue.
           b.   #Jane didn't bring an umbrella. She brought a blue umbrella.
           c.   #Jane didn't bring any umbrellas. Every umbrella she brought was blue.

Internal anaphora *141*

The sentences in (32) follow pattern (B), and again are infelicitous.

(32) a. #Either Jane brought an umbrella, or the umbrella she brought was blue.
b. #Either Jane brought an umbrella, or she brought a blue umbrella.
c. #Either Jane brought some umbrellas, or every umbrella she brought was blue.

But the sentences in (33), which follow pattern (C), are fine.

(33) a. Either Jane didn't bring an umbrella, or the umbrella she brought was blue.
b. Either Jane didn't bring an umbrella, or she brought a blue umbrella.
c. Either Jane didn't bring any umbrellas, or every umbrella she brought was blue.

For the DRT theorist, the (a) sentences in each set do not necessarily require an account different from the anaphora examples, for in some versions of DRT, definite descriptions may be treated just like pronouns with descriptive content[8]. Their interpretation requires an accessible discourse referent, just like an ordinary pronoun. But even for the DRT theorist, neither the (b) sentences nor the (c) sentences involve any anaphora. Nonetheless, the pattern of felicity and infelicity is clearly similar.

The contrast between (32b) and (33b) is familiar from the discussion of entailing disjunctions in Chapter One. (32b) is infelicitous because one disjunct entails the other. Adding negation to the first disjunct, as in (33b), eliminates that problem. The contrast between (32c) and (33c) is similar, although here we cannot directly invoke entailment. *Every umbrella Jane brought was blue* does not entail that there is an umbrella that Jane brought. However, this is an implicature of normal uses of the sentence. (If Jane brought no umbrellas then the sentence is trivially true, hence uninformative, so why say it?) The context update induced by an utterance of the sentence will, in normal circumstances, involve eliminating any worlds in which Jane brought no umbrellas. Hence (32c) is just like an entailing disjunction in the relevant respect. (33c) is fine, though, because the first disjunct expresses the negation of what is implicated by the second.

The infelicity of the sentence sequences in (31b-c) is also a matter of sensible content. If the first sentence of (31b) is uttered sincerely, then the second is obviously false. In Gricean terms, the sequence necessarily involves a violation of the Maxim of Quality: one of these sentences must be one that the speaker believes to be false.(With the right intonation, and a presupposition that there is something very special about blue umbrellas, this sequence could make sense as meaning something like: "Jane didn't bring *any old* umbrella. She brought a BLUE umbrella." But if we make sense of the sequence in this way, then the disjunction in (32b) also makes sense.) Similarly, if the first sentence of (31c) is uttered sincerely, then the second sentence can only be trivially true and its utterance involves a violation of the second submaxim of Quantity. In context update terms, it involves a failure of Relevant Informativity.

Now let's go back to the definite descriptions in the (a) sentences. Setting aside the DRT treatment of definite descriptions as anaphors, these cases are entirely parallel to the (b) and (c) cases. On the Russellian view, the descriptions entail the existence of a satisfier, that is, *the umbrella Jane brought was blue* entails that Jane brought an umbrella. Hence, (32a) is ruled out because it is an entailing disjunction, while (33a), which isn't an entailing disjunction, is fine. (31a) is odd because the first sentence denies what is entailed by the second; they cannot be simultaneously true. On the Fregean/Strawsonian view of descriptions as referring expressions, descriptions presuppose the existence of a referent, which, in this case, would be an umbrella that Jane brought. (The Russellian view is also compatible with the assumption that definite descriptions presuppose the existence of a satisfier, which is the view I will adopt here.) On the Fregean/Strawsonian view, (31a) is odd because of presupposition failure: the first sentence denies what the second presupposes. In the terms we have adopted, the second sentence will be infelicitous because the context produced by updating with the first sentence will not entail the presupposition of the second. (32a) is ruled out for the same reason as other disjunctions in which the content of the first disjunct is presupposed by the second, as discussed in Chapter Three. (If the presupposition is in the context prior to assertion of the disjunction, then the first disjunct is known to be true; if accommodation is required, global accommodation will produce a context in which the

Internal anaphora 143

first disjunct is known to be true, and local accommodation will produce an entailing disjunction.) But (33a) is fine, like other disjunctions whose first disjunct negates the presupposition of the second.

My claim is that the pronouns in both (29) and (30) are anaphoric on the indefinites in the preceding disjunct, and that on this interpretation are equivalent to the definite descriptions in the (a) sentences of (32) and (33). What is wrong with (29) is not that the anaphora is not possible. What is wrong is that the resulting sentence violates basic felicity requirements, in just the same way that the parallel sentence with non-anaphoric NPs does. This claim extends to the sentence sequence in (28). I repeat all of the relevant examples below:

(28)　#Jane didn't bring an umbrella. It was blue.

(29)　#Either Jane brought an umbrella, or it was blue.
(30)　Either Jane didn't bring an umbrella, or it was blue.

(32a)　#Either Jane brought an umbrella, or the umbrella she brought was blue.
(33a)　Either Jane didn't bring an umbrella, or the umbrella she brought was blue.

The claim is consistent with speaker intuitions about sentences like (28) and (29). Speakers have no difficulty in saying what these pronouns mean, and almost always gloss them as the corresponding definite descriptions. There is a clear contrast here with examples like (34). Informants will generally say that the pronoun in this case doesn't "refer" to anything.

(34)　#Every man came in. He sat down.

As speakers seem not to have any difficulty in saying what the pronoun in sentences like (35) means, there seems no reason to say that the pronoun is uninterpretable:

(35)　Either he doesn't have an umbrella, or he doesn't want to use it.

This felicity-based approach to anaphora "failure" has been hinted at in the literature by both Heim (1990) and Neale (1990). Heim raises the possibility of this approach in her discussion of a pragmatic E-type treatment of anaphora[9], where she notes that her proposal allows for anaphoric links in the following sentences, even though "there are no anaphoric readings available intuitively."

(36)   #John owns no sheep$_i$ and Harry vaccinates them$_i$.
(37)   #John doesn't own a car$_i$, and he drives it$_i$ on Sunday.

Heim goes on to discuss the way in which Evans (1977) rules out such cases. He proposes two semantic restrictions on the applicability of the E-type pronoun rule, which rule out certain kinds of NP in certain contexts as antecedents for E-type pronouns. But, Heim notes, "we don't need to follow Evans in this respect: the antecedency relations he rules out by means of [semantic restrictions] are already ruled out as presupposition failures" (p.174).

On the version of the E-type analysis that Heim considers, E-type pronouns are interpreted as definite descriptions constructed from the antecedent clause, and these descriptions are assumed to be referring expressions. Thus, they don't entail the existence of a satisfier, but they do presuppose it. So, for instance, (36) is interpreted as (38). (Exactly how this interpretation is derived will become clear later.)

(38)   #John owns no sheep and Harry vaccinates the sheep John owns.

If the first disjunct of (38) is true, then the description in the second fails to denote: hence, the peculiarity of the sequence.

Heim points out that there is no presupposition failure in the parallel disjunction:

(39)   John owns no sheep or Harry vaccinates them.

Hence, the disjunction is allowed.

Neale makes essentially the same point. With respect to examples like (36) and (37), he says:

> The syntactical and semantical rules of the language should not conspire to block [such] examples; they are perfectly well-formed. The problem

Internal anaphora 145

is simply that, in the normal course of things, it would make no practical sense to use these sentences ... Consider [(36)]: the anaphoric pronoun will come out as ["the donkeys John owns"], so the sentence as a whole will be straightforwardly contradictory[10] (p.232).

To spell out this felicity-based approach, I turn now to the E-type account of anaphora which I shall adopt.

4.3.2. The E-type account of anaphora
4.3.2.1. A brief overview of E-type accounts

The term *E-type* goes back to Evans (1977, 1980), who coined it as a name for pronouns which are dependent for their interpretation on a quantificational NP, but are not bound by this NP. As I, like Evans, have been taking indefinites to be expressions of existential quantification, all of the pronouns discussed in this chapter fall under Evans's characterization. Some further examples of E-type pronouns are given in (40-42):

(40)   Jane owns a cat. She takes good care of *it*.
(41)   If Jane gets a cat, she will take good care of *it*.
(42)   Everyone who owns a cat should take good care of *it*.

Evans argues that E-type pronouns are referential expressions whose reference is fixed via a definite description constructed from the content of the pronoun's antecedent clause. Roughly, he analyzes E-type pronouns as referring to that object, or those objects, which verify the antecedent clause.

Other authors have argued that E-type pronouns simply go proxy for definite descriptions. That is, the semantic value of an E-type pronoun simply is the value of some definite description. This is the most commonly discussed version of the E-type account. Among the most developed proposals along these lines are those of Cooper (1979) and Neale (1990), but the suggestion appears in a variety of sources, including Karttunen (1971) and Davies (1981). In the linguistic literature, the term *E-type account* or *E-type analysis* is used as a general name for any account in which pronouns of the relevant class are treated as semantically complex[11]. In most such accounts, though, the pronouns are taken to be related in some way to definite descriptions.

Proponents of E-type accounts differ in the semantics they assume for definite descriptions. Cooper and Neale both adopt the Russellian view of definite descriptions, according to which a sentence containing a definite description asserts the existence and uniqueness of a satisfier of the description. The denotation of a definite description *the F*, on this view, is that of the following logical expression:

(43) $\lambda P \exists x[F(x) \;\&\; \forall y[F(y) \rightarrow x=y] \;\&\; P(x)]$

Heim (1990), on the other hand, in giving her E-type account, assumes a Fregean treatment of definite descriptions as referential expressions. On this view, sentences containing definite descriptions do not assert the existence of a satisfier, but presuppose it. A sentence containing a definite description therefore entails the existence of a satisfier as it can be true only if the presupposition is true.

The assumptions about the semantics of descriptions have some consequences for the predictions of the E-type analysis. A strict Russellian, for example, will be committed to uniqueness/universality being part of the truth conditional content of an E-type pronoun, as uniqueness is part of the truth conditional content of a description. However, the adoption of an E-type analysis does not commit one to any particular view of the semantics of definite descriptions. The analysis is compatible with viewing descriptions as quantificational, as referential, or as ambiguous between the two, as presupposing or as non-presupposing.[12] In my exposition, I will follow Neale in assuming a Russellian semantics for definite descriptions[13].

E-type accounts are also distinguished from one another in the means used to determine the content of the description denoted by the E-type pronoun. Broadly, a distinction can be made between *structural* E-type accounts and *pragmatic* E-type accounts. Structural E-type accounts derive the content of the description, in one way or another, from the structure and content of the clause containing the pronoun's antecedent. Evans's original account is a structural account, as is Neale's. Pragmatic E-type approaches rely primarily on salient aspects of the context to provide the content of the description. Cooper (1979), for instance, translates E-type pronouns as Russellian definite descriptions containing a free variable over properties. He assumes that this variable is assigned a value by the context. Heim (1990) sketches a pragmatic account (adopted in Stone (1992) and Chierchia (1995)), according to which E-type pronouns denote the value of some contextually-given function for an argument which may itself be provided by the context.

There are difficulties associated with both types of E-type account. Pragmatic E-type accounts, being inference-based, suggest that a pronoun should be able to refer to any individual (actual or possible) made salient by the context. However, there are data which suggest that the possible interpretations for an E-type pronoun are syntactically constrained in some way, as Heim (1990) discusses. These data include the difference between (44) and (45), first presented in Heim (1982) as evidence against a Cooper-style theory of E-type anaphora:

(44) Every man who has a wife sits next to her.
(45) Every married man sits next to her.

As Heim says, "the two phrases [*man who has a wife* and *married man*] mean the same, so understanding one should put the listener into the same psychological state as understanding the other. Hence the pronouns in [(44)] and [(45)] should have exactly the same range of available readings." As they do not, Heim concludes that "psychological salience of an appropriate function [or property] is not sufficient for a pronoun to receive an anaphoric reading; certain formal properties of the preceding text seem to be relevant as well."

On the other hand, context and contextual inferences do often play a role in determining the interpretation of a pronoun. We will encounter some such examples later in this chapter, and in the next. This, of course, creates difficulties for structural E-type accounts, which tend to undergenerate possible readings. To allow for contextual effects, structural accounts must generally make some allowances for modifications in the descriptive content derived from the linguistic context. (Neale, though, argues that the effects of context on E-type pronouns simply mirror the effects of context on explicit definite descriptions, and so do not constitute an argument against the E-type account he proposes.) The account I will adopt is a structural account, largely based on that of Neale, so I will have to contend with the difficulties caused by contextual effects. However, as we will see, the structural account makes accurate predictions with respect to many core cases.

4.3.2.2. Presentation of the E-type account

The syntactic framework I assume in developing this account is that of Government and Binding Theory (Chomsky 1981, 1986a, 1986b), although my syntactic representations will often be greatly simplified for the sake of perspicuity. The crucial assumption which I take over from this theory is that the level of syntactic representation which serves as input to the semantic component is Logical Form (LF), which is derived from S-Structure by applications of Move α. In particular, I assume that at LF, all scope-taking expressions move to a syntactic position which determines their semantic scope. Of most relevance to us is the LF movement of quantificational NPs (QNPs), which I assume to undergo Quantifier Raising (QR). QR adjoins an NP to the minimal IP which dominates its base position, leaving a coindexed trace in the extraction site. As I take both definite and indefinite NPs to be QNPs, I assume that these, too, undergo QR. I assume, following Heim and Kratzer (1998), that application of QR is marked syntactically by adjoining the index of the raised NP to the IP from which the NP is extracted. I will call sentence constituents of the form [i IP] *indexed IPs*. The process of QR produces structures like (47), which is the LF of sentence (46). Note that subscripts on nodes indicate co-indexing. Other numbering is for identification only.

(46)   George loves a woman.

(47)

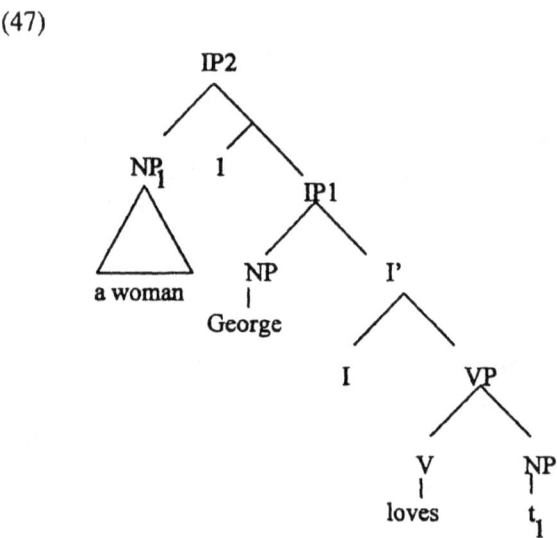

Internal anaphora

(48) shows a linear representation of the same structure.

(48)   [$_{IP2}$ [$_{NP1}$ a woman] [1 [$_{IP1}$ George loves t$_1$]]]

I will not interpret these structures directly, but proceed by providing translations into a type theoretic language with lambda abstraction. The translation language is quite standard, so the representations should be fairly transparent. The syntax and semantics of the translation language are given in full in the Appendix. Following Chierchia and McConnell-Ginet (1990), I call the translation of a sentence into this language its *logical form*, or *semantic logical form*. This, of course, is to be distinguished from the syntactic LF. It is the logical forms of antecedent clauses which will provide the interpretations of E-type pronouns.

I adopt a Generalized Quantifier treatment of quantified NPs. On this view, determiners such as *a*, *the*, *every* and *most* denote relations between sets or, in functional terms, functions whose domain and range are the set of functions from individuals to truth values. (In the definitions which follow, I utilize the set theory terminology.) The first argument of this relation is provided by the denotation of the N-bar. Adopting terminology from Heim (1982), we will call this argument the *restrictor* of the QNP. The second argument of the relation is provided, roughly speaking, by the predicate with which the QNP combines. However, as QNPs always undergo raising at LF, this predicate is not the VP, but the denotation of the indexed IP. This second argument we will call the *nuclear scope* of the QNP.

The logical forms of LFs will be derived via the following translation procedure:

(49)   *Translation Procedure*

Let α′ abbreviate "the translation of α into the translation language."

A. Translations for terminal nodes
i. *Lexical items:*
    If α is a non-pronominal lexical item, then α′ is a constant of the appropriate type. Special note: The translations of determiners are constants of type $\langle\langle e,t\rangle,\langle\langle e,t\rangle,t\rangle\rangle$.

ii. *Special lexical items (Logical constants):*
   a. or' = $\vee$
   b. NEG' = $\neg$

iii. *Traces*
   $t_i' = x_i$

B. Translations for non-terminal nodes
   Let α be a non-terminal node:
i. If α is a non-branching node with daughter β, then $\alpha' = \beta'$.
ii. If α is a branching node with daughters β and γ, and $\beta' \in ME_{\langle a,b \rangle}$ and $\gamma' \in ME_a$, then $\alpha' = \beta'(\alpha')$.
iii. If α is an indexed IP [i IP], then $\alpha' = \lambda x_i$ IP'

A few comments are in order with respect to the rules above. In applying rule A.i. I make the usual assumptions about the types to which syntactic categories correspond. In particular, I assume that intransitive verbs and nominal predicates are of type $\langle e,t \rangle$, and transitive verbs are of type $\langle e, \langle e,t \rangle \rangle$. Proper names, I take to be expressions of type e. I will generally represent the translations of proper names by a lower case letter (e.g. Jane' = j.) As I am not concerned here with the composition of predicates, I will treat complex predicates such as VPs containing PPs or adverbials as unanalysed units. In addition, I will freely substitute functional constants with the equivalent lambda abstracts where this aids perspicuity.

Rule A.ii.a. says that *or* is translated with the logical symbol "$\vee$," which has the semantics of logical inclusive disjunction. The preceding chapters, in particular Chapter Two, constitute arguments that this is all we need to assume about the semantics of *or* in order to account for its behavior. Unlike *or*, however, "$\vee$" is solely a sentential connective. In the next chapter, we will introduce a cross-categorial treatment of *or* as Boolean join. At the level of the clause, Boolean join is equivalent to inclusive disjunction. As we will discuss only clausal disjunctions in this chapter, I delay the more complex treatment until it is needed.

The rules in section B provide a type-driven translation procedure for non-terminal nodes. These rules are based in part on the type-driven interpretation rules in Heim and Kratzer (1998). Rule B.iii. says that indexed IPs are translated by abstracting over the variable x_i which is the translation of the trace of QR.

The determiners, including *a* and *the*, are translated as constants of type $\langle\langle e,t\rangle,\langle\langle e,t\rangle,t\rangle\rangle$, and I take these constants to have more or less the interpretations offered in Barwise and Cooper (1981). Specifically, I adopt a Russellian semantics for definite and indefinite descriptions. I take the truth conditions of sentences in which a definite description has widest scope to be as shown in (50). The truth conditions of sentences in which indefinite descriptions have widest scope are as shown in (51). For comparison, I show in (52) the truth conditions of sentences in which QNPs formed with *every* have widest scope.

(50) $[\text{the}'(P')(Q')]^c = 1$ iff $[P']^c \cap [Q']^c \neq \varnothing$ and $|[P']^c| = 1$

(51) $[a'(P')(Q')]^c = 1$ iff $[P']^c \cap [Q']^c \neq \varnothing$

(52) $[\text{every}'(P')(Q')]^c = 1$ iff $[P']^c \subseteq [Q']^c$

The superscripted "c" attached to the interpretation brackets indicates that the interpretation function is relativized to a context c. I take it that when we say *Every woman is wearing a hat*, we are quantifying over a restricted domain of women. Similarly, when we say *the woman is wearing a hat*, I assume that we are asserting the existence of a unique hat-wearing woman in a particular domain. I assume that this restriction is contextually given. Just what the mechanisms of domain restriction are is an unresolved issue which lies well beyond the scope of this inquiry. (For discussion of this topic, see Von Fintel (1994)). However, I do assume that the same mechanisms of domain restriction apply in the interpretation of E-type pronouns.

This concludes the preliminaries. Let's turn now to the central points of the E-type account itself.

An E-type pronoun, by definition, has a quantificational NP (QNP) as antecedent. It is not the job of the semantics to say how a hearer selects an antecedent for a given pronoun, but it will be important to have a way of formally marking the antecedent-anaphor relation. To do this, I will adopt a suggestion made by Heim (1990): I assume that antecedent-anaphor relations are determined at LF by co-indexing. In constructing LFs, we freely index NPs, in accordance with certain syntactic well-formedness constraints. The antecedent of a pronoun is that NP with which the pronoun is co-indexed. If a pronoun is co-indexed with a QNP which does not bind it, then the pronoun receives an E-type interpretation.

Once the antecedent has been identified, we can identify the *antecedent clause*, which I define as follows:

(AC)   Definition of Antecedent Clause
       The *antecedent clause* for a pronoun P co-indexed with a quantified NP Q_i occurring in an LF φ is the minimal IP contained in φ that dominates Q_i.

Because E-type pronouns always have QNP antecedents, and because QNPs always adjoin at LF to the IP in which they originate, the antecedent clause of the E-type pronouns we consider here will always be of the form $[_{IP} [_{NP} \text{Det } \bar{N}]$ [i IP]]^{14}. To take a concrete example, consider (53), in which the pronoun is co-indexed with the QNP *a woman*. The antecedent clause of the pronoun is the highest IP in (54). (In (54), I have again given the syntactic representation in the form of a tree, and linearly, using labeled bracketing. From now on, I will generally use just the linear form.)

(53)   A woman$_i$ is singing. She$_i$ has a fine voice.

(54a)

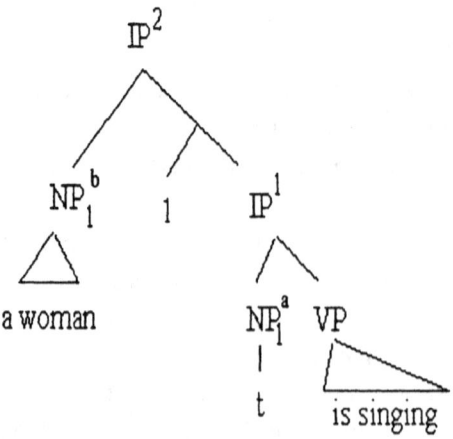

Internal anaphora   153

b. [$_{IP2}$ [$_{NP1}$ a woman][$_{IP1}$ 1 [t$_1$ is singing]]]

The logical form of such a structure will always be of the form:

(55)   Det'(F')(G')

where F' is the translation of the N-bar of the QNP, and G' is the translation of the indexed IP[15]. Let's see how this is derived by the translation procedure:

(56)
i. NP$_1$^{a}' = x_1
ii. VP' = is-singing'
iii. IP1' = VP'(NP$_1$^{a}') = is-singing'(x_1)
iv. [1 IP1]' = λx_1.is-singing'(x_1)
v. NP$_1$^{b}' = a'(woman')
vi. IP2' = a'(woman')(λx_1.is-singing'(x_1))

We now give a translation rule for E-type pronouns. The rule says that the translation of the pronoun is that of a definite description. The content of this description is derived by λ-abstraction over the conjunction of the restrictor and the nuclear scope of the antecedent QNP. More precisely:

(PR)   *Pronoun Rule*
If α is an E-type pronoun with antecedent clause φ whose logical form is Det'(F')(G'), then α' = the'($\lambda x.F'(x)\&G'(x)$).

4.3.3. A felicity-based solution to the internal anaphora puzzle

We can now apply the E-type account to the internal anaphora cases. On this account, there is nothing to prevent pronouns in one disjunct from being anaphoric on a QNP in another. However, in some cases, as discussed above, this anaphora will result in entailing disjunctions, which are ruled out for independent reasons. Let's begin, in fact, with these cases.

We return to the original example (2):

(2)   #Either Jane has a car$_i$, or it$_i$'s in the shop.

The pronoun *it* is given as co-indexed with the indefinite *a car*. By (AC) above, the antecedent clause of the pronoun will be the smallest IP dominating the indefinite at LF. The LF of the first disjunct of (2) is given in (57).

(57)   [$_{IP2}$ a car$_1$ 1 [$_{IP1}$ Jane has t$_1$]]

IP2 is the minimal IP dominating *a car*, and so is the antecedent clause for the pronoun. The logical form of this clause is (58):

(58)   a'(car')(λx_1.has'(x)(j))

The clause thus has the kind of logical form required by the Pronoun Rule. By this rule, the translation for the pronoun is (59):

(59)   the'(λx.car(x) & λx_1.[has'(x_1)(j)](x)) =
        the'(λx.car(x) & has'(x)(j))

This is also the translation for the description *the car that Jane has*. The disjunction, then, is equivalent to the sentence in (60).

(60)   #Either Jane owns a car, or the car Jane owns is in the shop.

More precisely, it has the logical form in (61)[16]:

(61)   a'(car')(λx_1.has'(x_1)(j)) $\lor$ the'(λx.car(x) & has'(x)(j))(λx_2.in-the-shop'(x_2)

Now, I have said that under my assumptions, the second of these disjuncts entails the first. Let us see that this indeed follows from the truth conditions I gave in (50) and (51). This is straightforward. Let us show that for any predicates F, G and P:

(62)   the'(λx.F'(x)&G'(x))(P') entails a'(F')(G')

Internal anaphora 155

By (50), $[\text{the}'(\lambda x.F'(x)\&G'(x))(P')]^c = 1$ only if $[\lambda x.F'(x)\&G'(x)]^c \cap [P']^c \neq \emptyset$. If this condition holds, then it must be the case that neither intersected set is itself empty, i.e. it must be the case that $[\lambda x.F'(x)\&G'(x)]^c \neq \emptyset$. If this is the case, then also $[\lambda x.F'(x)]^c \cap [\lambda x.G'(x)]^c \neq \emptyset$. By (51), these are just the conditions under which $[a'(F')(G')]^c = 1$. Hence, (62) holds.

We thus see that the cross-disjunct anaphora in (2) is straightforward, but results in a disjunction in which one disjunct entails the other, and which thus violates Simplicity.

(1) differs from (2) only in the presence of negation in the first disjunct. But because of the negation, the disjuncts will not entail one another:

(1)   Either Jane doesn't have a car$_i$, or it$_i$'s in the shop.

As before, we begin by identifying the antecedent clause of the pronoun, that is, the minimal IP dominating *a car*. The LF of the first disjunct is:

(63)   [$_{IP3}$ NEG [$_{IP2}$ a car$_1$ 1 [$_{IP1}$ Jane has t$_1$]]]

I am assuming that negation is an operator whose LF position determines its semantic scope with respect to other scope bearing expressions in the clause. Here, negation is adjoined at the highest position. It must be higher than the indefinite *a car*, because the sentence means that it is not the case that there is a car which Jane owns. It does not mean that there is a car which is not owned by Jane, which is the interpretation that would result from adjoining negation below the indefinite.

In this case, it is not the LF of the entire disjunct which constitutes the antecedent clause for the pronoun, but the constituent IP2. This is the minimal IP dominating the antecedent QNP. IP2 is identical to the LF of the first disjunct of (2), which was the antecedent clause for the pronoun in that example. As the pronouns in (1) and (2) have identical antecedent clauses, they have identical translations. The logical form of the entire disjunction is thus as in (64a), which is identical to the logical form of (64b):

(64) a. ¬[a'(car')(λx₁.has'(x)(j))]∨the'(λx.car(x)& has'(x)(j))(λx₂.in-the-shop'(x₂))
   b. Either Jane doesn't have a car or the car Jane has is in the shop.

Obviously, there is no entailment between the disjuncts in this case. Indeed, the disjunction meets all of the felicity conditions on disjunction, and hence is acceptable. The internal anaphora puzzle is thus solved without postulating any special constraints on anaphora itself. The constraints which render sentence (2) infelicitous are the felicity conditions on disjunction, which themselves are motivated in terms of general conversational principles.

The internal anaphora puzzle was originally posed with a sentence involving a negative QNP, and not sentential negation. For completeness, let me show that the account given extends straightforwardly to this case. The original example, due to Barbara Partee, is given in (65):

(65) Either there's no bathroom in this house, or it$_i$'s in a funny place.

The first disjunct of (65) is a *there*-insertion sentence. The precise structure of such sentences is somewhat controversial, but the niceties of the syntactic debate are not relevant here. What is relevant for our purposes is the basic structure of the LF. Whatever the details, the NP *no bathroom* moves to the subject position (either replacing *there* or adjoining to it) and then moves again by QR to adjoin to the IP. The result is shown in (66):

(66) [$_{IP2}$ no bathroom$_1$ 1 [$_{IP1}$ t$_1$ is in this house]]

(66), then, will be the antecedent clause for the pronoun in (65). Its logical form is given in (67):

(67) no'(bathroom')(λx₁.in-the-house'(x₁))

Again following the Pronoun Rule, the translation for the pronoun comes out as (68), which is identical to the translation of *the bathroom which is in this house*. The sentence as a whole thus has the logical form in (69):

(68) the'(λx_1.bathroom'(x)& in-this-house'(x))
(69) no'(bathroom')(λx_1.in-the-house'(x_1)) ∨
the'(λx.bathroom'(x)& in-this-house'(x))(λx_1.in-a-funny-place'(x_1)

This is equivalent to "either there's no bathroom in this house, or the bathroom which is in this house is in a funny place," just as desired.

4.3.4. Summary

The internal anaphora puzzle turns out to be a puzzle about disjunction, not about anaphora. The solution is quite simple: anaphora is possible across disjunction, but in some cases, the anaphora will produce an entailing disjunction. Such disjunctions are infelicitous for the reasons discussed in Chapter Two.

But not all theories of anaphora make it possible to articulate the felicity-based solution. As we saw in the previous section, when anaphora is accounted for as variable-sharing, or as dynamic binding, allowing anaphora across disjuncts becomes problematic, for it is then not possible to evaluate the disjuncts independently. On the E-type account of anaphora, pronouns are dependent for their interpretation on aspects of the linguistic context (the antecedent clause), but the clause in which the pronoun appears nonetheless expresses a complete proposition. Hence, in the case of disjunctions, we can ask whether the propositions expressed by the disjuncts are appropriately related, even when one disjunct contains a pronoun with an antecedent in another.

The effects of the E-type account can be replicated in DRT through the use of accommodation[17]. But the data constitute a challenge to pure variable-sharing/dynamic binding theories of anaphora.

4.4. FURTHER DATA

The E-type account I have adopted does impose constraints on possible anaphora. In order for a given QNP to serve as antecedent to a pronoun, the minimal IP containing the QNP must have an appropriate structure and logical form. In section 4.4.1., I will present further internal anaphora data, which, I will argue, need to be explained in terms of the structural constraints on anaphora.

In sections 4.4.2. and 4.4.3., I'll discuss two different kinds of apparent counter-examples to the E-type account. I will argue that what is involved in these cases is not E-type anaphora. Although these data raise a number of questions, they do not constitute a challenge to the E-type account given.

4.4.1. Narrow scope antecedents

Observe first the contrast between our old example (1), and example (70):

(1)   Either Jane doesn't have a car$_i$, or it$_i$'s in the shop.
(70) #Either most people don't have a car$_i$, or it$_i$'s in the shop.

The only difference between the two is that the first disjunct of (1) contains only one QNP – the intended antecedent – while the first disjunct of (70) contains two QNPs, with the intended antecedent taking narrow scope.

Because the antecedent in (70) has narrow scope, the logical form of the minimal IP dominating it will be an open sentence containing a free variable. This is easily demonstrated. (71) gives the LF of the first disjunct of (70):

(71)   [$_{IP4}$ most people$_2$ 2 [$_{IP3}$ NEG [$_{IP2}$ a car$_1$ 1 [$_{IP1}$ t$_2$ have t$_1$]]]]

The relative scopes assumed here reflect the normal interpretation given to the clause: most people are such that it is not the case that there is a car that they own. The minimal IP dominating *a car*, the intended antecedent, is IP2, which has the logical form:

(72)   a'(car')(λx$_1$.has'(x$_1$)(x$_2$))

The variable x$_2$ is free in this expression.

Now, suppose we use this to construct a translation for the pronoun, and determine the logical form of the entire second disjunct using this translation. What we will get is (73):

Internal anaphora

(73)   the'(λx.car'(x) & has'(x)(x_2))(λx_1.in-the-shop'(x_1))

The free variable is carried over, with the result that the pronoun-containing clause itself translates into an open sentence. Following Neale (1990: 246), I assume that such interpretations are ruled out. An E-type pronoun thus cannot have an antecedent clause which contains a free variable[18].

This structural constraint accounts for a fairly robust intuition that anaphora between a pronoun in one disjunct and a narrow scope QNP in another is not possible. Here are some further examples.

(74)   #Either no student attended a seminar$_i$, or it$_i$ was very dull.
(75)   #Either several chairwomen didn't write a report$_i$, or it$_i$ was misplaced.

The account given for the infelicity of these examples is quite different from the felicity-based account given for examples like (2):

(2)   #Either Jane has a car$_i$, or it$_i$'s in the shop.

(74) and (75) are infelicitous because the pronoun they contain is uninterpretable. Structural constraints rule out an E-type interpretation, and as there is no context, there is no way to use material from the non-linguistic context to interpret them. However, the impossibility of anaphora here has nothing to do with disjunction *per se*. Anaphora between a narrow scope indefinite and a pronoun in a conjoined or concatenated sentence is also impossible:

(76)   #No student attended a seminar$_i$. It$_i$ was very dull.

The constraints we observe in (70), (74) and (75) are constraints affecting anaphora *generally*. There is thus no evidence from these examples that anaphora across disjunction is restricted by anything other than the felicity conditions of disjunction and the structural constraints which affect all instances of E-type pronouns.

4.4.2. Non-E-type unbound anaphora

In the following example, the pronoun in the second disjunct apparently can be understood as anaphoric on the narrow scope indefinite in the first:

(77)   Either no one brought a corkscrew$_i$, or it$_i$'s in the picnic basket.

However, given the conclusions of the previous section we would not expect any E-type interpretation for the pronoun to be available, as the intended antecedent has narrow scope with respect to another QNP.

It is not the case that indefinites under the scope of a *no*-NP can always be accessed by E-type pronouns, as illustrated by (74) above, and by (78).

(78)   #Either no one brought a book, or it's in the picnic basket.

So we do not want to explain this case in terms of the structure or of the quantifiers it contains, but rather in terms of its content.

What seems to distinguish (77) is the expectation that there would be one and only one corkscrew at a picnic. When someone says that no one brought a corkscrew, they mean that no one brought the one corkscrew that was expected to be brought. In contrast, when someone says that no one brought a book, they (generally) did not expect any particular book to be brought in the first place. Perhaps, then, the pronoun in (77) does not receive an E-type interpretation, but in some sense refers to the expected corkscrew.

Kripke (1977) and Lewis (1979b) both raise the possibility that an indefinite description might have the effect of raising the salience of an individual presumed to meet the description. In this way, indefinites might "pave the way for referring expressions that follow" (Lewis, p. 243). Neale (1990: 199) points out that the E-type account he proposes does not rule out the possibility of there being other strategies for the interpretation of unbound pronouns, and suggests that "referential and [E]-type accounts of unbound anaphora are complementary rather than competing."

Lewis's example of an indefinite "paving the way" for a referring expression is the sequence:

(79)   A cat$_i$ is on the lawn; he$_i$ looks like a stray to me.

Internal anaphora 161

Here, he suggests, the pronoun refers to the cat that prompted the utterance of the first sentence, this being, no doubt, a particular cat. In the case of the disjunctive example, though, it seems less straightforward to say what the pronoun might refer to. After all, it is seemingly the *absence* of any corkscrew which prompts the utterance.

Some recent semantic treatments of specific indefinites suggest a way to produce referential effects without saying that the pronoun in (77) refers. Reinhart (1995) suggests that the indefinite article, in some cases, denotes a variable over choice functions. A choice function is a function which takes as argument a set of individuals, and returns as value an individual from that set. The argument of the choice function denoted by the indefinite article is provided by the denotation of the N-bar. The indefinite NP as a whole thus denotes the value of a choice function for that argument. When the indefinite article has a choice function interpretation, the denotation of the NP is an individual.

Kratzer (1995) adopts this treatment for specific indefinites, with one modification. While Reinhart assumes that the choice function variables may be bound by freely inserted existential operators, Kratzer suggests that the choice function variable is assigned a value – a particular function – in context. In this sense, the indefinite article is like an unbound pronoun: it denotes a variable whose value is fixed by the context. As before, the argument of the function is given by the denotation of the N-bar. So, for example, when the indefinite article is understood in this way, the NP *a corkscrew* denotes $f(\text{[corkscrew]})$, where f is some contextually given choice function. Applied to the denotation of *corkscrew*, the function will return some member of that denotation. In other words, $f(\text{[corkscrew]})$ is some specific corkscrew.

Suppose that we take the indefinite in (77), repeated here, to have a choice function interpretation:

(77)   Either no-one brought a corkscrew, or it's in the picnic basket.

We can then take the interpretation of the pronoun to be identical to the interpretation of the indefinite: the pronoun, in other words, is interpreted as a copy of its antecedent. So the sentence comes out as something like this:

(80)   Either no-one brought $f([\text{corkscrew}])$, or $f([\text{corkscrew}])$ is in the picnic basket.

Assuming that the value of f is the same in each case, the value of the pronoun will be identical to the value of the indefinite: whatever member of the set of corkscrews is returned as the value of f.

Treating the pronoun in (77) as a copy of its antecedent makes it much like a pronoun anaphoric on an ordinary referential antecedent like a proper name. These, we assume, refer to whatever their antecedent refers to. The simplest way to represent this co-reference is to assign the pronoun the semantic value of its antecedent. This is just what I am suggesting here. Evans (1977) also recognizes that some instances of unbound pronouns are best treated as copies of their antecedents, as originally suggested by Geach (1962) for examples like:

(81)   A man who takes his tax form to his accountant is wiser than *one* who takes *it* to his psychic.

Evans takes Geach to be correct in treating the italicized pronouns in (81) as "pronouns of laziness," which essentially go proxy for a repetition of their antecedents.

Treating certain unbound pronouns as pronouns of laziness also provides an account of another set of apparent counterexamples to the claims of the E-type account. These examples involve specific readings of a syntactically narrow scope indefinite, as in:

(82)   Either several chairwomen didn't sign a (certain) report$_i$, or it$_i$ was misplaced and never got to the director.

The pronoun in this sentence is interpretable only if the indefinite is given a "specific" reading. On this reading, the sentence as a whole is paraphrasable as:

(83)   A certain report was not signed by several chairwomen, or that certain report was misplaced and never got to the director.

If we assume this reading to be produced by scoping out the indefinite, we get the LF in (84) for the first disjunct:

Internal anaphora   163

(84) [$_{IP4}$a report$_1$ 1[$_{IP3}$several chairwomen$_2$ 2[$_{IP2}$NEG [$_{IP1}$t$_2$ signed t$_1$]]]]

Now, if the pronoun in the second disjunct is an E-type pronoun anaphoric on *a report*, its interpretation would be the description:

(85) the'(λx.report'(x) & [several'(chairwomen')(λx$_2$.¬sign'(x)(x$_2$))])

paraphrasable as "the report that several chairwomen didn't sign." This is not the actual interpretation of the pronoun. Indeed, assigning the pronoun this interpretation would result in an entailing disjunction, for the disjunction as a whole would be equivalent to:

(86) There is a report that several chairwomen didn't sign, or there is a unique report that several chairwomen didn't sign that was misplaced.

We can solve this problem by assuming that the indefinite in the first disjunct receives a choice function interpretation, and that the pronoun is a pronoun of laziness, interpreted as a copy of its antecedent. This gives us, roughly:

(87) Either several chairwomen didn't sign *f*([report]), or *f*([report]) was misplaced and never got to the director.

So the pronoun will straightforwardly pick out the same object as the specific indefinite antecedent.

There is a further set of counterexamples which might also be amenable to a treatment along these lines. Consider the following (based on an example from Kamp and Reyle (1993)):

(88) Either Jane owns a Porsche which I have seen race past our house several times this morning, or George owns it.

This sentence has the form of those which were ruled out as entailing disjunctions. If the pronoun is given an E-type interpretation, the second disjunct will come out as "George owns the Porsche which Jane owns which I have seen race past our house several times this morning." On this reading, it entails the first disjunct. However, as Kamp and Reyle observe, the sentence is felicitous only because the indefinite lends itself to a specific reading. If the descriptive content of the indefinite is reduced, so is the felicity of the example:

(89)   ?Either Jane owns a Porsche, or George owns it.

As these indefinites seem to be required to be specific, we can assume that they are interpreted as choice functions, and that the pronouns in these examples are pronouns of laziness. But the issue is complicated by the fact that plural NPs can also license this kind of anaphora:

(90)   Either Jane has bought several jazz records, or she's borrowed them.

We could again treat the pronoun as a pronoun of laziness, interpreted as a copy of its antecedent. Then the sentence would have the same interpretation as:

(91)   Either Jane has bought several jazz records, or she's borrowed several jazz records.

But this does not quite capture the intuitive interpretation of (90), which is something like:

(92)   There are several jazz records which Jane has either bought or borrowed.

To analyze (90) in the way suggested for (88), we would have to posit something like a choice-function interpretation for plural NPs. This could be implemented by assuming a function which takes as argument a set of sets, and returns a single member of that set as value. However, to consider whether such a treatment of plural NPs is desirable lies outside the scope of the current work.

The point of this discussion is to acknowledge that the E-type strategy is only one of the strategies available for interpreting unbound anaphoric pronouns. The claim the E-type theory makes is that unbound pronouns may be interpreted as definite descriptions, and when they are so interpreted, the description is constructed in the manner prescribed by the account. I think the "copy" strategy a good candidate for another interpretation strategy; and there may be more. It is not, however, my intention to attempt here a complete theory of unbound anaphora.

The examples discussed in this section are compatible with the claim made in the earlier part of the chapter with respect to the core examples of internal anaphora. These, I argued, do not show that anaphora across disjunction is ruled out, but merely show the workings of the felicity conditions on disjunction. In the previous section (4.4.1.), I showed that where pronouns are to be interpreted as E-type, structural constraints prevent anaphora in some cases. But this is not due to any special property of disjunction. The examples discussed in this section indicate that anaphora across disjunction is freer even than allowed by the E-type strategy, as other interpretation strategies for pronouns may be available when the E-type strategy is not. Disjunction itself, then, is no obstacle to the formation of anaphoric relations.

4.4.3. Pleonastic pronouns

In this final section, I will discuss another set of examples which raise an interesting problem for the syntax of disjunction and the syntax-semantics interface. Solving this problem lies outside the scope of the current investigation, but as it involves what at first blush looks like anaphora across disjunction, it warrants discussion here.

The problematic examples are of the following type:

(93) Several people didn't eat at all, or they brought their own food.
(94) Most people in this building don't own a car, or they park elsewhere.

First, an observation about the judgments. I myself find these sentences quite peculiar, as did some of my informants. A number of other informants, though, have told me that they find them acceptable, although (to varying degrees) slightly awkward. Judgments vary from example to example, even when the structure is the same. However, all of my informants, to the extent that they are able to interpret the sentences at all, agree on the interpretation, so these facts are quite robust.

Next, before we proceed, I need to say something about the interpretation of plural E-type pronouns. Following Neale (1990), I will assume that plural E-type pronouns may be interpreted as plural descriptions. Let "the_p'" be the translation of the plural definite article. The truth conditions of a sentence containing in which a plural description has widest scope are given in (95).

(95) $[the_p'(F')(G')]^c = 1$ iff $[F']^c \subseteq [G']^c$ and $|[F']^c| > 1$

i.e. iff all F's in the context are G and there is more than one F.

Whether a description is semantically singular or plural is determined by the syntactic number of the N-bar: *the boy* is a singular description, and *the boys* is plural. Similarly, the syntactic number of an E-type pronoun will, in most cases, determine the number of the description. In general, a singular pronoun is interpreted as a singular description, and a plural pronoun as a plural description. The syntactic number of the pronoun is, in turn, determined by the syntactic number of the antecedent. So far, I have looked only at singular pronouns anaphoric on singular indefinites, as in (96):

(96)   A soprano is singing. She has a lovely voice.

If we make the antecedent plural, the pronoun, too, must be plural:

(97)   a. Some sopranos are singing. They have lovely voices.
        b. Several sopranos are singing. They have lovely voices.
        c. Many sopranos are singing. They have lovely voices.

The plurality of the pronoun and of its antecedent does not affect the way the translation of the pronoun is constructed. In each case, *they* will translate as the definite description constructed from the logical form of its antecedent clause, which in these examples is the entire first sentence. *They*, in each of these examples, is translated as:

(98) $the_p'(\lambda x.soprano'(x)\ \&\ singing'(x))$

Because *they* is plural, the pronoun is translated with "the_p'" rather than "the'".

Plural pronouns do raise a number of complications, and I will return to them briefly at the end of Chapter Five. For our current purposes, though, we can simply assume that E-type pronouns, whether singular or plural, are assigned an interpretation in the same way. The only difference is that plural pronouns are interpreted as plural descriptions.

Returning now to the problematic examples, it is quite easy to see that the sentences *don't* mean what I would predict them to mean, should the pronouns be E-type. I will concentrate on example (94), repeated here.

(94)   Most people in this building don't own a car, or they park elsewhere.

Suppose that this pronoun is indeed an E-type pronoun anaphoric on *most people*. In this case, the antecedent clause for the pronoun would be the LF of the entire first disjunct, i.e.:

(99)   [$_{IP4}$ most people$_1$ 1 [$_{IP3}$ NEG [$_{IP2}$ a car$_2$ 2 [$_{IP1}$ t$_1$ own t$_2$]]]]

The logical form of this clause is:

(100)   most$'$(people$'$)(λx_1. ¬[a$'$(car$'$)(λx_2.own$'$(x$_2$)(x$_1$))])

Applying the Pronoun Rule to construct a translation for the pronoun from this clause, the second disjunct will come out as:

(101)   the$_p'$(λx.person$'$(x) & ¬[a$'$(car$'$)(λx_2.own$'$(x$_2$)(x))])(λx_1.park-elsewhere$'$((x$_1$))

i.e., "the people who don't own a car park elsewhere." But this is clearly not what the second disjunct means. So either the pronoun is not an E-type pronoun, or I have failed to give the correct rules for constructing an interpretation for E-type pronouns.

It looks like I might get the right interpretation for the pronoun by treating it as E-type but by somehow preventing negation from getting into the description. It's hard to see how I might do that without invoking some rather ad hoc and construction specific rules, which is of course precisely what I want to avoid. However, I will not need to try. Because interpreting the pronoun as the negation-less version of the description also does not give the right truth conditions for the sentence. On this revised E-type proposal, the second disjunct would be equivalent to "the people who own a car park elsewhere." For the sentence as a whole to be true, then, it would have to be the case that either most people don't own a car, or else all the people who own a car park it elsewhere. These, however, are not the correct truth conditions for the sentence, as is shown by the following case. Suppose that there are 20 people in the building. Of them, 15 own a car. 5 of the car owners park in the building's parking lot, and the remaining 10 park elsewhere. The question is whether our sentence, repeated here, is true in the situation described:

(94)   Most people in this building don't own a car, or they park elsewhere.

My informants agree that it is. However, the truth conditions given by the revised E-type proposal are not met. It is not the case that most people in the building don't own a car: only 5 of the 20 don't own a car. Nor is it the case that all the people who own a car park elsewhere: 10 of them do, but 5 do not. So the truth conditions of the sentence are not those given by the revised E-type proposal.

If the pronoun is not E-type, then what is it? Perhaps it is a pronoun of laziness, as discussed in the previous section. If so, the second disjunct would be interpreted as "most people in the building park elsewhere." However, the judgment about the case just described is incompatible with this interpretation. In the situation given, it is not the case that most people don't have a car, and it is not the case that most people park elsewhere. So if the pronoun were a copy of the antecedent, the sentence should be false in the case given. But intuitively, it's not.

By virtue of what, then is the sentence true? The reported judgments indicate that it is true by virtue of the fact that the people who don't own a car, together with the people who park elsewhere, amount to most of the people. In other words, the interpretation of the sentence is:

(102)   Most people are such that either they don't own a car or they park elsewhere.

All of my informants agree that this is a correct paraphrase of the sentence.

The judgments are, I think, rather delicate, so it might be helpful to look at another example:

Internal anaphora 169

(103)   Nearly all of my friends don't smoke or they're planning to quit.

The truth conditions of the sentence are captured by the paraphrase in (106), not by (104) or (105).

(104)   Nearly all of my friends don't smoke, or the friends of mine that smoke are planning to quit.
(105)   Nearly all of my friends don't smoke, or nearly all of my friends are planning to quit.
(106)   Nearly all of my friends are such that either they don't smoke or they are planning to quit.

This discussion shows that the pronouns in (93), (94) and (103) are not E-type pronouns: they do not go proxy for any description. Consequently, the sentences do not constitute counter-examples to the interpretation rules I have given for E-type pronouns.

However, the question of what these pronouns are remains unresolved. Indeed, there is something odd about the paraphrases I have given for the sentences in question. They don't look like paraphrases of clausal disjunctions at all. They are the paraphrases we would expect for phrasal disjunctions. For instance, (107b) is a correct paraphrase of the most salient reading of (107a)[19].

(107)   a.   Several people ate or drank.
        b.   Several people are such that either they ate or they drank.

The category disjoined in (107a) is at least a VP, but not an IP. As the verbs are marked for tense, the category is presumably larger than VP, including whatever functional head carries the tense morphology. Let's just assume that this functional head is I. The LF structure of (107a) is thus something like (108). (I suppress here the IP-adjoined index.)

(108)   [$_{IP}$ most people$_1$ [$_{IP}$ t$_1$ [$_{I'}$ ate or drank]]]

In (108), it's clear that the subject NP takes syntactic scope over the disjunction. This scopal relation is reflected in the paraphrase in (107b). But in sentences (93), (94) and (103) we have what looks like an IP disjunction. Nonetheless, in the interpretation, the subject of the first disjunct seems to take scope over the whole disjunction, which itself acts like a VP or I-bar disjunction, and not a clausal disjunction. In other words, although the sentences are syntactically IP disjunctions, they are interpreted as I-bar disjunctions. The pronoun apparently makes no contribution to the interpretation of the sentence.

To get some idea of what might be going on here, compare our original sentence (93) with (109). The only difference between the two is that the second does not contain *they*, and so is syntactically as well as semantically an I-bar disjunction.

(93)   Several people didn't eat at all or they brought their own food.
(109)   ?Several people didn't eat or brought their own food.

Most of my informants find (109) less felicitous than (93). The same is true of the following pair:

(110)   Almost all the guests didn't come by car or they parked in the parking garage.
(111)   ?Almost all the guests didn't come by car or parked in the parking garage.

The problem, I think, is that when we encounter such sentences, we have a strong preference to interpret the negation of the first clause as having scope over the disjunction as a whole. This is, in fact, what often happens. Consider, for instance:

(112)   He hasn't left or notified the landlord.

The most natural (perhaps only) interpretation of (112) is (113), with negation interpreted as having wide scope over the disjunction, rather than having scope only over *left*. Syntactically, this means that the sentence is being parsed as a VP disjunction, as shown in (114). (The syntactic representations given here are rough approximations, as I am ignoring questions of the location of tense and aspect, and syntactic movement of these morphemes or features.)

(113)   NOT[he has left or notified the landlord]

(114)

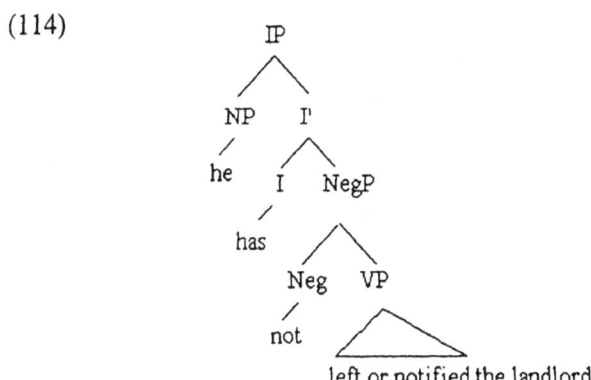

However, in principle the surface string (112) could also be associated with the structure in (115):

(115)

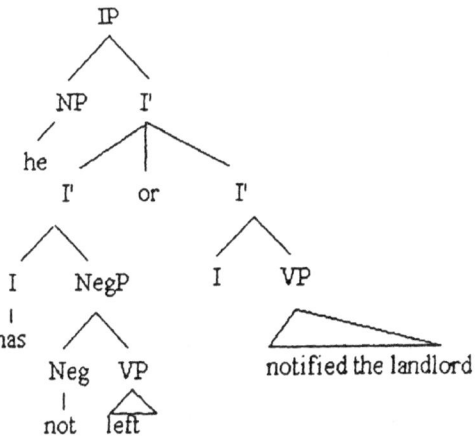

In this structure, what is disjoined is the I-bar. The negation is located inside the left disjunct, and does not take scope over the disjunction as a whole. The interpretation of the structure is:

(116)   Either he has not left or he notified the landlord.

But this interpretation just doesn't seem to be available for (112).

There are a couple of reasons why this might be. One possibility is that (115) is ruled out for syntactic reasons. Perhaps the asymmetry between the disjuncts is for some reason dispreferred. Another possibility is that (115) is allowed, but is, essentially, a non-obvious structure. The idea is something like this: In processing a sentence like (112), the hearer will not know that what she is hearing is a disjunction until she reaches *or*. Suppose that she constructs a representation for the sentence as she hears it. When she hears the *or*, she has to decide where to attach the branch. The phrase *notified the landlord* can be interpreted as a VP which "shares" the I head containing *hasn't* with the first VP. For the other interpretation, the hearer must "back-up" to the I-bar, and posit an empty I head for the second disjunct. The idea is that there is a kind of minimal attachment effect here: it is easier, on line, to construe (112) as a VP disjunction than as an I-bar disjunction, and so the latter interpretation is strongly dispreferred.

Support for an explanation along these lines is provided by the interpretation of (117), in which the order of disjuncts of (112) is reversed. There is no difficulty whatsoever in understanding the negation in (117) as having scope only within the second disjunct. In this sentence, there is no choice but to disjoin at the I-bar level, as the two disjuncts clearly do not share the auxiliary *hasn't*.

(117)   He notified the landlord or hasn't left.

Similarly, if there are clues in the surface structure that the disjunction is at the I-bar level, that interpretation becomes much more easily available. One way to do this is to introduce *either*, as in (118):

(118)   He either hasn't left or informed the landlord.

(118), in fact, cannot be interpreted as a VP disjunction at all. The effect is even stronger if both *either* and *else* are used:

(119)   He either hasn't left or else informed the landlord.

Either also improves examples (109) and (111). Compare:

(109) ?Most people didn't eat or brought their own food.
(120) Most people either didn't eat or brought their own food.

(111) ?Almost all the guests didn't come by car or parked in the parking garage.
(121) Almost all the guests either didn't come by car or parked in the parking garage.

As Larson (1985) shows, *either* marks the scope of a disjunction, essentially functioning as a left bracket which indicates where the disjunction begins[20]. The minimal attachment effect is eliminated, as a hearer knows as soon as she encounters *either* that what is to come is a disjoined structure.

When the second disjunct has an overtly filled I head, we are once again forced into an I-bar disjunction interpretation, as in (122):

(122) He hasn't left or has informed the landlord.

Again, it is obvious why this should be. The only way for there to be two I heads is for the I-bar to be disjoined. So again, the hearer is compelled to derive this structure.

Now, what does all of this have to do with the puzzling reading of sentences like (93)? (I repeat the example here.)

(93) Several people didn't eat at all or they brought their own food.

We noted above that this has the interpretation:

(123) Several people are such that either they didn't eat at all or they brought their own food

which is in fact the interpretation we would expect for (109), interpreted as an I-bar disjunction:

(109) Most people didn't eat at all or brought their own food.

But now we have observed that it is hard to get the I-bar-disjunction interpretation of such sentences, because of the minimal attachment effect. (It is not clear whether or not a VP disjunction construal is possible here. In this example, two different heads – *didn't* and *brought* – are marked for tense. A VP disjunction construal would require both heads to acquire their tense features from the same functional head.) The suggestion, then, is that the pronoun in (93) does not, in fact, turn the sentence into a clausal disjunction. It is something like a pleonastic, which is inserted in order to ensure that the negation is interpreted inside the first disjunct.

The data discussed here raise two separate questions. The first is why sentences like (111) are less than fully acceptable.

(111)   Almost all the guests didn't come by car or parked in the parking garage.

The ill-formedness appears to be a matter of processing, as the same sentence with the disjuncts reversed is perfectly acceptable. The order of the disjuncts cannot be relevant to syntactic well-formedness *per se*, but there appears to be some processing difficulty associated with the syntactic structure needed for the sentence. Certainly, there is no semantic issue here, for the string, once parsed, can be interpreted.

The second question is how sentences like (110) come to be interpreted in the way that we observed:

(110)   Almost all the guests didn't come by car or they parked in the parking garage.

This subdivides into two subordinate questions. The first is why the pronoun doesn't get the predicted E-type interpretation. I assume, in fact, that this interpretation is available, but was never suggested by any of my informants because this interpretation of the pronoun would make the sentence, overall, nonsensical. The interpretation would be equivalent to:

(124)   Almost all the guests didn't come by car or the guests who didn't come by car parked in the parking garage.

So, as far as the E-type account is concerned, there is nothing much to be explained.

What is hard to explain is how the surface IP disjunction is mapped to the I-bar disjunction interpretation that is observed. I have suggested that the reason this structure is used to express the I-bar disjunction is that the surface string we would expect to use for this interpretation is ill-formed for some reason. But explaining the mapping from the surface structure to the interpretation is an issue in the syntax/semantics interface, which I cannot address further here. What is clear, though, is that there is nothing further to be accounted for by a theory of pronoun interpretation.

4.5. CONCLUSION

The main goal of this chapter has been to argue that there are no special constraints on establishing anaphoric relations across disjunction. In the literature to date, examples like (125) have frequently motivated the claim that anaphora is blocked by disjunction.

(125)   #Either Jane owns a car, or it's in the shop.

I have argued that there is no difficulty in interpreting the pronoun in (125) as anaphoric on the indefinite, an argument supported by robust speaker intuitions. The infelicity arises because the interpretation of the pronoun results in entailment between the disjuncts, which is ruled out independently. (125) is ruled out, not because of a failure of anaphora, but because of a violation of the general felicity conditions on disjunction.

Cases like (126) contrast with (125):

(126)   #Most people don't own a car, or it's in the shop.

The infelicity of (126) *is* due to a failure of anaphora. However, it is not the disjunction which makes anaphora impossible, but the general difficulty of establishing anaphoric relations between a pronoun and a narrow scope QNP. The internal anaphora data thus do not support the claims of dynamic semantic theories that disjunction is a "static" operator, and that disjunction must be given a complex semantic representation in order to account for its interaction with anaphora.

The secondary goal of the chapter has been to present a structural E-type account of certain cases of unbound anaphora. One of the consequences of the E-type account is that clauses containing a pronoun, although dependent for their interpretation on the content of the antecedent clause, express complete propositions and can be assigned truth conditions independently of the linguistic context. In this, it differs from the variable-sharing/dynamic binding account of anaphora, on which a clause containing an anaphoric pronoun whose antecedent lies outside of it cannot be assigned truth conditions independently. This consequence is important in the overall account of internal anaphora, which makes reference to the logical relations between the propositions expressed by the disjuncts.

NOTES

1. The static negation of a sentence is defined as follows:
   (i) $\neg S = \uparrow \neg \downarrow S$

Sentences are interpreted as functions from propositions to truth values, or as sets of propositions. $\downarrow$ is an operator which applies to a sentence denotation to give back its truth conditional content. $\uparrow$ is an operator which applies to a an expression of type t and gives back its dynamic-semantic denotation i.e. the set of propositions with which it is compatible.

2. It turns out that $\neg\neg S = \uparrow\neg\neg\downarrow S = \uparrow\downarrow S$. Thus with respect to truth conditional content, double negation is cancelable, but dynamic properties are not preserved. That is, $S \neq \uparrow\downarrow S$. (Compare, in standard Montague Grammar, $S \neq {}^{\wedge\vee}S$.) $\uparrow\downarrow S$ is always a static expression.

3. Dynamic negation is defined using function application: Let p be a variable of type $\langle s,t\rangle$. Then $\underline{\neg}S = \lambda p(S(p))$.

4. The intuition underlying this objection has been debated, the question being whether the uniqueness/universality implied by the second disjunct is part of its truth conditional content or is merely an implicature. See Kadmon (1987) for extensive discussion.

5. A function g is an extension of f iff the domain of f is included in the domain of g, and for every $a \in \text{dom}(f)$, $f(a) = g(a)$. (I.e. g assigns a value to anything that f does, and assigns it the same value as f does.) g may differ from f in assigning values to additional variables which are not in the domain of f. The truth conditions have to be given in terms of extensions of f because the disjuncts may contain discourse referents not in any of the superordinate DRSs.

6. Krahmer and Muskens actually state the rule in terms of what they call the *anti-extension* of K_1. The anti-extension of a DRS is identical to the extension of the negation of that DRS. For the purposes of presentation, formulation in terms of the negation of K_1 is equivalent.

7. The close connection between accessibility relations and the semantics of DRS conditions is pointed out by Geurts (1994: 11). In general, in order for referent-sharing between two sub-DRSs K_1 and K_2 to produce the effects of anaphora, the semantics must require that K_1 and K_2 always be evaluated with respect to embedding functions which agree on the shared domain of K_1 and K_2.

8. This treatment of definites is central to Heim (1982). Kamp and Reyle (1993) also adopt this treatment, although with significant

reservations.

9. Heim (1990) is a detailed comparison of E-type and variable-sharing accounts of anaphora. In the course of the paper, she sketches out a possible pragmatic E-type account, which she goes on to reject, and then a possible structural E-type account. Neither is offered as a definitive account, but is given for the purposes of discussion.

10. For Neale, the result is contradiction rather than presupposition failure because he assumes a Russellian semantics for definite descriptions.

11. E-type accounts are generally contrasted with dynamic binding/variable-sharing accounts of anaphora, in which pronouns are treated as variables.

12. Frege treated definite descriptions as referential; Russell proposed the quantificational treatment. More recently, arguments that definite descriptions are ambiguous between these two have been given by Peacocke (1975), Hornsby (1977) and Wilson (1991).

13. As is clear from the previous chapter, I also assume that definite descriptions presuppose the existence of a satisfier. In adopting this "mixed" view of descriptions, I follow Gazdar (1979).

14. It is not strictly true that QNPs always adjoin to IP. There is some evidence that they may adjoin to VP. If in these cases the subject also originates in [Spec, VP], adjunction to VP would produce structures isomorphic to the IPs I assume. To allow for this case, we could define the antecedent clause as the minimal Complete Functional Complex containing the antecedent (see Chomsky 1986). For simplicity of exposition, I will maintain the simplifying assumption that QR always adjoins to IP.

15. At least, this is true for the cases to be considered in this chapter. It is not true for the cases I will discuss in Chapter Five. This will be one of the motivations for reformulating the theory later on.

16. Given my assumption that type mismatches between verbs and their arguments are resolved by QR, I must also assume that E-type pronouns, which are expressions of type $\langle\langle e,t\rangle,t\rangle$, raise at LF. Consequently, the nuclear scope of the pronoun/description is provided by the indexed IP which results from raising of the pronoun.

17. I gave a felicity-based account within a DRT framework in Simons (1996).

18. Although this is true for the basic case, there are some additional complications. I will discuss the issue in more detail in Chapter Five,

section 5.4.3.
    19.   (107a) may also have a reading equivalent to:
        "Several people ate or several people drank."
This is not relevant to the point I am making, and I will ignore it.
    20.   Larson attributes this view of *either* to Quine (1976).

CHAPTER FIVE
External Anaphora

5.1. INTRODUCTION

In the preceding chapter I argued that to account for internal anaphora, some kind of E-type account is required. A variable-sharing/dynamic binding treatment of this anaphora is possible only at the cost of significantly complicating the semantics of disjunction. The E-type account, on the other hand, provides an adequate account of the data without introducing any semantic complexity in the analysis of *or*.

In this chapter, I develop a revised version of the E-type account presented in Chapter Four. Much of the chapter will be devoted to exploring the consequences of the new proposal. The motivation for the revised account will be provided by a new set of anaphora data involving pronouns outside of a disjunction anaphoric on NPs inside a disjunction. Following Groenendijk and Stokhof (1990), I call this *external anaphora*.

The antecedents of external anaphors are NPs which are disjoined or which are contained in disjoined clauses, as in (1) and (2)[1]:

(1)   A soprano or an alto will sing. She will be accompanied on the piano.
(2)   A soprano will sing, or an actress will recite a monologue. Then she will lead the audience in the national anthem.

In these examples, the pronoun is not anaphoric on one or the other of the indefinites, but is dependent for its interpretation on the disjunction as a whole. It means something like "the person who sings (performs)." In other cases, a following pronoun cannot be interpreted in this way, but may be interpreted as dependent on a particular NP, as in (3) and (4):

(3)   Jane or George will sing. HE is an interesting performer.
(4)   Jane will sing or George will recite a monologue. HE is an interesting performer.

I will begin the chapter with a discussion of the data, focusing in particular on the availability of each kind of interpretation with different types of NP antecedent (section 5.2). We will find that the first kind of interpretation is possible when the antecedents are quantificational NPs, including ordinary indefinites and definites. The second kind of interpretation is available when the antecedents are proper names, specific indefinites, or definite descriptions.

The next question is how each of these interpretations is derived. My central concern will be with the first kind of interpretation. I will suggest that in examples like (1) and (2), the pronouns are E-type pronouns with multiple antecedents. These examples will motivate the revision of the E-type account, as the account as given in Chapter Four cannot be applied to these data. The new account, presented in section 5.4., provides a set of recursive rules for deriving the interpretation of an E-type pronoun on the basis of the content of the antecedent clause. Section 5.5. will be concerned with exploring this new proposal, and applying it to the external anaphora data.

The remaining questions are how the interpretation of the pronoun is derived in examples like (3) and (4), and what the relation is between the properties of the antecedent NPs and possible readings of following pronouns. This will be the subject of section 5.6. In section 5.7., I will review some other treatments of the external anaphora data. Finally, in section 5.8., I will briefly discuss some residual issues raised by the new E-type proposal.

5.2. THE BASIC DATA

5.2.1. Anaphora to a disjunction of NPs

Examples (5) and (6) provide further illustration of a pronoun anaphoric on a disjunction of indefinites. The disjunction may occur in either subject or object position of its own clause.

(5)   Either a soprano or an alto will sing. She will perform Mozart.
(6)   George will sing either an aria or a ballad. It will have German lyrics.

As observed, the pronouns in these examples are in some sense anaphoric on the disjunction as a whole. The pronoun in (5), for example, is naturally paraphrased as "the person who sings" or "the soprano or alto who sings." I suggest that the pronoun is an E-type pronoun simultaneously anaphoric on both disjuncts. I will call such readings of pronouns *disjunctive E-type readings*. Note that no other anaphoric interpretation is available for the pronouns in these examples. Thus, the pronoun in (5) is not paraphrasable as "the soprano" or as "the alto."

It might be thought that anaphora to one of the NP disjuncts is ruled out in (5) because of an unresolvable ambiguity: there is no way to determine whether the pronoun is intended as anaphoric on *a soprano* or on *an alto*, and so neither is possible. However, anaphora to one of the subordinate NPs is ruled out even when there is no problem of ambiguity, as in (7).

(7)   Either a soprano or a bass will sing. #He will perform Mozart.

Any ambiguity would be resolved here by the gender clash between *he* and *a soprano*, but nonetheless, the pronoun cannot be understood as anaphoric on *a bass*. Moreover, as the two antecedents of the pronoun differ in gender, *he* cannot be given a disjunctive E-type interpretation, as an E-type pronoun is required to agree in gender with its antecedent or antecedents. So the pronoun in this case is not felicitous under any interpretation. I have found, however, that speakers who accept *they* as a gender-neutral singular anaphor also accept (8) with the disjunctive E-type interpretation.

(8)   Either a soprano or a bass will sing. They'll perform Mozart.

Disjunctions of other quantificational NPs also license external anaphora under a disjunctive E-type reading:

(9)   Either several altos or many sopranos left the choir. They were unhappy with the conductor.

They is paraphrasable as "the altos or sopranos who left the choir"[2].

Examples (5-9) contrast with cases in which one or both indefinites are replaced by proper names, as in (10-12). In these cases, the pronoun cannot be given a disjunctive E-type interpretation. This is not surprising, as E-type pronouns are pronouns anaphoric on quantificational NPs. (I will return to this issue later in the chapter.) A pronoun following a disjunction of proper names can, however, be interpreted as anaphoric on a particular subordinate NP, as long as there is no ambiguity. I will call this the *single-antecedent* reading of the pronoun.

(10)   Either Jane or Maud will sing. #She'll perform Mozart.
(11)   Either Jane or a soprano will sing. #She'll perform Mozart.
(12)   a. Either Jane or George will sing. HE is a very interesting performer.
        b. Jane and George will sing. HE is a very interesting performer.

To make the single-antecedent reading natural, the pronoun needs to be slightly stressed. (Strong contrastive stress is not necessary; the pronoun simply must not be de-accented.) Whatever the reason for this, the same holds in the case of anaphora to a subordinate NP in a conjunction such as (12b).

In the previous chapter, I discussed a number of cases involving "specific" indefinites, indefinites used in such a way as to indicate that the speaker has in mind (or intends to speak of) a particular individual satisfying the description. Specific indefinites pattern with proper names in the way they license external anaphora: they do not support disjunctive E-type readings of a following pronoun, but can serve independently as antecedents to a single-antecedent pronoun provided, again, that there is no ambiguity. In the following examples, I have given the indefinites heavy descriptive content, which facilitates a specific reading. This is not essential.

(13) The concert will be opened by a famous mezzo who started her career as a violist, or a young soprano who recently sang at the Met. #She will perform Mozart.
(14) The concert will be opened by a famous mezzo who started her career as a violist, or a young Welsh baritone who recently sang at the Met. HE is a very interesting performer.

Disjunctions of definite NPs allow both disjunctive E-type readings (example 15) and single-antecedent readings (example 16) for a following pronoun. As before, single-antecedent readings are available only when there is no ambiguity. Hence, the infelicity of (17):

(15) Either the soprano or the alto will sing. She'll perform Mozart.
(16) Either the soprano or the bass will sing. HE has a fine voice.
(17) Either the soprano or the alto will sing. #SHE has a fine voice.

In examining these data, we have to be careful to distinguish between two different ways in which an anaphor clause (the clause containing the anaphor) may be infelicitous. Sometimes, an anaphor clause is infelicitous because the pronoun cannot be interpreted in any appropriate way. These are the cases I am interested in. In other examples, an anaphor clause is infelicitous because the clause or sequence as a whole does not make sense. This distinction is familiar from Chapter Four. With respect to the current case, the distinction becomes apparent in the following examples:

(18) Jane or George will sing.
    a. ?HE will perform Mozart.
    b. HE is a very interesting performer.

(19) A soprano or an alto will sing.
    a. She will perform Mozart.
    b. ??She is a very interesting performer.

I have already shown that an external pronoun following a disjunction of proper names may be anaphoric on a particular disjunct. This is what we see in (18b), which says of George that he is a very interesting performer. Now, (18a) is quite odd as a continuation of (18), but in this case it is not because there is anything wrong with the anaphora. The anaphora works in just the same way, so that (18a) says of George that he will sing Mozart. But this is an odd thing to say, because the previous sentence conversationally implicates that as far as the speaker knows, it is possible that George will not sing at all.

The infelicity of (19) is similar. The pronoun in (19a) is a disjunctive E-type pronoun anaphoric on *a soprano or an alto*, and the sentence as a whole is equivalent to "the soprano or alto who sings will perform Mozart," which is perfectly coherent. But if the pronoun in (19b) is interpreted in the same way, the result is not terribly coherent. We end up saying "the soprano or alto who sings is a very interesting performer," which is odd. Being an interesting performer is something we can say only of a specific individual, but the interpretation of the pronoun rules out the speaker having a particular individual in mind. So once again, it is not the anaphora itself which renders the sentence infelicitous, but the content of the assertion as a whole.

5.2.2. Clausal disjunction

The pattern of anaphora to clausal disjunctions is very similar to what we have already seen. Clausal disjunctions which contain indefinites support external anaphora, with the pronoun receiving a disjunctive E-type interpretation. The pronoun in (20), for example, is paraphrasable as "the soprano who sings or actress who performs a monologue." (21) is another example of this kind. Other quantificational NPs, including definites, can give rise to this reading, as illustrated in (22-23). With proper names or specific indefinites, the disjunctive E-type reading disappears, but the pronoun may be understood as anaphoric on a particular NP in one of the disjuncts (examples 24-26).

(20) For the final act, either a soprano will sing or an actress will perform a monologue. Then she will lead the audience in the national anthem.

(21) Either a squirrel has got into the attic, or a bird is building a nest up there. We'll have to get it out.

External anaphora 187

(22) For the final act, either several sopranos will sing or two actresses will perform a dialogue. Then they will lead the audience in the national anthem.

(23) For the final act, either the soprano will sing or the actress will perform a monologue. Then she will lead the audience in the national anthem.

(24) Either Jane will sing or Maud will play the piano. #Then she'll lead the audience in the national anthem.

(25) Either a famous mezzo who started her career as a violist will sing, or a young pianist who won the Rubinstein competition a couple of years ago will play. #She'll probably do several encores.

(26) Either Jane will sing or George will play the piano. HE is a very interesting performer.

In Chapter Four, I discussed the unavailability of anaphora to narrow scope QNPs. That constraint emerges here too. The antecedents of a disjunctive E-type pronoun must have wide scope within their respective clauses. The pronoun in (27) thus cannot be anaphoric on the indefinites in the disjunction:

(27) Either every soprano admires a bass, or every alto admires a tenor. #He has wonderful breath control.

The effects of scope are also seen in the following contrast:

(28) Either a soprano will sing an aria, or an actress will recite a monologue.
    a. Then she will lead the audience in the national anthem.
    b. ?It'll be in German.

(29) Either an aria will be sung by a soprano, or a monologue will be recited by an actress.
    a. #Then she will lead the audience in the national anthem.
    b. It'll be in German.

These examples will be treated in section 5.5.2.

As I observed in the introduction, the data raise three different questions: First, how is the disjunctive E-type reading derived? Second, how is the single-antecedent reading derived? And third, what properties of the antecedent NPs affect the availability of each reading?

5.3. A FIRST REFORMULATION OF THE E-TYPE ACCOUNT

The E-type account as formulated in Chapter Four cannot be applied to the cases of external anaphora. This is because the definition of antecedent clause presupposes that a given pronoun can have only one NP antecedent, and the pronoun rule applies only when the antecedent clause has the logical form [Det'(F')(G')]. I begin by repeating the relevant rules from Chapter Four:

(AC)   *Definition of Antecedent Clause*
       The *antecedent clause* for a pronoun P co-indexed with a quantified NP Q_1 occurring in an LF φ is the minimal IP contained in φ that dominates Q_1.

(PR)   *Pronoun Rule*
       If α is an E-type pronoun with antecedent clause φ whose logical form is Det'(F')(G'), then α' = the'(λx.F'(x)&G'(x)).

Let's now see why these rules fail to apply to the cases we are concerned with here.

In an example like (30), the interpretation of the pronoun depends on the content of the entire disjunction.

(30)   Either a squirrel has got into the attic, or a bird is building a nest up there. We have to get it out.

I suggest that this is because the pronoun is anaphoric on both of the indefinite NPs *a squirrel* and *a bird*. To allow for this on the indexation view I am adopting, I must (i) posit an LF which represents the entire two sentence string in (30) and (ii) allow the pronoun to be co-indexed with both indefinites. To implement this, I assume, following Heim (1982), that strings of sentences may be grouped together under a text node, as in

(31). (Something like this assumption is needed in any structural E-type treatment of cross-sentential anaphora.)

(31)

I assume further that co-indexation is possible across sentence boundaries, and that a single pronoun may be co-indexed with more than one NP. I follow Heim (1990) in assuming that indexation is free. Many possible indexations will lead to uninterpretability, but these need not be ruled out directly. They are syntactically licensed, but never emerge because they cannot be used.

There are two ways in which a pronoun could be co-indexed with multiple antecedents. The antecedents may share a single index, which is also shared by the pronoun; or the pronoun may be assigned two different indices. It is not important here that we choose between these options. Indeed, if co-indexation is free, there is no reason to assume one of these possibilities over the other. In my representations, I will assign the antecedents distinct indices and assume the pronoun is multiply indexed.

Having allowed for the possibility of a pronoun having more than one antecedent, we must reformulate the definition of antecedent clause. This is straightforward. The revised formulation is given in (AC_1).

(AC_1) *Antecedent Clause: Revised Definition*
The *antecedent clause* for a pronoun P co-indexed with quantified NPs $Q_1...Q_n$ occurring in an LF φ is the minimal IP contained in φ that dominates $Q_1...Q_n$.

With the revised definition, a pronoun will still have a single antecedent clause, but that clause must contain all of the NP antecedents of the pronoun.

As an illustration, let us apply the new definition to example (30), repeated here:

(30)   Either a squirrel has got into the attic or a bird is building a nest up there. We have to get it out.

The LF of the disjunction is given in (32). If the pronoun is coindexed with both of the indefinites in the disjunction, then by (AC_1), its antecedent clause is the entire disjunction, as no lower IP dominates both of the antecedents:

(32)

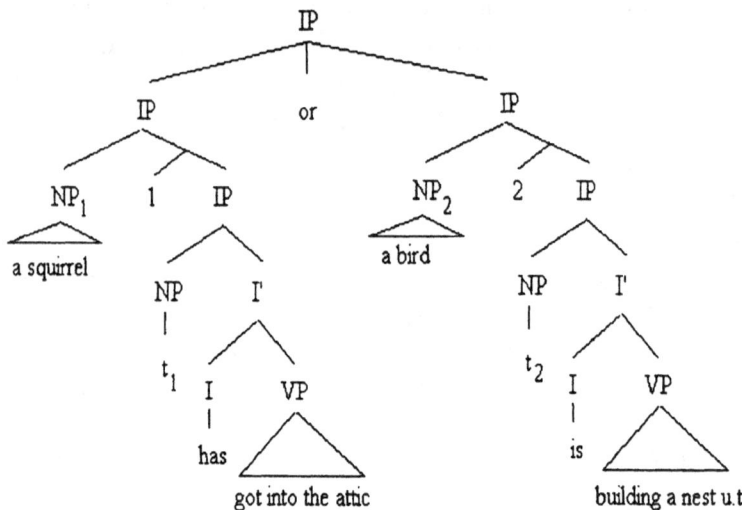

We get the same effect with NP disjunctions like the first sentence in (33), whose LF is given in (34):

(33)   A squirrel or a bird has got into the attic. We have to get it out.

(34)

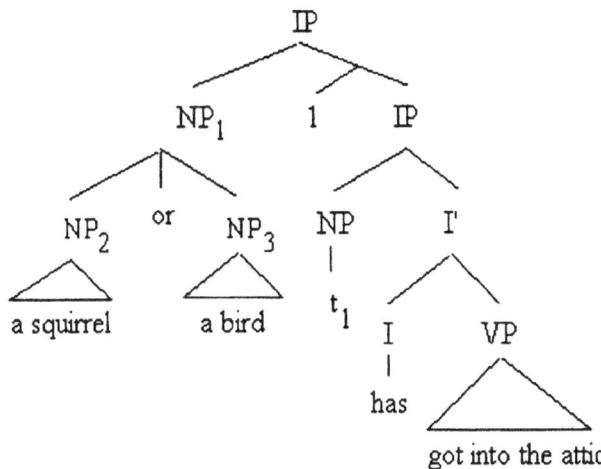

Once again, if the pronoun *it* in the second sentence of (33) is co-indexed with both disjuncts then its antecedent clause is the whole sentence. (In fact, even if the pronoun is co-indexed with only one disjunct, the antecedent clause will still be the whole sentence. This is a point to which we shall return later.)

The Pronoun Rule (PR) constructs a translation for E-type pronouns on the basis of the logical form of the antecedent clause. However, the translation language and procedure adopted in Chapter Four do not provide for the translation of NP disjunctions as in (32). At this point, then, I introduce a new disjunction operator into this language. At the same time, I will introduce a conjunction operator, although this will not be of use until later in the chapter.

The two operators are based on the Generalized Disjunction and Conjunction operators of Partee and Rooth (1983). Building on a proposal in Montague (1973), Partee and Rooth provide a cross-categorial treatment of disjunction and conjunction using the two recursively defined operators "⊔" (generalized disjunction) and "⊓" (generalized conjunction). When these operators conjoin expressions of type t, they are identical to the sentential connectives "∨" and "&," respectively. This constitutes the base case for the recursive definition. All other occurrences of "⊔" and "⊓" are defined in terms of the base case.

I incorporate these two operators into the translation language adopted in Chapter Four. First, we state which types of expressions can be conjoined by the operators (definition of conjoinable type). Then, we introduce a new translation rule for disjunctive and conjunctive expressions which makes use of the new operators. Finally, we define the semantics of the operators.

(35) *Recursive Definition of Conjoinable Type*
    i.   t is a conjoinable type.
    ii. If b is a conjoinable type, then for any a, <a, b> is a conjoinable type.

(36) *Translation Rule for Disjunction and Conjunction*
If α and β are expressions of category A, of conjoinable type a, with translations α' and β', then [α or β] has the translation [α'⊔β'], also of type a, and [α and β] has the translation [α'⊓β'], of type a.

(37) *Semantics of* ⊔ *and* ⊓
    i.   In D_t, "⊔" is equivalent to "∨" and "⊓" is equivalent to "&."
    ii. Let b be a conjoinable type and let f, g ∈ $ME_{<a,b>}$.
       Then f⊔g is that function in $D_{<a,b>}$ which maps any element x of D_a onto the element f(x) ⊔ g(x) of D_b and
       f⊓g is that function in $D_{<a,b>}$ which maps any element x of D_a onto the element f(x) ⊓ g(x) of D_b.
       i.e. f ⊔ g ≡ λu [f(u) ⊔ g(u)]
            f ⊓ g ≡ λu[f(u) ⊓ g(u)]

The following equivalences, which can be derived from (37), provide useful shortcuts in working out translations:

(38)   i.   φ ⊔ ψ = λz [φ(z) ⊔ ψ(z)], where φ and ψ are of the same type, and z is a variable of appropriate type not occurring free in either φ or ψ.
       ii. [φ ⊔ ψ](x) = φ(x) ⊔ ψ(x)
       iii. λvφ ⊔ λvψ = λv [φ ⊔ ψ]

We can now use the new operator to provide logical forms for (32) and (34). These are given in (39) and (40) respectively:

(39) $a'(\text{squirrel}')(\lambda x.\text{has-got-into-the-attic}'(x)) \sqcup a'(\text{bird}')(\lambda x.\text{is-building-a-nest-up-there}'(x))$ [3]

(40) $[a'(\text{squirrel}') \sqcup a'(\text{bird}')](\lambda x_1.\text{has-got-into-the-attic}'(x_1))$

Neither of these matches the logical form required for application of (PR). (PR), in fact, is a construction-specific rule. It applies when a pronoun is co-indexed with a single, non-conjoined NP occurring in a simple sentence. To extend the account to external anaphora, we must give two further construction-specific rules: one for the case of clausal disjunction, and one for the case of NP disjunction. The rules we need are as follows:

(PR: IP disj)
  If α is an E-type pronoun with antecedent clause φ whose logical form is $[\text{Det}_1'(F')(G') \sqcup ... \sqcup \text{Det}_n'(P')(Q')]$, then:
  $\alpha' = \text{the}'(\lambda x.[F'(x)\&G'(x)] \sqcup ... \sqcup [P'(x)\&Q'(x)])$

(PR: NP disj)
  If α is an E-type pronoun with antecedent clause φ whose logical form is $[\text{Det}_1'(F') \sqcup ... \sqcup \text{Det}_n'(P')](Q')$, then:
  $\alpha' = \text{the}'(\lambda x.[F'(x) \sqcup ... \sqcup P'(x)]\&Q'(x))$

Following these rules, we arrive at the translations below for the pronouns in (30) and (33), repeated here:

(30) Either a squirrel has got into the attic, or a bird is building a nest up there. We have to get it out.
  $it' = \text{the}'(\lambda x.[\text{squirrel}'(x) \& \text{has-got-into-the-attic}'(x)] \sqcup [\text{bird}'(x) \& \text{is-building-a-nest-up-there}'(x)]$

(33) A squirrel or a bird has got into the attic. We have to get it out.
  $it' = \text{the}'(\lambda x.[\text{squirrel}'(x) \sqcup \text{bird}'(x)] \& \text{has-got-into-the-attic}'(x))$

These are the translations we are after for the pronouns, but the method of arriving at them is, to echo Heim (1990), pedestrian. For every sentence type which might appear as antecedent clause to an E-type pronoun, a distinct interpretation rule is needed. Pronouns anaphoric on conjoined NPs or NPs inside a conjunction will need another pair of rules, at least. This seems unsatisfactory. In the following section, I will propose a method for arriving at the content of the description which departs far more significantly from Neale's proposal than this, and which offers a compositional way to derive the interpretation of an E-type pronoun.

5.4. A COMPOSITIONAL STRUCTURAL E-TYPE ACCOUNT

5.4.1. Presentation

The structural E-type accounts proposed by Evans (1977, 1980), by Neale (1990) and (in passing) by Heim (1990) all suffer from the same lack of generality. They do not offer general principles for deriving the interpretation of an E-type pronoun from the content of the antecedent clause, but only construction-specific rules. The output of these rules is intuitively plausible. The definite descriptions which are given as the interpretations of E-type pronouns are just those which naive informants will give as paraphrases. But those informants, surely, are applying some general principle of interpretation. There is something which they are able to extract from an antecedent clause which they recognize as providing content for a following pronoun.

The content of a definite description is always a one-place property, the denotation of a predicate. It is this one-place property that we extract from an antecedent clause when we construct an interpretation for an E-type pronoun. The grammar determines that the pronoun is interpreted as a description. What the hearer must do is only to identify the property which gives the description its content. So what appears to be rule-governed is the process of going from a clause (an IP) to a one-place property.

To get to this property, we use the content of property-denoting expressions which the clause contains to construct a new, composite property. An E-type pronoun anaphoric on the NP *many sopranos* occurring in the clause *many sopranos sang* will be interpreted as "the sopranos who sang." So from this antecedent clause we have apparently recovered the property of being a soprano who sang. We arrive at this property because the clause is itself constructed from the predicate-containing expression *many sopranos* and the predicate *sang*. From the expression *many sopranos* we recover the property of being sopranos or of "soprano-hood." From the expression *sang* we recover the property of being something that sang. The subject-predicate structure of the antecedent clause tells us to combine these properties to give the composite property of being a soprano who sang.

The central idea of the proposal, then, is to have a set of rules for determining what I will call the *recoverable property* of any LF expression. As I am working within a system of indirect interpretation (interpretation via a translation language) I do not give these rules directly, but give a set of rules for determining the predicates which express the relevant property in the translation language. I call this the *recoverable predicate* of an expression. Recoverable predicates are determined on the basis of the translations of LF expressions. The central idea is that the predicate we recover mirrors in its structure the structure of the antecedent clause. Consequently, when the antecedent clause is disjunctive, so is the predicate.

I limit myself here to providing rules for determining the recoverable predicates of expression types for which I have already given translation rules. In a system of direct interpretation, an isomorphic set of rules could be given to determine the recoverable property of LF expressions on the basis of their denotation.

(RP) *Rules for determining recoverable predicates*

For any LF node α let α' be the translation of the subtree dominated by α and let α^P be the recoverable predicate of that subtree.

(RP:1) $\overline{N}^P = \overline{N}'$
(RP:2) $[_{NP} \text{Det } \overline{N}]^P = \overline{N}^P$
(RP:3) $[i \text{ IP}]^P = [i \text{ IP}]'$
(RP:4) $[_{IP} NP_i [i \text{ IP}]]^P = NP_i^P \sqcap [i \text{ IP}]^P$
(RP:5) $[_{XP} XP_1 \text{ or } ... \text{ or } XP_n]^P = XP_1^P \sqcup ... \sqcup XP_2^P$

(RP:1) and (RP:2), taken together, ensure that the recoverable predicate of quantificational NPs (including definites and indefinites) is the translation of the $\overline{N}$. Note that the determiner itself plays no role in fixing the recoverable predicate, so *a soprano*, *many sopranos*, and *every soprano* all determine the same recoverable predicate. (Again, I am setting aside the possible complications introduced by plurality.) (RP:3) is the rule for the recoverable predicate of an IP from which an NP has been extracted by QR. The recoverable predicate of this structure is identical to its translation, which is derived by lambda abstraction over the translation of the NP trace. (RP:4) uses the generalized conjunction operator (meet) to combine the recoverable predicate of the extracted NP with the recoverable predicate of the IP from which it is extracted to give the recoverable predicate of the higher IP. Finally, (RP:5) gives a cross-categorial rule for determining the recoverable predicate of any disjoined constituent, using the generalized disjunction operator.

To illustrate how these rules work, I give in (42) the calculation of the recoverable predicate of *many sopranos sang*, assuming the LF in (41):

(41) $[_{IP2} [_{NP1}\text{many sopranos}] 1 [_{IP1} t_1 \text{ sang }]]$

(42)
i. $IP2^P = NP1^P \sqcap [1 \text{ } IP1]^P$ (by (RP:4))
ii. $NP1^P = \overline{N}^P = \overline{N}' = \text{soprano}'$ (by (RP:1) and (RP:2))
iii. $[1 \text{ } IP1]^P = [i \text{ } IP]' = \lambda x_1.\text{sang}'(x_1)$ (by (RP:3))
iv. $IP2^P = \text{soprano}' \sqcap \lambda x_1.\text{sang}'(x_1)$ (by (RP:4))
     $= \lambda z.\text{soprano}'(z) \sqcap \lambda x_1[\text{sang}'(x_1)](z)$
     $= \lambda z.\text{soprano}'(z) \sqcap \text{sang}'(z)$ (by λ-conversion)
     $= \lambda z.\text{soprano}'(z) \text{ \& sang}'(z)$ (by definition of "⊓")

This property – the property of being a soprano who sang – is what we want to use in constructing the interpretation of any E-type pronoun for which this IP is the antecedent clause. We can now give the interpretation rule for E-type pronouns in terms of the recoverable property of their antecedents:

(PR)   *Pronoun Rule (revised)*
       If α is an E-type pronoun with antecedent clause φ, then
       $\alpha' = \text{the}'(\varphi^P)$

We now apply this rule to produce the interpretation for the pronoun in (43):

(43) Many sopranos$_i$ sang. They$_i$ were wonderful.
(44) they' = the'(λz.soprano'(z) & sang'(z))

The only additional consideration is to ensure that the description matches the pronoun in number. I will simply add this requirement as a condition to (PR), as follows:

(PR), revision:
(i) If α is a singular E-type pronoun with antecedent clause φ, then
    α'=the'(φ^P)
(ii) If α is a plural E-type pronoun with antecedent clause φ, then
    α'=the$_P$'(φ^P)

This is the only interpretation rule for E-type pronouns; we do not need a different rule for pronouns occurring in different environments. Nor are the rules for deriving recoverable properties construction-specific. Hence, the proposal offers a greater degree of generality than the proposal of Chapter Four.

5.4.2. Comparison with Chapter Four account

Before applying the new proposal to the external anaphora data, let us verify that it provides an adequate treatment of the internal anaphora data discussed in Chapter Four, and treated with the simpler E-type account. In fact, in all cases in which the Chapter Four proposal is applicable, (i.e., cases in which an E-type pronoun has a single antecedent contained in a simple clause), the predictions of the two proposals are the same. In all of these cases, the antecedent clause is of the form in (45a), with the semantic logical form in (45b). (46a-b) give a particular example with this form:

(45) a. [$_{IP}$ [$_{NPi}$Det $\bar{N}$] [i IP]]
     b. Det'($\bar{N}$')(λx_i.IP')

(46) a. [$_{IP}$ [$_{NPi}$ many sopranos][i [$_{IP}$ t$_i$ sang]]]
     b. many'(soprano')(λx_i.sang'(x_i))

According to the Pronoun Rule of Chapter Four, an E-type pronoun with an antecedent clause of the form in (45) has the interpretation:

(47) the'$(\lambda x.\overline{N}'(x)$ & $\lambda x_i.IP'(x))$

For the specific example in (46), this gives us:

(48) the'$(\lambda x.\text{soprano}'(x)$ & $\text{sang}'(x))$

The new proposal produces the same result. The recoverable property of an IP of the form in (45) is the meet of the recoverable predicate of the NP and the recoverable property of [i IP]. So for any sentence φ of this form:

(49) $\varphi^P = NP^P \sqcap [i\ IP]^P = \overline{N}' \sqcap [i\ IP]'$

Inserting this property into a definite description gives us:

(50) the'$(\overline{N}' \sqcap [i\ IP]')$

And (50) is always equivalent to:

(51) the'$(\lambda x.\overline{N}'(x)$ & $[i\ IP]'(x))$

which is identical to (47).

Going through this calculation with the example, we have that:

(52) [many sopranos sang]^P = soprano' $\sqcap \lambda x_i.\text{sang}'(x_i)$
      $= \lambda x.\text{soprano}'(x) \sqcap \text{sang}'(x)$
      $= \lambda x.\text{soprano}'(x)$ & $\text{sang}'(x)$

the very same property which appears in the description in (48).

5.4.3. Narrow scope antecedents

The new account makes the same predictions as the earlier one also with respect to anaphora to a narrow scope QNP. Just as before, such anaphora will be ruled out due to the occurrence of a free variable in the translation

External anaphora   199

of the pronoun. I will go through an example to illustrate how this arises on the new proposal. As I mentioned in the previous chapter, there are some additional complications, which I will go on to discuss here.

In the following example, if the indefinite is understood as having narrow scope, the pronoun cannot be interpreted as anaphoric on it:

(53)   Every soprano admires a bass$_1$. #He$_1$ has wonderful breath control.

Consider, then, how the derivation of an interpretation for this pronoun would proceed if it were so interpreted. First, we identify the antecedent clause of the pronoun on the basis of the LF in (54):

(54)   [$_{IP3}$ every soprano$_2$ 2 [$_{IP2}$ a bass$_1$ 1 [$_{IP1}$ t$_2$ admires t$_1$]]]

The minimal IP dominating *a bass* is IP2. Because t$_2$ is not bound inside IP2, the translation of IP2 contains a free variable, and so too does the recoverable predicate of IP2, as shown by the calculation in (55). The same variable will be free in the definite description constructed from this property.

(55)
(i)   IP2^P = [a bass$_1$]^P ⊓ [1 [$_{IP1}$ t$_2$ admires t$_1$]]^P
(ii)   [a bass$_1$]^P = bass'
(iii)   [1 [$_{IP1}$ t$_2$ admires t$_1$]]^P = λx_1.admire'$(x_1)(x_2)$
(iv)   IP2^P = bass' ⊓ λx_1.admire'$(x_1)(x_2)$
             = λx.bass'(x) ⊓ admire'$(x)(x_2)$
             = λx.bass'(x) & admire'$(x)(x_2)$

In Chapter Four, I simply assumed, following Neale (1990), that an E-type pronoun cannot have a translation which contains a free variable, and that where such a translation is the only one available, the pronoun is unacceptable. The intuition underlying this is that a sentence containing such a pronoun would be uninterpretable. However, we do not necessarily want to rule out free variables from all sentences of the translation language. Deictic pronouns, for example, are naturally translated as free variables. These variables would be interpreted via an assignment function, presumably an element of the contextual parameter c to which interpretations are relativized. This assignment function would also provide an interpretation for a free variable in the translation of an E-type pronoun.

But if this happens, the value assigned to the variable as part of the translation of the pronoun will differ from the value it will be assigned in the denotation of the *sentence* containing the clause from which the property is derived, where the pronoun is bound. Thus, the description will not "match" the clause from which it is constructed. But a recoverable predicate which contains a free variable which is also free in the denotation of the sentence (say, a variable introduced as the denotation of a deictic pronoun) could be used to construct a translation for an E-type pronoun. So let us say that E-type pronouns whose antecedent clause contains an *incidentally* free variable are ruled out, and hence anaphora to a narrow scope QNP is generally not possible.

However, it is not the case that anaphora to a narrow scope QNP is never possible. Anaphora to an indefinite under a universal is possible in certain kinds of sentence sequences. Such cases are discussed extensively in Roberts (1987). Where anaphora is possible, the discourse usually relates to a generic or script-like situation (see Poessi and Zucchi 1992), as in the following:

(56) Every chess-set comes with a spare pawn. It is taped to the lid of the box. (Sells)
(57) Every graduate went up to the dais. She took her diploma and returned to her seat. (Poessi and Zucchi)

There seems to be a general consensus that such examples involve a special mechanism, and are not to be assimilated to standard cases of cross-sentential anaphora (see, for example, Chierchia (1995: 9)). The E-type account I am proposing predicts that anaphora to narrow scope indefinites should be a special case, as indeed it seems to be.

There is a further complication, though, which arises with sentences containing multiple definites or multiple indefinites, as in (58) and (59):

(58) A man$_1$ I know loves a woman$_2$. He$_1$ lives in Paris. She$_2$ lives in Vienna.
(59) The man who lives upstairs$_1$ loves the woman who lives downstairs$_2$. He$_1$ is from Paris. She$_2$ is from Vienna.

The NPs in the first sentence of each example are syntactically scoped relative to one another, so whichever pronoun is anaphoric on the narrow scope indefinite must, on our current assumptions, contain a free variable. However, both pronouns in each example are quite natural, and neither has the flavor of the telescoping examples discussed above. Both appear to receive an interpretation straightforwardly on the basis of the antecedent clause.

Notice, first, that the syntactic scope of the NP antecedents in these examples does not affect the interpretation of the sentence in which they occur. Although definites and indefinites must be syntactically scoped with respect to one another, their syntactic scope has no semantic effect. Thus, whether the subject or the object has wide scope in (58) and (59), the interpretation is the same. Let's focus on (58). It has the two possible LFs in (60):

(60) a. [$_{IP3}$ a man$_1$ 1 [$_{IP2}$ a woman$_2$ 2 [$_{IP1}$ t$_1$ loves t$_2$]]]
     b. [$_{IP3}$ a woman$_2$ 2 [$_{IP2}$ a man$_1$ 1 [$_{IP1}$ t$_1$ loves t$_2$]]]

Given this, we would expect both sequences in (61) to be possible, as indeed they are:

(61) a. A man$_1$ loves a woman. He$_1$ lives in Paris.
     b. A man loves a woman$_2$. She$_2$ lives in Vienna.

To allow anaphora to *a man*, we assume the LF (60a), which gives *a man* wide scope. To allow anaphora to *a woman*, we assume the LF (60b), which gives *a woman* wide scope. We can choose whichever allows for maximal interpretability of the string as a whole, because the interpretation of the first sentence is unaffected.

Fox (1995) has argued that inverse scope relations are possible only when the difference in syntactic scope produces a difference in interpretation. To derive the LF in which the object has wide scope over the subject, a longer move is needed than in the derivation of the LF in which the object has narrow scope. For this reason, he argues, objects are given wide scope only when this has a semantic effect. Semantically vacuous scope changes are ruled out by economy considerations. However, in the case of (61b), inverse scope in the first sentence is required in order to produce an interpretation for the anaphor sentence.

This observation, though, still does not explain why anaphora to *both* indefinites is possible, as in the string in (58). Whichever LF we choose, one of the indefinites must have narrow scope, and hence should not allow for anaphora. The answer, perhaps, is that we do not have to choose one LF from which to construct a recoverable predicate, and hence an interpretation for the pronoun. Suppose that the antecedent of an E-type pronoun is identified inside a sentence S which has only one interpretation, but multiple semantically equivalent LFs. In this case, the interpretation of the pronoun may be constructed from any of these LFs. Suppose that S has more than one interpretation, and multiple LFs associated with each interpretation. First, we select an interpretation for S, and eliminate from consideration any LFs not associated with this interpretation. The interpretation of the pronoun may then be constructed on the basis of any of the remaining semantically equivalent LFs. In (58), then, the pronoun *he* is interpreted with the predicate recovered from the LF in (60a), while the pronoun *she* is interpreted with the predicate recovered from the LF in (60b).

Examples (58) and (59) are of the type which a variable-sharing/ dynamic binding theory deals with very straightforwardly. As I made clear in Chapter Four, it is not my intention to argue that the E-type strategy is the only strategy of pronoun interpretation, and I am not committed to giving an E-type account of the anaphora in these examples. I discussed in Chapter Four the possibility of a "copy" strategy of interpretation, and I do not rule out the possibility that dynamic binding is also available. (Chierchia (1995) advocates a "mixed" system incorporating both dynamic binding and an E-type strategy, although the E-type account he adopts is a pragmatic one. Similarly, Kadmon (1987) incorporates something like an E-type strategy into DRT by allowing for quite extensive accommodation.) However, as I argued in Chapter Four, there is no straightforward way to treat internal anaphora in disjunctions with a variable-sharing/dynamic binding approach. And as I will show in the next section, the E-type account is successful in treating the relevant cases of external anaphora.

5.5. APPLICATION TO THE EXTERNAL ANAPHORA DATA

5.5.1. Anaphora to a disjunction of NPs

Recall that disjunctive E-type anaphora is possible to disjunctions of (non-specific) indefinites, definites, and other quantificational NPs, as in:

(62) A soprano or an alto will sing. She will perform Mozart.
(63) The soprano or the alto will sing. She will perform Mozart.
(64) Some sopranos or several altos will sing. They will perform Mozart.

The derivation of this reading is quite straightforward. I will use (62) as my illustration.

The LF of the first sentence of (62) is given in (65)[4]:

(65) $[_{IP2} [_{NP3}$ a soprano$_1$ or an alto$_2] [3 [_{IP1} t_3$ will sing $]]]$

Assuming the pronoun in the second sentence of (62) to be coindexed with both NP disjuncts, its antecedent clause is IP2. The recoverable predicate of this clause is calculated in (66):

(66)
i. $IP2^P = NP3^P \sqcap [3\ IP1]^P$
ii. $NP3^P = [_{NP}$ a soprano$]^P \sqcup [_{NP}$ an alto$]^P$
   $=$ soprano$' \sqcup$ alto$'$
   $= \lambda x.\text{soprano}'(x) \sqcup \text{alto}'(x)$
   $= \lambda x.\text{soprano}'(x) \vee \text{alto}'(x)$
iii. $[3\ IP1]^P = [3\ IP1]' = \lambda x_3.\text{will-sing}'(x_3)$
iv. $IP2^P = [\lambda x.\text{soprano}'(x) \vee \text{alto}'(x)] \sqcap [\lambda x_3.\text{will-sing}'(x_3)]$
   $= \lambda z[[\lambda x.\text{soprano}'(x) \vee \text{alto}'(x)](z) \sqcap [\lambda x_3.\text{will-sing}'(x_3)](z)]$
   $= \lambda z[[\text{soprano}'(z) \vee \text{alto}'(z)] \sqcap \text{will-sing}'(z)]$
   $= \lambda z.[\text{soprano}'(z) \vee \text{alto}'(z)]\ \&\ \text{will-sing}'(z)$

We now insert this predicate into a definite description, to give the translation of the pronoun:

(67) she$' = $ the$'(\lambda z.[\text{soprano}'(z) \vee \text{alto}'(z)]\ \&\ \text{will-sing}'(z))$

The anaphor sentence as a whole thus has the logical form:

(68) the'(λz.[soprano'(z) $\vee$ alto'(z)] & will-sing'(z))(λx_1.will-perform-Mozart'(x_1))

i.e., "the soprano or alto who will sing will perform Mozart."

It will make no difference whether the NP disjunction is in subject or object position (provided it is not under the scope of some other QNP). If the disjunction occurs in object position, it will still be adjoined to its IP at LF, and the calculation of the recoverable predicate will proceed in parallel fashion. So, for example, (69) will have the LF in (70), from which we recover the predicate in (71):

(69) George loves a soprano or an alto. She sings Mozart beautifully.
(70) [$_{IP2}$ [$_{NP3}$ a soprano$_1$ or an alto$_2$] [3 [$_{IP1}$George loves t$_3$]]]
(71) λx.[soprano'(x) $\vee$ alto'(x)] & loves'(x)(g)

This predicate denotes the property of being a soprano or alto loved by George.

So far, I have been assuming that a disjunctive E-type pronoun is co-indexed with each of the disjunct NPs. However, identical results would be achieved by assuming that the pronoun is simply co-indexed with the disjunctive NP itself. It is the antecedent *clause* which determines the interpretation of the pronoun. The minimal IP dominating each of the disjuncts is always identical to the minimal IP dominating the disjunction, so we can simply assume that disjunctive E-type pronouns are co-indexed with the disjunctive NP.

There is a further consequence of the fact that it is the antecedent clause, and not the antecedent itself, which determines the interpretation of the pronoun. This is that whether a following E-type pronoun is co-indexed with one disjunct, some subset of the disjuncts, all disjuncts, or the disjunctive NP itself, the antecedent clause will be the same, and hence the interpretation of the pronoun would be the same. This provides an explanation for the observation made in section 2 that non-specific indefinites and QNPs (although not definites) do not license what I called *single-antecedent* anaphora. Thus, it is not possible to interpret the pronoun *he* in (72) as anaphoric on *a bass*:

(72) A soprano or a bass₁ will sing. #He₁ will perform Mozart.

Given the observation just made, this constraint has a structural explanation. Assuming that in this case there is no strategy other than the E-type to link the indefinite with the pronoun, there is no interpretation available for the pronoun other than "the soprano or bass who will sing." An E-type pronoun can be co-indexed with an indefinite disjunct. But this co-indexation will produce just the same result as co-indexation with the disjunction as a whole. Single-antecedent anaphora to a quantificational disjunct is thus ruled out by the nature of the rules for interpreting E-type pronouns.

5.5.2. Anaphora to clausal disjunctions

We are still engaged in the project of accounting for the disjunctive E-type interpretation of external pronouns. I turn now to pronouns anaphoric on indefinites or other QNPs contained in clausal disjuncts. I begin with the cases which work out straightforwardly: pronouns anaphoric on QNPs which have wide scope in their clauses. In 5.5.2.2., I turn to some more complex cases involving narrow scope QNPs.

5.5.2.1. Basic case

Let's begin with the example in (73):

(73) A soprano will sing, or an actress will recite. Then she will lead the audience in the national anthem.

Assume that *she* is co-indexed with the two indefinites, *a soprano* and *an actress*. Assume further that the first sentence of (73) has the LF in (74). The antecedent clause of the pronoun is the minimal IP which dominates both antecedents, which in this case is IP5, the highest IP. We thus calculate the recoverable predicate of this clause in order to determine the translation of the pronoun. The calculation is given in (75). (From now on, I will allow myself to skip some of the steps in these calculations.)

(74)

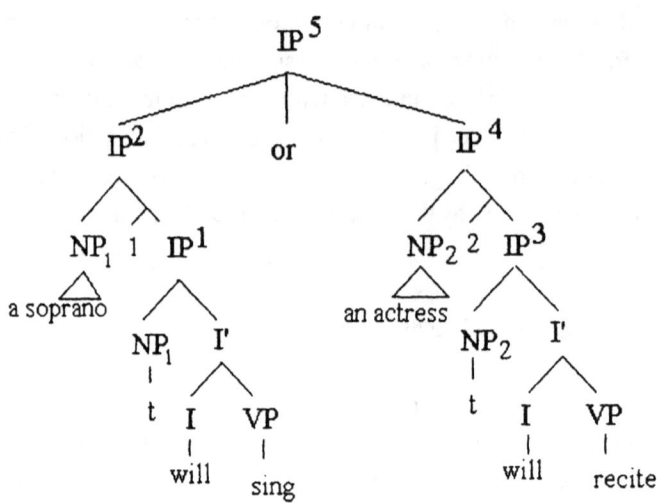

(75)
i. $IP5^P = IP2^P \sqcup IP4^P$
ii. $IP2^P = NP1^P \sqcap [1\ IP1]^P$
   $= soprano' \sqcap \lambda x_1.will\text{-}sing'(x_1)$
   $= \lambda x.soprano'(x)\ \&\ will\text{-}sing'(x)$
iii. $IP4^P = NP2^P \sqcap [2\ IP3]^P$
   $= actress' \sqcap \lambda x_2.will\text{-}recite'(x_2)$
   $= \lambda y.actress'(y)\ \&\ will\text{-}recite'(y)$
iv. $IP5^P = [\lambda x.soprano'(x)\ \&\ will\text{-}sing'(x)] \sqcup [\lambda y.actress'(y)\ \&\ will\text{-}recite'(y)]$
   $= \lambda z.[soprano'(z)\ \&\ will\text{-}sing'(z)] \vee [actress'(z)\ \&\ will\text{-}recite'(z)]$

This, then, is the predicate we will use in constructing the translation of the pronoun, giving:

External anaphora

(76)   the'(λz.[soprano'(z) & will-sing'(z)] $\vee$ [actress'(z) & will-recite'(z)])

i.e. "the soprano who will sing or actress who will recite." Thus, the anaphor clause comes out as equivalent to "Then the soprano who will sing or actress who will recite will lead the audience in the national anthem," as desired.

As with disjunctions of indefinite NPs, indefinites and other QNPs contained in clausal disjuncts cannot serve as antecedents to single-antecedent pronouns. (77), for example, is infelicitous, and in (78), *they* cannot be interpreted as anaphoric on *some tenors* alone.

(77)   A soprano will sing Mozart, or a tenor$_i$ will sing Schubert. #He$_i$ will be accompanied on the piano.
(78)   Some sopranos will sing Mozart, or some tenors$_i$ will sing Schubert. #They$_i$ will be accompanied on the piano.

In the previous section, I pointed out that the absence of single-antecedent readings to disjunctions of indefinites has a structural explanation: even if a pronoun were co-indexed with only one disjunct, the interpretation derived would be the disjunctive E-type reading. The same does not apply in these cases. Consider (79), the LF of the first sentence in (77). A pronoun co-indexed with *a soprano* would have IP2 as its antecedent clause and, by the now familiar procedure, would be interpreted as "the soprano who will sing Mozart." Similarly, a pronoun co-indexed with *a tenor* would have IP4 as its antecedent clause and would be interpreted as "the tenor who will sing Schubert." A pronoun co-indexed with both indefinites would have IP5 as its antecedent clause and, interpreted in parallel fashion to the pronoun in (73), would be interpreted as "the soprano who will sing Mozart or tenor who will sing Schubert." So, in principle, it seems that all three readings should be available for a following pronoun (assuming gender features match).

(79)

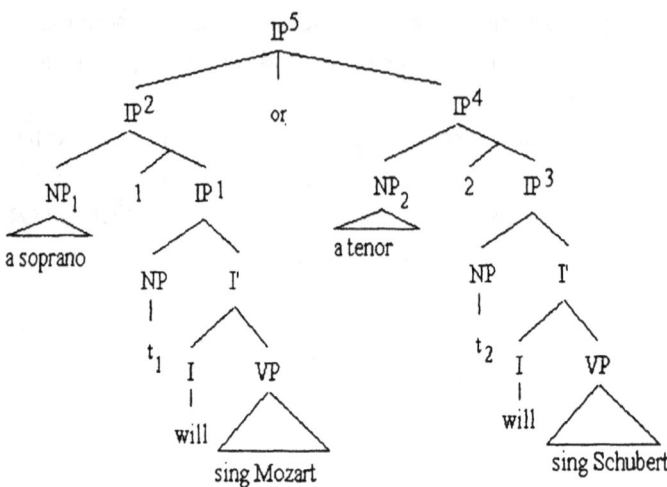

However, we can explain the absence of single-antecedent readings in pragmatic terms. Notice that the following string is as infelicitous as (77) above:

(80)   Either a soprano will sing Mozart or a tenor will sing Schubert. The tenor who will sing Schubert will be accompanied on the piano.

In (80), there is a conflict between the content of the first sentence and the presuppositions of the second. The definite description in the second sentence presupposes (and entails) the existence of a (unique) tenor who will sing Schubert. This presupposition will not be satisfied in the context, as update by the first sentence will produce a context containing some worlds in which a soprano sings but no tenor does. Moreover, as the disjunction conversationally implicates that the speaker does not know that there will be a tenor who sings, the presupposition cannot be accommodated without attributing peculiar conversational practices to the speaker.

(80) is, of course, equivalent to the result of interpreting the pronoun in (77) as an E-type pronoun anaphoric on *a tenor*. The interpretation is thus not ruled out by any structural considerations, but by considerations of felicity. Any case in which a pronoun is interpreted as anaphoric on an indefinite inside a disjunct will result in presupposition failure. In being interpretable but pragmatically ill-formed, (77) is like the examples of infelicitous internal anaphora discussed in Chapter Four, such as:

(81)   #Either Jane owns a truck, or it's in the shop.

Such examples are infelicitous, not because the anaphora is not possible, but because the anaphora produces an entailing disjunction.

Presupposition failure also accounts for the impossibility of anaphora in (82):

(82)   Either the wind is knocking things about in the attic, or a squirrel has got in, or a bird is building a nest up there. #We have to get it out.

Suppose that *it* were co-indexed with *a squirrel* and with *a bird*. Then its antecedent clause would be the IP dominating *a squirrel has got in or a bird is building a nest up there*, and the pronoun would be interpreted as "the squirrel that has got in or bird that is building a nest up there." This definite description presupposes the existence of something satisfying the description. But this presupposition is not satisfied, as the context to which the anaphor sentence is added will contain worlds in which there is no animal in the attic. Hence, the reading is ruled out.

The same may happen even when the "additional possibility" is not included in the disjunction itself, as in (83):

(83)   One possibility is that an attic window has broken and the wind is blowing things about. But perhaps a squirrel has got in there, or a bird is building a nest in the rafters. #We have to get it out.[5]

Because of the content of the first sentence, the context to which the anaphor sentence is added does not entail that there is something (bird or squirrel) in the attic. Consequently, the presupposition of the anaphor clause is not satisfied.

I have now given two different accounts of the absence of single-antecedent readings for external pronouns. In the previous section, I suggested that single-antecedent anaphora to a disjunction of QNPs is ruled out structurally. In this section, I have argued that single-antecedent anaphora to an QNP contained in a clausal disjunction is formally possible, but pragmatically ill-formed. I am thus positing different explanations for the infelicity of (84) and (85):

(84) A soprano or a tenor will sing. #He will be accompanied on the piano.
(85) A soprano will sing Mozart or a tenor will sing Schubert. #He will be accompanied on the piano.

This initially does not seem ideal, as the two cases seem parallel. It seems that we ought to be able to derive the interpretation "the tenor who will sing" for the pronoun in (84), and then rule it out as a matter of presupposition failure. However, the formal system I have set up does not allow for this, as I explained above.

Still, given that the account I am proposing is structure-sensitive, it is to be expected that synonymous but structurally distinct expressions will have distinct treatments. It is not out of the question that the failure of anaphora in (84) and (85) have different causes. Of course, if anaphora were structurally possible in (84), it would still be ruled out by presupposition failure. But this does not entail that no other constraint applies.

I will return briefly to this point in section 5.8.3., where I will sketch the changes that would be needed to allow for anaphora to a particular disjunct. As we will see, what is required is something not significantly different from the construction-specific rules I started out with in section 5.3. But rather than returning to that form of the account, I continue to explore the results and consequences of the current proposal.

5.5.2.2. Narrow scope antecedents

We have seen above that anaphora to a narrow scope QNP in a simple clause is generally ruled out because the antecedent clause, and hence the resulting description, would contain a free variable. (More precisely, the description would contain a variable which is free in the description but corresponds to a variable which is bound in the denotation of the sentence containing the antecedent clause.) It also turns out that anaphora to NPs contained in a clausal disjunction is possible only when the antecedents have wide scope within their clauses. Once again, this is due to a formal constraint, which is best illustrated by working through an example.

Consider, then, example (86):

(86)   Either every soprano admires a bass, or every alto admires a tenor.

The most natural interpretation of this is the one in which the indefinite in each clause has narrow scope. This reading is paraphrased in (87).

(87)   Either every soprano is such that there is some bass she admires, or every alto is such that there is some tenor she admires.

Now, keeping this reading for the disjunction in mind, observe that it is not possible to interpret the pronoun *he* in (88) as anaphoric on the indefinites:

(88)   Either every soprano admires a bass, or every alto admires a tenor. #He has wonderful breath control.

Let's now see why this is.

The relevant reading of the disjunction is derived from the LF in (89). (Note that of the possible LFs for the surface string, this is the only one which will give rise to the interpretation we are considering.)

(89)

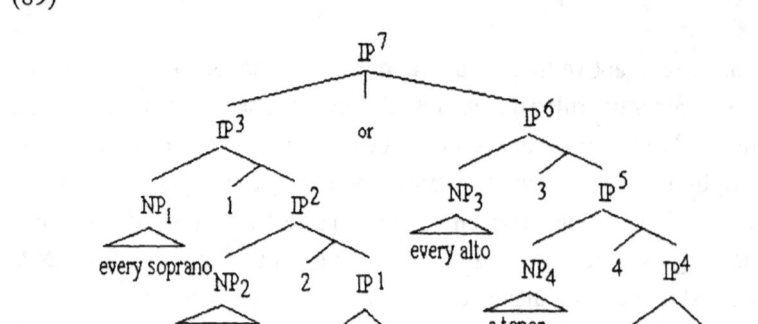

Now, suppose that the pronoun in (88) were co-indexed with *a bass* and with *a tenor*. Its antecedent clause would be IP7, the whole sentence. The recoverable predicate of this clause is calculated in (90):

(90)
i. $IP7^P = IP3^P \sqcup IP6^P$
ii. $IP3^P = NP1^P \sqcap [1\ IP2]^P$
   $= soprano' \sqcap [1\ IP2]'$
   $= soprano' \sqcap \lambda x_1.IP2'$
   $= soprano' \sqcap \lambda x_1.a'(bass')(\lambda x_2.admires'(x_2)(x_1))$
   $= \lambda x[soprano'(x)\ \&\ a'(bass')(\lambda x_2.admires'(x_2)(x))]$
iii. $IP6^P = NP3^P \sqcap [3\ IP5]^P$
   $= alto' \sqcap [3\ IP5]^P$
   $= alto' \sqcap \lambda x_3.IP5'$
   $= alto' \sqcap \lambda x_3.a'(tenor')(\lambda x_4.admires'(x_4)(x_3))$
   $= \lambda y[alto'(y)\ \&\ a'(tenor')(\lambda x_4.admires'(x_4)(y))]$
iv. $IP7^P = \lambda z[[soprano'(z)\ \&\ a'(bass')(\lambda x_2.admires'(x_2)(z))] \vee$
   $[alto'(z)\ \&\ a'(tenor')(\lambda x_4.admires'(x_4)(z))]]$

External anaphora 213

The predicate derived denotes the property of being a soprano who admires a bass or an alto who admires a tenor. Inserting this predicate into a definite description gives an expression equivalent to "the soprano who admires a bass or alto who admires a tenor." This, though, is not the description we were after. Even though the pronoun is co-indexed with the narrow scope NPs, the only interpretation that can be derived for it is the interpretation we would want for a pronoun anaphoric on the wide-scope NPs. But due to the gender (and number) conflict between the wide scope NPs and the pronoun, the pronoun cannot be assigned the derivable interpretation, and so is simply infelicitous.

The effect we see here is just like that discussed earlier with respect to co-indexing with one disjunct of an NP disjunction. The co-indexation is, in effect, nullified by the interpretation rules for the pronoun, which make reference to the recoverable predicate of the antecedent clause. It is the structure and content of the antecedent clause which determine the available interpretations for the pronoun.

With some effort, the disjunction in (88), repeated here, can be understood with the indefinites having wide scope, i.e with the interpretation paraphrased in (91)[6].

(88) Either every soprano admires a bass, or every alto admires a tenor. He has wonderful breath control.

(91) Either there is a bass who is admired by every soprano or there is a tenor who is admired by every alto.

When the disjunction is so understood, anaphora is possible in (88). This is as expected. The relevant reading of the disjunction is derived from the LF in (92) below. The antecedent clause of the pronoun will again be the whole sentence, but now the intended antecedents have widest scope within their respective IPs.

(92)

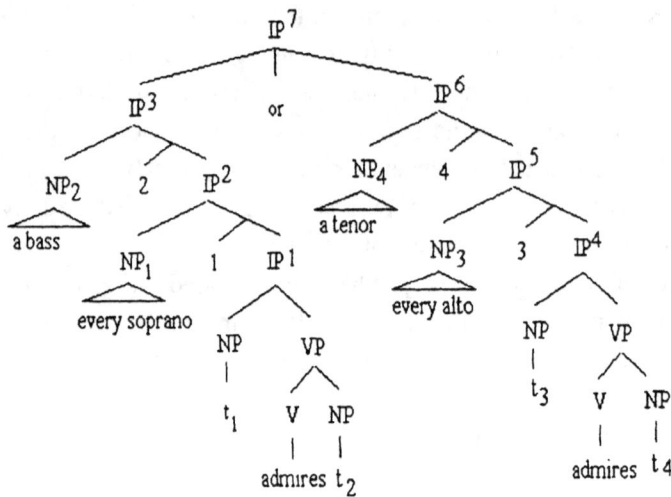

The recoverable predicate of IP7 is:

(93) λx[[bass'(x) & every'(soprano')(λx₁.admires'(x)(x₁)] ∨
      [tenor'(x) & every'(alto')(λx₃.admires'(x)(x₃)]]

which denotes the property of being a bass admired by every soprano or a tenor admired by every alto. This property provides an appropriate interpretation for the pronoun *he*.

The observation that disjunctive E-type anaphora to indefinites contained in a clausal disjunction is possible only when the indefinites have wide scope in their clause thus follows from the interpretation rule for E-type pronouns.

The effect of scope also provides an explanation for a contrast noted at the end of section 5.2.2.:

(94) Either a soprano will sing an aria, or an actress will recite a monologue.
    a. Then she will lead the audience in the national anthem.
    b. ?It'll be in German.

(95) Either an aria will be sung by a soprano, or a monologue will be recited by an actress.
    a. #Then she will lead the audience in the national anthem.
    b. It'll be in German.

The interpretation for the pronoun in (94a) is derived straightforwardly by assuming *a soprano* and *an actress* to have wide scope in their respective clauses. Assuming *she* to be co-indexed with both of these NPs, the antecedent clause of this pronoun will be the entire disjunction, whose recoverable predicate is:

(96) $\lambda x[[\text{soprano}'(x) \& \text{a}'(\text{aria}')(\lambda x_i.\text{will-sing}'(x_i)(x))] \vee [\text{actress}'(x) \& \text{a}'(\text{monologue}')(\lambda x_j.\text{will-recite}'(x_j)(x))]]$

This gives an appropriate interpretation for *she*.

The string in (94b) is a little odd, although possible. To derive an appropriate interpretation for the pronoun in this case, we must assign wide scope to the object NPs of each disjunct, contrary to the indication of surface order. We have already seen (section 5.4.3.) cases where we must assume inverse scope relations to account for anaphora to narrow scope indefinites, as in:

(97) A soprano will sing an aria. It will be in German.

I pointed out that there is generally a preference to preserve at LF the surface hierarchy among QNPs. To get the right interpretation for the pronoun in (94b) we must posit inverse scope in two adjacent clauses, and this, presumably, is responsible for the slight oddity of the string.

In (95), each disjunct of (94) is passivized. The content of the disjuncts is the same, but their structure quite different. For this discussion, we need to begin by looking at the *pre*-LF structure of the sentence, which I show in (98).

(98)

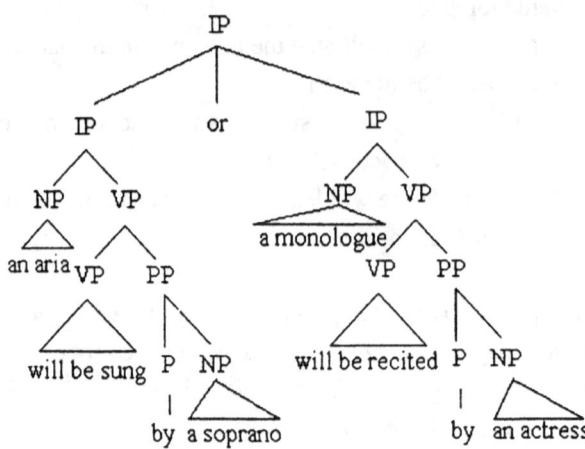

At LF, the subject of each disjunct (*an aria*, in the first, and *a monologue*, in the second) will move by QR to adjoin to its IP. But what about the NP in the *by*-phrase? Being quantificational, it too must raise. There are three options: it could adjoin either to the VP, to the IP below the QR-ed subject, or to the IP above the QR-ed subject. Now, if the NPs *a soprano* and *an alto* are to be antecedents for the E-type pronoun *she* in (95a), each of them must raise to the highest position. Just as in the previous example, this would involve a longer move than necessary to obtain what is in fact the only reading of the sentence. Moreover, in the case of the passive, there is a further obstacle to this derivation. Raising to the highest sentential position correlates in some way with assignment of the status of topic. But from a communicative perspective, the point of a passive is to demote the agent argument and make the *theme* argument the topic of the sentence. Raising the NP of the *by*-phrase above the derived subject thus counters the communicative effect of the passive structure, and so will be strongly dispreferred. This explains why the attempted anaphora in (95a) is really impossible, while that in (94b) is, although rather odd, at least possible.

Examples (94) and (95) are suggestive of a possible correspondence between the formal notion of recoverable property and the intuitive notion of "aboutness." A passive sentence differs from its active counterpart in the way in which its content is presented. In the active disjuncts of (94),

External anaphora 217

the subjects are presumably the topics, the content that the disjunct is "about." The disjunction as a whole is "about" the possible performers, rather than the possible performances. In the passive disjuncts in (95), the surface subject, again, is the topic, but now the topic is what is to be performed. So here, the disjunction as a whole is "about" the performance, not about the performers. This difference is matched by the possibilities of anaphora: (94) can serve as an antecedent clause for a pronoun relating to the performers, and (95), for a pronoun relating to what is to be performed.

5.5.3. Summary

In this section, we have seen how the revised E-type account can be applied to the external anaphora data. The account produces intuitively correct interpretations for those pronouns which I called disjunctive E-types. These pronouns are assumed to be simultaneously co-indexed with multiple antecedents or perhaps, in the case of anaphora to NP disjunction, co-indexed with the disjunction itself. The account also provides explanations for the absence of disjunctive E-type anaphora to narrow scope QNPs in different disjuncts, and of single-antecedent anaphora to QNPs (other than definites) contained in a disjunction.

With respect to disjunction, no special assumptions have been made at all. I have relied throughout on Partee and Rooth's cross-categorial semantics. This semantics, which is based on the idea that disjunction of all categories involves Boolean join, is mirrored in the rule for deriving the recoverable property of disjunctive expressions.

5.6. THE SINGLE-ANTECEDENT READING

In the previous section, I showed why E-type readings to particular disjuncts are ruled out in the case of antecedents which generally give rise to E-type readings. In this section, I will turn to the cases in which single-antecedent readings do arise. There will be two questions to answer: How are single-antecedent readings for external pronouns derived? And what characterizes the kinds of NPs which allow for disjunct specific readings?

5.6.1. Derivation of single-antecedent readings

There are three kinds of NPs which clearly give rise to disjunct specific readings: proper names, specific indefinites, and definite descriptions. Examples (99-101) are illustrations:

(99)   a.   Jane or George will sing. HE has a fine voice.
           b.   Jane will sing Mozart or George will sing Schubert. HE has a fine voice.

(100) a.   A soprano who recently sang at the Met or a tenor who got rave reviews in Italy will sing. HE has a fine voice.
           b.   A soprano who recently sang at the Met will sing Mozart or a tenor who got rave reviews in Italy will sing Schubert. HE has a fine voice.

(101) a.   The soprano or the tenor will sing. HE has a fine voice.
           b.   The soprano will sing Mozart or the tenor will sing Schubert. HE has a fine voice.

In each of the examples above, *he* is anaphoric on the masculine name or NP in the preceding disjunction.

In the case of proper name antecedents, there seems to be nothing puzzling about the anaphora. A pronoun anaphoric on a referential antecedent may simply co-refer with the antecedent. There is no reason why occurrence of the antecedent in a disjunction should affect co-reference. In the examples in (99), George is referred to. The fact that the speaker does not know that George will sing does not affect reference. To represent co-reference formally, let's assume that the pronoun is translated as a copy of its antecedent.

Given that the pronouns in (99) receive a co-reference interpretation, it is clear why they cannot simultaneously be anaphoric on more than one antecedent. An expression cannot refer simultaneously to distinct referents. And the pronouns cannot be given an E-type interpretation for, by definition, an E-type pronoun is one whose antecedent is a QNP, an expression consisting of a determiner and a restrictor. Note that it is not semantic type that is relevant. A proper name can also be treated as a generalized quantifier, an expression of type $\langle\langle e,t\rangle,t\rangle$. Viewed as expressions of this type, proper names denote the set of properties (sets of individuals) to which the individual they denote belongs. When proper names are conjoined, they must be assigned this type, as expressions of type e are not conjoinable by the Partee and Rooth semantics. But this does not suffice to make them potential antecedents to E-type pronouns[7].

In section 4.4.2. of Chapter Four, I discussed a number of examples involving specific indefinites. I suggested adopting Reinhart and Kratzer's choice-function treatment of specific indefinites, and argued that pronouns anaphoric on them could be treated as copies of their antecedents. This produces the effect of co-reference. The same treatment can be applied to the examples in (100). The pronoun can be translated as a copy of the specific indefinite antecedent, and thus will co-refer with it. Once again, it is clear that the pronoun can only be a copy of one antecedent, hence this kind of interpretation ensures that the pronoun can have only one antecedent.

The train of thought can be extended to the case of definite NP antecedents, as in (101). Given the Russellian treatment of definites which I have adopted, I cannot say that the pronouns in these examples co-refer with their antecedents, as I do not take the definite antecedents to refer at all. However, let us suppose that these pronouns, too, can be translated as copies of their antecedents when they have only one. This gives the correct result.

One might think that as definite NPs are of the right kind to serve as antecedents to E-type pronouns, the single-antecedent reading in (101) could be derived by the E-type strategy, assuming the pronoun to be co-indexed with only one antecedent. However, this produces incorrect results, even in the clausal disjunction case. Consider again:

(101) b. The soprano will sing Mozart or the tenor will sing Schubert. HE has a fine voice.

Suppose *he* were interpreted as an E-type pronoun anaphoric on *the tenor*. Its antecedent clause would then be *the tenor will sing Schubert*. By the now familiar calculation, the recoverable predicate of this clause turns out to be $\lambda x[\text{tenor}'(x) \;\&\; \text{will-sing-Schubert}'(x)]$. Inserted into a definite description, this gives us something equivalent to "the tenor who will sing Schubert." But this interpretation once again leads to a failure of presupposition. The disjunction itself presupposes the existence of both a soprano and a tenor, but is compatible with the tenor not singing at all (on the relevant occasion). Hence, the context updated with the disjunction will not satisfy the presupposition of the description derived by the E-type strategy. So the interpretation of the pronoun in (101b) cannot be E-type, given current assumptions. Moreover, my current assumptions also preclude treating the pronoun in (101a) as an E-type pronoun dependent on a single disjunct, as E-type anaphora to a single NP disjunct is ruled out structurally. I conclude, then, that single-antecedent anaphora is *not* an instance of an E-type interpretation.

The question that remains is what it is that proper names, specific indefinites and definite descriptions have in common which allows them to serve as antecedents for single-antecedent anaphora of this kind. The answer one wants to give is that these expressions are referring, but as I observed above, the assumption of a Russellian semantics for definite descriptions excludes this answer.

But even if definite descriptions are not actually referring expressions, they can certainly be *used* to refer, along with proper names and specific indefinites. This point is familiar from Kripke (1977). Thus, the fundamental intuition is that any expression which can be used to refer can provide an antecedent for a pronoun which, by some means, refers to whatever the antecedent is used to refer to. And it is when a disjunction contains such an expression that single-antecedent readings of external pronouns are possible. I have suggested that this kind of pseudo-coreference could be captured by translating the pronouns as copies of their antecedents. Whether or not this is correct, the general point holds: disjunctive E-type pronouns are indeed E-type, and arise only when the antecedents are of a type which, in general, give rise to E-type readings. Single-antecedent pronouns, on the other hand, are not E-type, but involve some kind of (pseudo-) co-reference. These pronouns are possible only with antecedents which generally allow for anaphora of this kind.

5.6.2. Maximal quantifier antecedents

I would like to return in this section to the issue of single-antecedent anaphora to definites, and bring up a difference between my E-type account and that of Neale (1990). In Chapter Four, I gave a rule for interpreting E-type pronouns based on that of Neale. I repeat that rule here:

(102)   *Chapter Four pronoun rule*
If α is an E-type pronoun with antecedent clause φ whose logical form is Det'(F')(G') then α' = the'(λx.F'(x) & G'(x))

But Neale's own rules (his $P5_a$ and $P5_b$, p.182) make reference not just to the form of the antecedent clause but also to the nature of the antecedent. He distinguishes between *maximal* and *non-maximal* quantifiers, the maximal quantifiers being those of the form *the F, the Fs, each F, every F*, and *all Fs*. The Chapter Four pronoun rule is equivalent to Neale's rule for pronouns anaphoric on a non-maximal quantifier. The rule for pronouns anaphoric on maximal quantifiers interprets the pronoun using only the content of the restrictor, more or less as follows:

(103)   *Pronoun rule for pronouns with maximal antecedents*
If α is an E-type pronoun anaphoric on a maximal quantifier, with antecedent clause φ whose logical form is Det'(F')(G') then α' = the'(λx.F'(x))

Now, in the cases which Neale actually discusses (where the antecedent clause is simple), distinguishing between maximal and non-maximal antecedents does not alter the predictions made. (As far as I can tell, Neale adopts the rule for maximal antecedents because he wants the description to be as simple as possible. See his rule P5, p.182.) Consider, for example, the string in (104):

(104)   The sopranos sang Mozart. They were wonderful.

It makes no significant difference whether *they* is interpreted as "the sopranos" (applying rule (103)) or as "the sopranos who sang Mozart" (applying rule (102)). Admittedly, the simpler description seems a more natural paraphrase of the pronoun, but that might be due simply to the redundancy of the more complex one.

However, in the case of definite antecedents contained in a disjunction, the rule we choose will affect the acceptability of the anaphora. Consider again (101b), repeated from above:

(101)   b.   The soprano will sing Mozart or the tenor will sing Schubert. HE has a fine voice.

I observed above that my current account excludes the possibility of treating *he* as an E-type pronoun anaphoric on *the tenor*, as this would result in a presupposition failure. Neale's rule (102) would produce the same interpretation, and thus the same result. But if we applied Neale's rule for pronouns with maximal antecedents, we would derive the interpretation "the tenor" for the pronoun. This is appropriate.

My revised E-type account does not allow for the kind of rules Neale gives, and so the option of distinguishing between maximal and non-maximal antecedents is not open to me. I have not needed such a rule, as I have argued that single-antecedent anaphora to definites is not E-type, but involves interpretation of the pronoun as a copy of the antecedent.

But what about other maximal quantifiers? If they give rise to single-antecedent readings, this would seem to indicate that we do, after all, need something like Neale's rule. And such readings seem to be possible. Consider:

(105)　Either every male student or every female student complained about this professor. They (fem) don't usually complain about anyone.

Now, as English does not have distinct pronouns for third person plural masculine and feminine, we cannot really test the judgment in English. However, I have asked speakers of languages which do make such a distinction (Spanish, Catalan and Arabic) for their judgments about translations of this sentence, and all have agreed that a feminine pronoun can be used to means something like "the female students." This seems to bear out the need for a special rule for pronouns with maximal antecedents. It also seems to indicate that E-type anaphora to a single disjunct of an NP disjunction is not, after all, ruled out.

However, there is a case to be made that the pronoun in (105) is not being given a standard E-type interpretation, but some kind of generic interpretation. There is a quite general tendency for plural pronouns with quantificational antecedents to receive this kind of interpretation. This is the case in (106):

(106)　Some students, but not many, attended the rally. They are apathetic about politics.

They cannot here mean "the students who attended the rally," for those students are presumably not apathetic. Nor can it mean "the students" on a strict interpretation of the description, for there are evidently some students who are not apathetic (those that attended the rally). The pronoun means "the students," with the description understood generically, in a way which allows for exceptions. And the judgments offered by informants are compatible with treating the pronoun in (105) in the same way.

Support for this view is provided by the observation that non-maximal pronouns can also, in certain circumstances, produce this effect. Consider:

(107) Either some male students or some female students complained about this professor. They (fem) don't usually complain about anyone.

The feminine pronoun seems to be possible here, again meaning something like "the female students."

Moreover, if we change the content of the anaphor clause to something which does not favor a generic interpretation of the pronoun, the felicity of the single-antecedent interpretation is much reduced:

(108) Either every male student or every female student complained about this professor. ??They (fem) said that he is lazy.

Interpretation of the pronoun as "the female students" is not ruled out pragmatically, for the explicit description can be used felicitously. (This implies that the there was a complaint made by some group of students and in addition the female students said that the professor was lazy.)

I conclude, then, that these examples do not motivate distinguishing between E-type pronouns with maximal and non-maximal antecedents.

5.6.3. Summary

Single-antecedent readings raise questions about pronominal co-reference which go beyond the purview of this dissertation. However, as far as external anaphora is concerned, we have reached several conclusions. First, disjunctive E-type interpretations are accounted for by the E-type proposal set out in this chapter. The proposal accounts for the interpretations observed, as well as for the distribution of disjunctive E-type versus single-antecedent interpretations of external pronouns. Essentially, disjunctive E-type pronouns occur with antecedents of the kind which generally do give rise to E-type anaphora (QNPs, including definite and indefinite descriptions) and are absent with proper names, which do not give rise to E-type anaphora. The second conclusion reached is that single-antecedent readings of external pronouns are not the result of an E-type interpretation strategy, but involve some kind of (possibly pseudo-) coreference.

5.7. OTHER APPROACHES TO EXTERNAL ANAPHORA

There has been little discussion of external anaphora in the literature, but it is worth pausing here to see how the analysis I have pursued in this chapter compares with the other proposals which have been made.

The earliest suggestion for a treatment of external anaphora is due to Rooth and Partee (1982). They adopt a variable-sharing treatment for external pronouns, along with a special variable-introducing semantics for disjunction. To account for the external anaphora facts, they suggest that disjunctions, like indefinites, might be treated as expressions which introduce into a representation a single free variable, which can later be used as the interpretation of a pronoun. Their proposal is motivated by the logical correspondence between indefinites and disjunctions: indefinites express existential quantification, and disjunctions are equivalent to existential quantification over a specified domain. In the theories of Kamp (1981) and Heim (1982), of course, indefinites are not viewed as inherently quantificational, but as expressions which introduce a variable and a condition which constrains its value. Rooth and Partee suggest that a disjunction $A \ or \ B$ could similarly be treated as introducing a single variable, along with the constraint that the value of the variable be either that of A or that of B.

The idea is to have a way of deriving (109b) as a translation for (109a):

(109)   a.   a soprano or an alto
        b. $\lambda P \ [P(x) \ \& \ [soprano'(x) \lor alto'(x)]]$

External anaphora 225

In this translation, both indefinites introduce the same variable, in apparent violation of the standard rule in DRT and FCS that indefinites must always introduce new variables. This violation is to be licensed by the rule for the translation of the disjunction itself. Because the indefinites share a variable, if a pronoun which follows "picks up" that variable, it will be interpreted as simultaneously anaphoric on both antecedents, or as anaphoric on the disjunction as a whole. This explains the anaphora in examples like:

(110) A soprano or an alto will sing. She will be accompanied on the piano.

Stone (1992) points out, however, that the approach cannot provide a general account of the external anaphora data, as it does not extend to external anaphora to NPs contained in a clausal disjunction. This is because the semantic type of the variable introduced by the disjunction is dependent upon the semantic type of the expressions disjoined[8]. A disjunction of clauses can only introduce a free variable of type t. There is thus no explanation for the anaphora in sequences like:

(111) A soprano will sing or an actress will recite. Then she will lead the audience in the national anthem.

For the pronoun *she* to be simultaneously anaphoric on *a soprano* and on *an actress*, the two NPs must share a variable. But as they themselves are not disjoined, they are not predicted to do so.

Nonetheless, the fundamental idea is quite intuitive, and emerges again in a different form in Kamp and Reyle's (1993) DRT account. Kamp and Reyle, of course, propose a variable-sharing treatment of external anaphora, but suggest an inference-based strategy for introducing the special variable. Their idea is that external anaphora is possible when the NP antecedents can be understood as giving "alternative characterizations of one and the same thing" (p.206). In such a case, we may introduce into the DRS an additional discourse referent which stands for this inferred object or individual, and it is this referent which provides the antecedent for an external pronoun.

To illustrate, they discuss the following example:

(112)   The barn contains a chain saw or a power drill. It makes an ungodly racket.

By their rule for disjunction, the first sentence of (112) gives rise to the DRS in (113)[9]:

(113)
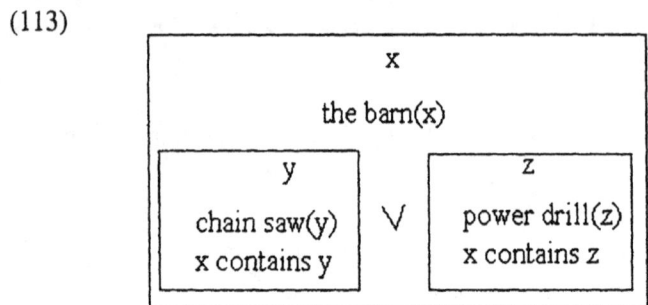

This provides no antecedent for the pronoun *it*. But from (113) we can infer the existence of some heavy-duty power tool inside the barn, which licenses the introduction of an additional discourse referent, as in (114):

(114)
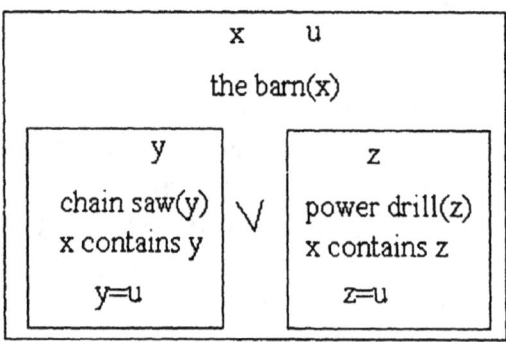

The external pronoun can now be identified with *u*, providing an interpretation equivalent to the disjunctive E-type interpretation I have given.

External anaphora

Like any inference-based account of anaphora, Kamp and Reyle's proposal overgenerates to some extent. In particular, it does not rule out disjunctive external anaphora to proper names. Consider:

(115)   Jane or Maud will sing. #She will be accompanied on the piano.

The first sentence will give rise to the DRS in (116):

(116)

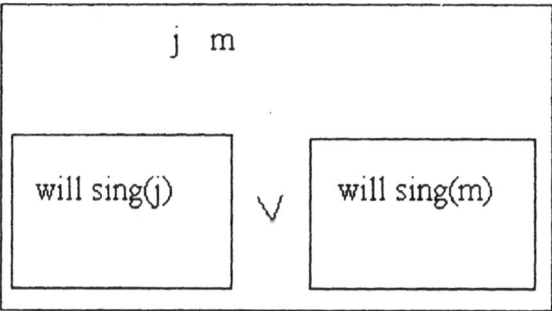

But from this, presumably, we can infer the existence of someone who will sing, which should allow us to turn (116) into (117):

(117)

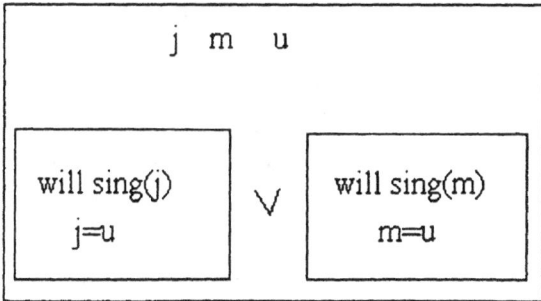

The infelicity of the anaphora in (115), though, indicates that this is not licensed. One could, of course, rule it out by fiat. Certainly, there is no way to rule it out in terms of differences between anaphora to indefinites and anaphora to proper names, as in this framework, there is no such difference.

The proposal of Stone (1992) is the closest to the E-type account I have given. Stone also assumes that external pronouns are E-types, but he adopts a version of the pragmatic E-type account suggested in Heim (1990). Stone adopts the general framework of situation semantics, in which a sentence is assumed to denote a set of situations, namely, the set of minimal situations in which the sentence is true[10]. The view of sentence denotations gives rise to a parallel notion of discourse context: the set of minimal situations denoted by the conjunction of the sentences uttered (i.e., the intersection of the denotations of these sentences). Incorporating Heim's suggestion into this framework, Stone treats E-type pronouns as denoting functions which map each situation in the discourse context to an individual. On any occasion of use, a pronoun denotes some function which is salient in the context applied to an argument provided by context or by the linguistic content of the anaphor clause.

The way this works for disjunction is as follows. Consider again the sentence:

(118) A soprano will sing or an actress will recite. Then she will lead the audience in the national anthem.

The first sentence denotes the union of the set of minimal situations in which a soprano will sing with the set of minimal situations in which an actress will recite. Assuming this sentence to be the first in the discourse, the context will consist of just the situations in that set. By virtue of its content, the sentence makes salient a particular function: a function from situations to the person who performs in that situation. This function is used to interpret the pronoun *she*. The anaphor sentence will thus be true if, for every situation in the context, the person who performs in that situation will lead the audience in the national anthem.

Once again, the account fails to distinguish between proper names and indefinites. If the first sentence of (118) makes salient a function from situations to people who perform, then surely (119) should do so too:

(119) Either Jane will sing or Maud will recite.

External anaphora 229

Because the pragmatic E-type account does not rely on any formal relation between an antecedent and the pronoun, it predicts that whenever the context makes salient a function appropriate for the interpretation of the pronoun, the pronoun should be interpretable as an E-type. So there is no explanation of why proper names should not be possible antecedents for E-type pronouns.

The fundamental intuition which underlies all of these accounts is that disjunctive sentences like (120) and (121) serve, in discourse, to introduce an individual of which the speaker is able to give only a disjunctive characterization. These sentences are, in some sense, about that individual. A disjunctive external pronoun is used to talk of the individual so introduced.

(120) A soprano or an alto will sing.
(121) A soprano will sing Mozart or an alto will sing Schubert.

The E-type account I have given reflects this same intuition. The recoverable property of the antecedent clause of disjunctive E-type pronouns is the very property which holds of the individual being introduced. The pronoun provides a way of speaking of the individual who bears this property.

The E-type account further reflects an intuitive distinction between (120-121), and the parallel proper name cases:

(122) Jane or Maud will sing.
(123) Jane will sing Mozart or Maud will sing Schubert.

(122) and (123) do not introduce an unidentified disjunctively-characterizable individual. Rather, they say something of Jane and Maud, who must be independently identifiable. This is reflected in the absence of an E-type interpretation for a pronoun anaphoric on the proper names.

5.8. FURTHER ISSUES FOR THE E-TYPE ACCOUNT

In the last two chapters, I have focused on a quite narrow set of anaphora data, my primary interest being to provide an account of the disjunction-related cases. Clearly, there are many other issues against which the E-type account I have proposed must be tested. In this final section I will bring up some of the problematic areas.

5.8.1. Inference-based anaphora

I will begin by setting aside a kind of anaphora for which I think there can be no completely formal linguistic account, exemplified in such cases as[11]:

(124) His leg was cancerous. He contracted it in Africa.
(125) I spent last summer in Indonesia. They are very dissatisfied with the present regime.
(126) Maud has remarried. He's an improvement over her last one.

Judgments about such examples tend to vary from speaker to speaker (and indeed from occasion to occasion). Undoubtedly, interpretation of the pronoun involves some kind of inference from the content of the previous discourse to individuals that we might speak about. This kind of inference process has been dubbed "bridging" by Clark (1977).

These observations are perfectly compatible with the view that the pronouns themselves denote definite descriptions whose descriptive content must be provided by context. In the case of E-type pronouns, the descriptive content is supplied by the recoverable property of the antecedent clause. In examples like (124-126), the content is supplied by the inferential process. (I do not think, though, that these examples constitute an argument that E-type pronouns *in general* should be treated pragmatically.) How this inference process proceeds is not a problem for semantic theory. The problem for semantics is to say what the linguistic form or content of the pronouns so interpreted is, and the definite description view seems plausible.

5.8.2. Interpretation of plural pronouns

The precise interpretation of certain plural pronouns is a matter for semantic theory to worry over. In my discussion, I have adopted Neale's treatment of plural pronouns in examples like (127):

(127) Some sopranos arrived late. They were held up in traffic.

External anaphora

They is interpreted as the plural definite description in (128). The truth conditions I assume (following Neale) for sentences containing plural descriptions are in (129):

(128) the$_p$'(λx.soprano'(x) & arrived-late'(x))
(129) [the$_p$'(F')(G')]^c = 1 iff [F']^c ⊆ [G']^c and | [F']^c| > 1

But not all cases of plural E-type pronouns can be assimilated to the singular case quite so straightforwardly. E-type pronouns anaphoric on a conjunction are a case in point. Consider:

(130) A soprano$_i$ and an alto$_j$ came late. They$_i$ were held up in traffic.

A natural paraphrase of *they* is "the soprano and the alto who came late." But this paraphrase uses two conjoined definite descriptions, rather than one. If we are to maintain a unified treatment of E-type pronouns as having the logical form "the'(F')" we must find a single definite description which will do the same job. Neither the singular nor the plural descriptions in (131) will do:

(131) a. the'(λx.soprano'(x) & alto'(x) & came-late'(x))
       b. the$_p$'(λx.soprano'(x) & alto'(x) & came-late'(x))

These descriptions hold only of individuals which are *both* sopranos and altos. What we need, rather, is a description which applies to plural individuals (or sets of individuals) and which attributes the property of having some atomic parts (or members) which are sopranos and some other atomic parts (or members) which are altos, all of which came late.

But it is not only E-type pronouns which require such an interpretation. The same kind of interpretation is needed for explicit definite descriptions like *the men and women*, as in:

(132) The men and women of this town believe in equal opportunity for all.

So the complication that is raised by E-type pronouns anaphoric on conjoined NPs is a problem raised independently by descriptions containing conjoined common nouns, and indeed by conjoined NPs in general. There is a substantial literature on the semantics of conjoined NPs, and I will not attempt any discussion of it here. The point is simply that although E-type pronouns with conjunctive antecedents do introduce new problems, these problems are not particular to the E-type theory, but belong to the set of questions to be answered by a theory of plural NPs.

In (130), the antecedent of the plural pronoun is a conjunction of NPs, which itself presumably has a plural denotation. But the antecedent of a plural pronoun is not always given by a single syntactic constituent. Consider:

(133)　First, a soprano will sing. Then two tenors will perform a duet. Then they will all sing together.

(134)　Jane has known Maud for years. Recently, she introduced her to George. They get along surprisingly well.

In both of these cases, the antecedent has to be constructed from distinct NPs which do not form a constituent and do not even occur in the same sentence. Modulo the problem discussed above, the E-type account can perhaps deal with (133) by treating the two sentences containing the antecedents as conjoined. (134) would require a different account, as the antecedents are proper names. The problem is compounded by examples like (135), in which a plural pronoun is anaphoric on both a proper name and a QNP:

(135)　Jane went on vacation with several friends. They had a wonderful time.

This problem, though, is again not specific to the pronominal arena. It arises also with overt definite descriptions, as in:

(136)　Jane went on vacation with several friends. The women had a wonderful time.

5.8.3. Anaphora to NP disjuncts and conjuncts

I'd like to return briefly to the matter of anaphora to NP disjuncts, and extend the discussion to NP conjuncts. Currently, the anaphora in (137) is ruled out by virtue of the rule for constructing recoverable predicates,

External anaphora

which makes reference to the antecedent clause, rather than the particular antecedent:

(137)   A soprano or a bass$_i$ will sing. #He$_i$ will be accompanied on the piano.

But in the case of conjoined NPs, it seems that anaphora to a single conjunct is possible:

(138)   A soprano$_i$ and a bass$_j$ will attend the festival. She$_i$ will sing Mozart and he$_j$ will sing Schubert.

If (137) is ruled out by virtue of the structure of the antecedent clause, then (138) should be too (unless both antecedents are treated as specific indefinites). This looks like a reason to re-formulate the rules to allow, in general, for anaphora to a subordinate NP in a conjunction or disjunction of NPs. The failure of anaphora in (137) could then be accounted for as a matter of presupposition failure, as discussed in section 5.5.2.1.

But such a reformulation will still leave the anaphora in (139) as a puzzle:

(139)   A soprano$_i$ and a bass$_j$ will sing a duet. Then she$_i$ will sing a Mozart aria and he$_j$ will sing some Schubert.

The pronoun *she* cannot be interpreted as "the soprano who will sing a duet" as the soprano alone does not sing a duet. If the pronouns here are E-type pronouns anaphoric on the subordinate NPs, their interpretation is unlike other E-type pronouns in being constructed only from the content of the $\bar{N}$. (This makes them like Neale's E-type pronouns with maximal antecedents, but the antecedents here are not maximal in Neale's sense.) So simply allowing anaphora to a subordinate NP will not solve the problems raised by anaphora to conjuncts. On the other hand, this is another case which a variable-sharing/ dynamic-binding account can deal with straightforwardly.

The reason I an unwilling to reformulate the rules to allow for anaphora to specific disjuncts (and conjuncts) is that the only plausible way I see to do so is to revert to the kind of construction-specific rules offered by Neale (and other existing structural E-type accounts).

Currently, the structure-sensitivity of the account falls out automatically from the use that is made of the recoverable predicate of the antecedent clause. The recoverable predicate mirrors the internal structure of the denotation of the clause; if the NP antecedents are separated by disjunction in the denotation, then this is reflected in the recoverable predicate, and hence in the denotation of the pronoun. If we revert to a rule which picks out individual antecedent NPs, then we will no longer be able to make reference to the antecedent clause in the same way. So we will be forced to stipulate the relation between the form of the denotation of the pronoun and the form of the antecedent clause. The kinds of rules we would need for the NP disjunction and clausal disjunction cases are given in (140) and (141):

(140)   *Rule for E-type pronouns with NP disjunct antecedents*
If α is an E-type pronoun with antecedents $NP_1...NP_n$ occurring as constituents of a disjunctive NP, NP_i, in a structure of the form $[_{IP}NP_i \,[i\, IP]]$, then:
$\alpha' = \text{the}'([NP_1^P \sqcup ... \sqcup NP_n^P](x) \,\&\, [i\, IP]^P(x))$

(141)   *Rule for E-type pronouns with antecedents in clausal disjuncts*
If α is an E-type pronoun with antecedents $NP_1...NP_n$, each occurring as the widest scope NP in a clause of the form $[_{IP}NP_i \,i\, IP]]$ occurring as a constituent of a disjoined clause, then:
$\alpha' = \text{the}'([NP_1^P \sqcap [1\, IP]^P](x) \sqcup ... \sqcup [NP_n^P \sqcap [n\, IP]^P])$

Such rules, like the rules proposed in section 5.3., are merely descriptive, and not explanatory. The more general proposal made in this chapter thus seems worth further exploration.

5.9. CONCLUSION

If there is any consensus in the current literature on anaphora, it is that no one theory can successfully account for everything. Heim (1990) demonstrates very elegantly that the two principal competitors in the field of anaphora, the variable-sharing/ dynamic-binding approach and the E-type approach, have complementary failings. Neither is clearly superior to the other, but there may well be reasons to assume that both are in operation, as does Chierchia (1995). Even the avowedly DRT-based proposals of Kadmon (1987) and Kamp and Reyle (1993) incorporate strategies which are essentially translations into the framework of an E-type proposal. Within the E-type literature, advocates of structural approaches (like Neale) acknowledge that the denotation of the pronoun may be affected by pragmatic considerations, while pragmatic E-type accounts that make no reference to structure are unable to account for certain structural effects. In the end, we seem forced to the conclusion that there are multiple strategies for the interpretation of pronouns. One appealing idea is that these strategies are arranged in a hierarchy, perhaps ordered by simplicity, and that in any given case, the simplest strategy which produces a reasonable interpretation is applied.

The E-type account argued for in this chapter extends the possible contexts of application of earlier structural E-type proposals. I have argued that this strategy is used to interpret disjunctive E-type pronouns. This has given us a treatment of external anaphora to disjunction, and a new approach to E-type anaphora.

NOTES

1. To understand the point of many of the examples in this chapter, you will need to know that sopranos and altos are generally female, and tenors and basses are generally male. For the purposes of the examples, assume that they always are.

2. Recall that I take plural E-type pronouns to be interpreted as plural descriptions. See discussion in Chapter Four, section 4.4.3. I will discuss plural pronouns further in section 5.8.2. of this chapter.

3. Here, I could have used "∨" in place of "⊔," as the conjoined expressions are of type t and in this domain the two operators are equivalent. I will usually adopt this simplification from now on.

4. Note that my assumptions require me to assign a distinct index to each of the disjoined NPs and to the disjunctive NP of which they are constituents. This could be avoided by assuming the other indexing strategy mentioned in section 5.3., by giving all of these NPs the same index. It could also be avoided by assuming that the pronoun is anaphoric on the disjunctive NP itself, as I will discuss below.

5. Notice that here a modal subordination reading (in the sense of Roberts 1987) is possible, if the anaphor sentence is changed to "We **would** have to get it out." Here, the anaphor sentence falls under the scope of the *perhaps* in the disjunction, and the presupposition must be satisfied just with respect to those worlds compatible with the supposition.

6. As will become apparent later, I am committed to this reading, which gives rise to disjunctive E-type anaphora, involving ordinary wide scope indefinites, and not specific indefinites.

7. It seems to be possible to construct some examples in which a pronoun with proper name antecedents gets something like a disjunctive E-type reading. Imagine the coach of the Chicago Bulls telling one of his players:
(i) If you get the ball, throw it to Jordan or Pippin. He'll dunk it.
One way to account for this example would be to say that in certain cases, proper names can serve as antecedents to E-type pronouns, providing, perhaps, the property of being identical to the bearer of the name. I think it more likely that the pronoun has an inference-based interpretation. (See section 8.1. below.) Certainly, what makes the anaphora possible is the salience of a relevant property shared by Jordan and Pippin, namely, the ability to dunk the ball. But the existence of such a property doesn't

guarantee the felicity of anaphora of this kind. Compare:
(ii) Don't foul Jordan or Pippin. #He's too tall.
The shared property of being tall doesn't suffice to license the anaphora here.

8. One of the difficulties in giving a precise formulation of Rooth and Partee's proposal is that their informal presentation suggests that disjunctions of indefinite NPs are to be treated differently from all other types of disjunction. In general, the type of the variable introduced by a disjunction is supposed to match the type of the expressions disjoined. So, for instance, a disjunction of intransitive verbs is to introduce a free variable of type $\langle e,t \rangle$ (or $\langle s,\langle e,t \rangle \rangle$). But in disjunctions of indefinites, which Rooth and Partee treat as generalized quantifiers of type $\langle \langle e,t \rangle ,t \rangle$, the free variable introduced is of type e, i.e. the same type of variable ordinarily introduced by indefinites in the Kamp/Heim framework.

9. Kamp and Reyle treat NP disjunctions as reductions of clausal disjunctions, and do not provide DRS construction rules for NP disjunctions which do not have clausal counterparts.

10. A minimal situation in which a proposition p is true is a situation in which p is true which has no sub-parts in which p is true.

11. Examples (124) and (125) adapted from Neale (1990: 210, fn22.), attributed to Paul Grice.

CONCLUDING REMARKS
GRICE, STALNAKER AND DYNAMIC SEMANTICS

Critiquing certain kinds of arguments in Ordinary Language Philosophy, Grice said.

> before we rush ahead to exploit the linguistic nuances which we have detected, we should make sure that we are reasonably clear what sort of nuances they are (1989: 237).

The same undoubtedly holds for attempts to *explain* linguistic nuances. What we have learnt from Grice is that there are different kinds of facts about linguistic meaning, for which different kinds of explanations are needed. Some facts are facts about conventional properties of expressions, which are to be accounted for by some theory of semantic content. Other facts are facts about the *use* of expressions; and for these an entirely different kind of explanation is needed. In "Logic and Conversation," Grice demonstrates the explanatory power of the idea that conversation is a process governed by certain principles of rational interaction, which speakers expect one another to abide by. Speakers expect one another to be truthful, relevant and informative. When an interlocutor appears to be otherwise, we attempt to understand their utterances in a way which makes them so. If we cannot do that, we will judge their utterances deficient.

Grice's theory gives us a way "to distinguish between the case in which an utterance is inappropriate because it is false or fails to be true, or more generally fails to correspond with the world in some favored way, and the case in which it is inappropriate for reasons of a different kind" (Grice 1989: 4). For Grice, the distinction was vital to the pursuit of philosophy. He believed that "a more or less detailed study of the way we talk ... is an indispensable foundation for much of the most fundamental kind of philosophizing" (1986: 58), but recognized that the conclusions to be drawn from pragmatic facts differ from those which can be drawn from semantic facts. For linguists, the distinction between different kinds of infelicity is crucial. The observation that a locution is syntactically well-formed but unacceptable does not mean that it is semantically deviant, and if the deviance lies elsewhere, we do not want our semantic theory to account for it.

Stalnaker takes up and elaborates on the distinction between semantic and pragmatic facts in his work on presupposition. He uses the notion of context change to characterize the goals of (certain kinds of) conversation, but understands context change as a process which is constrained and regulated by Gricean principles. Stalnaker suggests that his theory of presupposition "may make it possible to explain some of the facts [about presupposition] in terms of general assumptions about rational strategy in situations where people exchange information or conduct argument" (1974: 205). He continues, "Where [such arguments] can be given, there is no reason to build specific rules about presupposition into the semantics" (206). Stalnaker insists that there is a distinction between the kinds of facts which are to be explained by a semantic theory, and the kinds of facts which are to be explained by a theory of conversation. Like Grice, he seems to take the view that any fact which *can* be attributed to general conversational principles *should* be.

Stalnaker's theory is, of course, much more than a restatement or reformulation of Grice's proposal. It goes further in providing a framework in which to elaborate on the often complex inter-relations between context and content which arise from the dual role that context plays, being "both the object on which speech acts act and the source of the information relative to which speech acts are interpreted" (1996: 280). At the same time, the theory allows for the investigation of the formal properties of contexts independently of propositions expressed in them. Ultimately, though, the Stalnakerian theory is designed to allow for explanations of context-related observations in terms of "what language is for [and] what it is supposed to do" (1996: 277).

Concluding remarks

In Dynamic Semantics, the mode of explanation is quite different. The premise on which these theories are built is that meaning (content) can be *identified* with context change. This immediately eliminates the distinction between propositional content and context change effect which is present in the Stalnakerian theory. Both File Change Semantics and Dynamic Montague Grammar allow for a way to recover propositional content from the context change potential (in DMG, from the dynamic value) of an expression. However, the very clear distinction which is possible in the Stalnakerian theory between constraints on propositional content and constraints on context change effects is lost. More generally, in Dynamic Semantics the tendency is to offer accounts of linguistic phenomena in terms of formal properties of context, without further enquiring into the question of why context should have just these formal properties and no others. For instance, we have seen that some dynamic semanticists explain the distinction between (1) and (2) by saying that negation renders a sub-context opaque to anaphora, while double negation does not, and by providing formal characterizations of context which reflect this:

(1) Jane doesn't own a truck. #It's red and it's parked in the drive.
(2) It's not true that Jane doesn't own a truck. It's red and it's parked in the drive.

But we have still to answer the question of why this is the case, and this seems to me to be answerable. If we have just denied the existence of an object fitting a particular description, we cannot sensibly go on to attribute properties to such an object, which is the case in (1). In (2), we *deny* the non-existence of an object fitting a particular description, so it is perfectly sensible to go on to make further claims about the satisfying object. We are left with the question of why speakers feel obliged to make sense, and expect one another to do so. But this is a question of a very different order, and is a question about something which seems more or less undeniable. So this seems to get us much closer to an explanation than the formal account does.

This is not to say that we should not view contexts as structured or otherwise complex entities. Indeed, I think it likely that there are linguistic facts which will only be explicable in terms of a more complex notion of context than Stalnaker's simple possible worlds model. But whatever model we work with, we must distinguish between those properties of context change which are due solely to formal properties of context, and those which are imposed by general principles of cooperative interaction. In attempting to account for the presupposition projection properties of disjunction and for the possibility of anaphora across disjunction in semantic terms, Dynamic Semantics fails to make this distinction and in doing so, oddly enough, conflates meaning and use in much the same way that the Ordinary Language Philosophers sometimes did. It was this very conflation that motivated Grice's "Logic and Conversation" in the first place.

In this dissertation, I have shown how general principles of conversation can be used with explanatory force within a context-change model. I have argued that certain properties of disjunctive sentences should be explained in terms of these principles, rather than by attributing to *or* complex lexically-given properties such as a complex CCP. I have distinguished between infelicities which are due to a violation of these principles, as in (3) and (4), and infelicities which are due to formal constraints on the construction of interpretations, as in (5) and (6):

(3) #Either Jane owns a truck$_i$, or it$_i$'s red.
(4) #Either Jane is in town, or George knows that she is.

(5) #Most people own a truck$_i$, or it$_i$'s red.
(6) #Jane$_i$ or Maud$_j$ will sing. Then she$_{i,j}$ will play the piano.

Whether or not the specific accounts are correct in their details, what is crucial is the distinction between these two kinds of infelicity, and the corresponding difference in the kind of account which should be given of them.

I think the project undertaken here can be usefully extended to the other logical operators. (Geurts (1997), for example, makes some similar arguments for the case of conjunction.) The context change framework and its realization in the various theories of Dynamic Semantics provides important insights into certain properties of language, which is undeniably context dependent in multiple ways. But in order for this framework to provide insight and explanation, we must not forget the Gricean injunction to distinguish meaning and use.

APPENDIX
Syntax and Semantics of Translation Language

SYNTAX

A. Set of Types
1. e is a type
2. t is a type
3. If a and b are types, then $\langle a,b \rangle$ is a type.
4. Nothing else is a type.

For any type a, let ME_a denote the set of expressions of type a.

B. Definition of Conjoinable Type
1. t is a conjoinable type.
2. If b is a conjoinable type, then for any a, <a, b> is a conjoinable type.

C. Basic Expressions of TL
1. For each type a, there is a set of *non-logical constants* of type a, Con_a. Non-logical constants consist of symbols of the object language followed by a prime.
2. For each type a, there is a set of *variables* of type a, Var_a.
   For each natural number n, $x_n \in Var_e$.

D. Syntactic Rules
1. For each type a, every variable and constant of type a is a member of ME_a.
2. For any types a and b, if $\alpha \in ME_{\langle a,b \rangle}$ and $\beta \in ME_a$ then $\alpha(\beta) \in ME_b$.
3. For any types a and b, if $\alpha \in ME_a$ and $\beta \in Var_b$ then $\lambda\beta[\alpha] \in ME_{\langle b,a \rangle}$.
4. If $\alpha, \beta \in ME_t$ then so are $\alpha \& \beta$ and $\alpha \vee \beta$.
5. For any type a, if $\alpha, \beta \in ME_a$ then so are $\alpha \cap \beta$ and $\alpha \cup \beta$.

SEMANTICS

Let $[\alpha]^c$ denote the interpretation of α relative to c. c is to be an "all-purpose" contextual parameter, and can be thought of as containing a set of indices including at least an index for an assignment function which assigns values to variables of any type.

A. Definition of Possible Denotations
Let E be the set of all entities and T be the set of truth values, and let D_a be the set of possible denotations for expressions of type a. Then:
1. D_e is E.
2. D_t is T.
3. For any types a and b, $D_{\langle a,b \rangle}$ is the set of all functions from D_a to D_b.

B. Basic Expressions
1. If $\alpha \in Var_a$ then $[\alpha]^c = c(\alpha)$.
2. If $\alpha \in Con_a$ then $[\alpha]^c$ is that member of D_a determined by the lexicon of English.

    e.g. $[loves']^c$ = that function g in $D_{\langle e, \langle e,t \rangle \rangle}$ s.t. for any $a \in E$, g(a) is that function in $D_{\langle e,t \rangle}$ s.t. for any $b \in E$, g(a)(b)=1 iff b loves a in c,
    or, equivalently,
    $[loves']^c = \{<b,a>: b \text{ loves } a \text{ in } c\}$

3. Denotations of determiners:
    i. $[a']^c$ = that function in $D_{\langle \langle e,t \rangle, \langle \langle e,t \rangle, t \rangle \rangle}$ s.t. for any α in $D_{\langle e,t \rangle}$, $g(\alpha)$ is that function in $D_{\langle \langle e,t \rangle, t \rangle}$ s.t. for any β in $D_{\langle e,t \rangle}$, $g(\alpha)(\beta) = 1$ iff there is an $a \in E$ s.t. $\alpha(a)=1$ and $\beta(a)=1$.

Or equivalently:
$[a'(F')(G')]^c = 1$ iff there is an $a \in E$ s.t. $[F]^c(a)=1$ and $[G]^c(a)=1$.

Or equivalently:
$[a'(F')(G')]^c = 1$ iff $[F]^c \cap [G]^c \neq \emptyset$

(The remaining definitions will be given only in set terminology.)

ii. $[the'(P')(Q')]^c = 1$ iff $[P']^c \cap [Q']^c \neq \emptyset$ and $|[P']^c| = 1$
iii. $[the_p'(F')(G')]^c = 1$ iff $[F']^c \subseteq [G']^c$ and $|[F']^c| > 1$
iv. $[every'(P')(Q')]^c = 1$ iff $[P']^c \subseteq [Q']^c$

C. Composition Rules
1. If $\alpha \in ME_{(a,b)}$ and $\beta \in ME_a$ then $[\alpha(\beta)]^c = [\alpha]^c([\beta]^c)$.
2. If $\alpha \in ME_a$ and $\beta \in Var_b$ then $[[\lambda\beta[\alpha]]^c$ = that function h in $D_{(b,a)}$ s.t. for all $k \in D_b$, $h(k) = [\alpha]^{c[k/\beta]}$, where $c[k/\beta]$ is the set of indices identical to c except that the assignment function included in c assigns k to the expression β.
3. For any $\alpha, \beta \in ME_t$,
   i. $[\alpha \& \beta]^c = 1$ iff $[\alpha]^c = 1$ and $[\beta]^c = 1$ and
   ii. $[\alpha \lor \beta]^c = 1$ iff at least one of $[\alpha]^c$ and $[\beta]^c$ equals 1.
4. i. For any $\alpha, \beta \in ME_t$, $[\alpha \cup \beta]^c = [\alpha \lor \beta]^c$ and $[\alpha \cap \beta]^c = [\alpha \& \beta]^c$
   ii. Let b be a conjoinable type and let $\alpha, \beta \in ME_{<a,b>}$.
   Then $[\alpha \cup \beta]^c$ = that function g in $D_{<a,b>}$ s.t. for any $x \in D_a$, $g(x) = [\alpha(x) \cup \beta(x)]^c$ and
   $[\alpha \cap \beta]^c$ = that function g in $D_{<a,b>}$ s.t. for any $x \in D_a$, $g(x) = [\alpha(x) \cap \beta(x)]^c$.

Bibliography

Aone, Chinatsu (1988). "Type-Shifting and Variable-Introducing Disjunction in English and Japanese." *WCCFL* 7.

Ball, Catherine (1986). "Metalinguistic Disjunction." *Penn Review of Linguistics*. Tenth Penn Linguistics Colloquium.

Barrett, R.B. and A.J. Stenner (1971). "On the Myth of Exclusive *Or*." *Mind* 80 (Vol.317): 116-121.

Barwise, J. and R.Cooper (1981). "Generalized Quantifiers and Natural Language." *Linguistics and Philosophy* 4: 159-219.

Beaver, David (1992). "The Kinematics of Presupposition." In P. Dekker and M. Stockhof (eds.). *Proceedings of the Eighth Amsterdam Colloquium*, ILLC, University of Amsterdam.

——— (1995a). *Presupposition and Assertion in Dynamic Semantics*. PhD dissertation, University of Edinburgh.

——— (1995b). "An Infinite Number of Monkeys." ILLC Research Report.

——— (1997). "Presupposition." In J. van Bentham and A. ter Meulen (eds.). *The Handbook of Logic and Language*. Amsterdam: Elsevier, and Cambridge, Mass: MIT Press.

Cann, Ronnie (1993). *Formal Semantics*. Cambridge, England: Cambridge University Press.

Carlson, Greg N. (1981). "Distribution of Free-Choice *Any*." *CLS* 17: 8-23.

Carlson, Lauri (1983). *Dialogue Games: An Approach to Discourse Analysis*. Boston: D. Reidel Publishing Company.

Chierchia, Gennaro (1992). "Anaphora and Dynamic Binding." *Linguistics and Philosophy* 15: 111-183.

―― (1995). *Dynamics of Meaning: Anaphora, Presuppositions and the Theory of Grammar*. Chicago: University of Chicago Press.

―― and Sally McConnell-Ginet (1990). *Meaning and Grammar*. Cambridge, Mass.: MIT Press.

Chomsky, Noam (1981). *Lectures on Government and Binding*. Dordrecht: Forest.

―― (1986a). *Knowledge of Language, its Nature, Origin and Use*. New York: Praeger.

―― (1986b). *Barriers*. Cambridge, Mass.: MIT Press.

―― (1995). *The Minimalist Program*. Cambridge, Mass.: MIT Press.

Clark, Herbert H. (1977). "Bridging." In Johnson-Laird, P.N. and P.C. Wason (eds.), *Thinking: Readings in Cognitive Science*. Cambridge: CUP, 411-420.

Cooper, Robin (1979). "The Interpretation of Pronouns." In F. Heny and H. Schnelle (eds.), *Syntax and Semantics* 10: *Selections from the Third Groningen Round Table*. New York: Academic Press, 61-92.

Davies, M. (1981). *Meaning, Quantification, Necessity*. London: Routledge and Kegan Paul.

Donnellan, Keith (1978). "Speaker Reference, Descriptions and Anaphora." In P. Cole (ed.), *Syntax and Semantics, Vol. 9: Pragmatics*. New York: Academic Press, 47-68.

Du Bois, John W. (1974). "Syntax in mid-sentence". *Berkeley studies in syntax and semantics, Vol. I*. Berkeley: Department of Linguistics and Institute of Human Learning, University of California.

―― (1977). "Pronouns, Quantifiers and Relative Clauses (I)." *Canadian Journal of Philosophy* 7: 467-536.

―― (1980). "Pronouns." *Linguistic Inquiry* 11(2): 337-362.

Fox, Danny (1995). "Economy and Scope." *Natural Language Semantics* 3: 283-341.

Gärdenfors, Peter (1988). *Knowledge in Flux: Modeling the dynamics of epistemic states*. Cambridge, Mass.: MIT Press.

Gazdar, Gerald (1979). *Pragmatics: Implicature, Presupposition and Logical Form*. New York: Academic Press.

Geach, P. (1962). *Reference and Generality*. Ithaca: Cornell University Press.

Geurts, Bart (1994). *Presupposing*. PhD dissertation, Universität Osnabrück.

——— (1997) "Dynamic Dido and Commutative Aeneas." In R. van der Sandt, R. Blutner and M. Bierwisch (eds.), *From Underspecification to Interpretation: Papers from the ASG Workshop*. ILL Working Paper 29, Institute for Logic and Linguistics, IBM Scientific Center, Heidelberg: 163-182.

Ginzburg, Jonathan (1997). "Querying and Assertion in Dialogue". Ms, Hebrew University of Jerusalem.

Girle, Roderic A. (1989). "*And/or* or *Or but not both* or both." *History and Philosophy of Logic* **10**: 39-45.

Grice, Paul (1967). "Logic and Conversation." Harvard: the William James Lectures (unpublished). Published in: Cole, P and J.L.Morgan (eds.) (1978). *Syntax and Semantics* Vol 3: *Speech Acts*. New York: Academic Press, 183-198.

——— (1978). "Further Notes on Logic and Conversation." In Cole, P (ed.) *Syntax and Semantics* Vol 9: *Pragmatics*. New York: Academic Press, 113-127.

——— (1986). "Reply to Richards." In R. Grandy and R. Warner (eds.), *Philosophical Grounds of Rationality*. Oxford: Oxford University Press.

——— (1989). *Studies in the Way of Words*. Cambridge, Mass.: Harvard University Press.

Groenendijk, Jeroen (1997). "Questions in Dynamic Semantics". Talk given at Conference on Semantics, Institute for Advanced Studies, Hebrew University of Jerusalem.

Groenendijk, Jeroen and Martin Stokhof (1982). "Semantic Analysis of *wh*-complements." *Linguistics and Philosophy* **5**: 175-233.

——— (1984). *Studies on the Semantics of Questions and the Pragmatics of Answers*. PhD Dissertation, University of Amsterdam.

——— (1990). "Dynamic Montague Grammar." In Laszlo Kalman and Laszlo Polos (eds.). *Papers from the Second Symposium on Logic and Language*. Budapest: Akademiai Kiado.

——— (1991). "Dynamic Predicate Logic." *Linguistics and Philosophy* **14**: 39-100.

Hausser, R. (1976). "Presupposition in Montague Grammar." *Theoretical Linguistics* **3**: 245-280.

Heim, Irene (1982). *The Semantics of Definite and Indefinite Noun Phrases*. PhD Dissertation, University of Massachussets at Amherst. Published by Garland, New York, 1989.

―――― (1983a). "File Change Semantics and the Familiarity Theory of Definiteness." In Bäuerle, R, Ch. Schwarze and A. von Stechow (eds.) *Meaning, Use and Interpretation of Language*. Berlin: de Gruyter, 164-198.

―――― (1983b). "On the Projection Problem for Presuppositions." *WCCFL* 2.

―――― (1990). "E-type pronouns and donkey anaphora." *Linguistics and Philosophy* 13: 137-177.

―――― (1992). "Presupposition Projection and the Semantics of Attitude Verbs." *Journal of Semantics* 9: 183-221.

―――― and Angelika Kratzer (1998). *Semantics in Generative Grammar*. Maldan, Mass.: Blackwell.

Higginbotham, James (1991). "Either/Or." *NELS* 21: 143-155.

Hintikka, Jaakko (1976). *The Semantics of Questions and the Questions of Semantics*. (=*Acta Philosophica Fennica*, Vol.28(4)). Amsterdam: North Holland Publishing Company.

Horn, Laurence (1972). *On the Semantic Properties of Logical Operators in English*. PhD dissertation, UCLA.

―――― (1985). "Metalinguistic Negation and Pragmatic Ambiguity." *Language* 61: 121-174.

―――― (1989). *A Natural History of Negation*. Chicago: University of Chicago Press.

Hornsby, J. (1977). "Singular Terms in Contexts of Propositional Attitude." *Mind* 86: 31-48.

Hurford, J.R. (1974). "Exclusive or Inclusive Disjunction. *Foundations of Language* 11: 409-411.

Jennings, R.E. (1994). *The Genealogy of Disjunction*. New York: Oxford University Press.

Kadmon, Nirit (1987). *On Unique and Non-Unique Reference and Asymmetric Quantification*. PhD Thesis, UMass.

Kamp, Hans (1973). "Free Choice Permission." *Proceedings of the Aristotelian Society* 74: 57-74.

―――― (1978). "Semantics versus Pragmatics." In Guenthner, F., and S.J. Schmidt (eds.). *Formal Semantics and Pragmatics for Natural Languages*. Dordrecht: Reidel Publishing Company.

—— (1981). "A Theory of Truth and Semantic Representation." In: J.A.G. Groenendijk, T.M.V. Janssen and M.B.J. Stockhof (eds.). *Formal Methods in the Study of Language*, Mathematical Centre Tract 135, Amsterdam: 277-322. Reprinted in J.A.G. Groenendijk et al., (eds.). *Truth, Representation and Information* (=GRASS Series No.2). Dordrecht: 277-322.

—— and Uwe Reyle (1993). *From Discourse to Logic*. Boston: Kluwer Academic Publishers.

Kaplan, David (1977). "Demonstratives. An Essay on the Semantics, Logic, Metaphysics and Epistemology of Demonstratives and other Indexicals." Unpublished ms, University of California, Los Angeles.

Karttunen, Lauri (1971). "Definite Descriptions and Crossing Coreference." *Foundations of Language* 7: 157-182.

—— (1973a). "Presuppositions of Compound Sentences." *Linguistic Inquiry* 4: 169-193.

—— (1973b). "Remarks on Presuppositions." In Murphy, J., A. Rogers and R. Wall (eds.). *Proceedings of the Texas Conference on Performatives, Presupposiitons and Conversational Implicatures*. Center for Applied Linguistics, Washington D.C.

—— (1974). "Presupposition and Linguistic Context." *Theoretical Linguistics* 1(1): 181-194.

—— (1976). "Discourse Referents." In J. McCawley (ed.), *Syntax and Semantics 7: Notes from the Linguistic Underground*. New York: Academic Press, 363-385.

—— (1977). "Syntax and Semantics of Questions." *Linguistics and Philosophy* 1: 3-44.

—— and Stanley Peters (1979). "Conventional Implicature." In C.-K Oh and D.A. Dineen, (eds.). *Syntax and Semantics* Vol. 11. New York: Academic Press.

Krahmer, Emiel and Reinhard Muskens (1994). "Umbrellas and Bathrooms". *Proceedings from Semantics and Linguistic Theory (SALT) IV*. Cornell University, Ithaca NY: CLC Publications.

Kratzer, Angelika (1989). "An investigation of the lumps of thought." *Linguistics and Philosophy* 12: 607-653.

—— (1995). "Scope or Pseudoscope: Are there Wide Scope Indefinites?" Ms., University of Massachusetts at Amherst.

Kripke, Saul (1977). "Speaker's Reference and Semantic Reference." In P.A. French et al. (eds.), *Contemporary Perspectives in the Philosophy of Language*. Minneapolis: University of Minnesota Press. Reprinted in A.P. Martinich (ed.), *The Philosophy of Language*. Oxford: Oxford University Press, 1985.

——— (ms). "Presupposition and Anaphora: Remarks on the Formulation of the Projection Problem." Princeton University.

Ladusaw, William (1980). "Affective *or*, factive verbs and negative polarity items." *CLS* 16.

Landman, Fred (1991). *Structures for Semantics*. Boston: Kluwer Academic Publishers.

Larson, Richard (1985). "On the Syntax of Disjunction Scope." *Natural Language and Linguistic Theory* 3: 217-264.

Legrand, Jean Ehrenkranz (1975). *Or and Any: The Syntax and Semantics of Two Logical Operators*. Unpublished dissertation, University of Chicago.

Levinson, S.C. (1983). *Pragmatics*. Cambridge: Cambridge University Press.

Lewis, David (1979a). "A Problem about Permission." In E. Saarinen et al. (eds.). *Essays in Honor of Jaakko Hintikka*. Dordrecht: Reidel Publishing Company.

——— (1979b). "Scorekeeping in a Language Game." In R. Bäuerle et al. (eds.). *Semantics from Different Points of View*. Berlin: Springer, 172-187. Also in *Journal of Philosophical Logic* 8: 339-359.

Liberman, Mark (1973). "Alternatives." *CLS* 9: 346-355.

Loewer, Barry (1976). "Counterfactuals with Disjunctive Antecedents." *Journal of Philosophy* 73: 531-537.

Massey, Gerald J. (1970). *Understanding Symbolic Logic*. New York.

McKay, Thomas and Peter van Inwagen (1977). "Counterfactuals with Disjunctive Antecedents." *Philosophical Studies* 31: 353-356.

Mitchell, D. (1962). *An Introduction to Logic*. London: Hutchison.

Montague, Richard (1973). "The Proper Treatment of Quantification in English" [=PTQ]. In J. Hintikka et al. (eds.) *Approaches to Natural Language*. Proceedings of the 1970 Stanford Workshop of Grmmar and Semantics. Dordrect: Reidel, 221-242.

Neale, Stephen (1990). *Descriptions*. Cambridge, Mass.: MIT Press.

Nute, Donald (1975a). "Counterfactuals." *Notre Dame Journal of Formal Logic* XVI (4): 476-482.

——— (1975b). "Counterfactuals and the Similarity of Worlds." *Journal of Philosophy* **72**, number 21: 773-778.
——— (1984). "Conditional Logic." In Gabbay, D. and F. Guenthner (eds.). *Handbook of Philosophical Logic*, Vol. II (387-439). D. Reidel Publishing Co.
Partee, Barbara and Rooth, Mats (1983). "Generalized Conjunction and Type Ambiguity." In R. Bäuerle, C. Schwarze, and A. von Stechow, (eds.). *Meaning, Use and Interpretation of Language*. Berlin: de Gruyter.
Peacocke, C. (1975). "Proper Names, Reference and Rigid Designation." In S. Blackburn (ed.), *Meaning, Reference and Necessity*. Cambridge: Cambridge University Press, 109-132.
Pellettier, Francis Jeffry (1977). "Or." *Theoretical Linguistics* 4: 61-74.
Poessi, Massimo and Sandro Zucchi (1990). "On Telescoping". *Proceedings of Semantics and Linguistic Theory (SALT) II*.
Reinhart, Tanya (1995). *Interface Strategies*. OTS, University of Utrecht.
Rescher, Nicholas (1964). *Introduction to Logic*. New York.
Richards, Thomas J. (1989). "*Or* and *And/or*: a Discussion." *History and Philosophy of Logic* **10**: 29-38.
Roberts, Craige (1987). *Modal Subordination, Anaphora and Distributivity*." PhD. Dissertation, University of Massachusetts at Amherst.
Roberts, Craige (1989). "Modal Subordination and Pronominal Anaphora in Discourse." *Linguistics and Philosophy* **12**: 683-721.
——— (1996). "Information Structure in Discourse: Towards an Integrated Formal Theory of Pragmatics." *OSU Working Papers in Linguistics* **49**: 91-136.
Rooth, Mats (1985). *Association with Focus*. Ph.D. dissertation, University of Massachusetts, Amherst.
——— (1992). "A Theory of Focus Interpretation." *Natural Language Semantics* **1**: 75-116.
——— and Barbara Partee (1982). "Conjunction, Type Ambiguity and Wide Scope 'Or'," in D. Flickenger, M. Macken and N. Wiegand (eds.). *Proceedings of the First West Coast Conference on Formal Linguistics*. Linguistics Department, Stanford University.
Salmon, Wesley C. (1984). *Logic*. New York.
Schwarz, Bernhard (1997). "On the Syntax of *either...or*." Ms., University of Massachusetts at Amherst.

Simons, Mandy (1996). "Disjunction and Anaphora." In T. Galloway and J. Spence (eds.), *Proceedings from Semantics and Linguistic Theory (SALT) VI*. Ithaca: CLC Publications, 245-260.

Soames, Scott (1979). "A Projection Problem for Speaker Presuppositions." *Linguistic Inquiry* 10: 623-666.

——— (1982). "How Presuppositions are Inherited: A Solution to the Projection Problem." *Linguistic Inquiry* 13: 483-545.

——— (1989). "Presupposition." In D. Gabbay and F. Guenthner (eds.). *Handbook of Philosophical Logic*. Boston: D.Reidel Publishing Company.

Sperber, Dan and Deidre Wilson (1986). *Relevance: Communication and Cognition*. Cambridge, Mass.: Harvard University Press.

Stalnaker, Robert (1972). "Pragmatics." In Davidson, D. and G. Harman (eds.). *Semantics of Natural Language*. Dordrecht: D.Reidel Publishing Company: 380-397.

——— (1973). "Presuppositions." *Journal of Philosophical Logic* 2: 447-457.

——— (1974). "Pragmatic Presuppositions." In Milton K. Munitz and Peter K. Unger (eds.), *Semantics and Philosophy*. New York: New York University Press.

——— (1975). "Indicative Conditionals." *Philosophia* 5(3): 269-286.

——— (1976). "Propositions." In McKay and Merrill (eds.). *Issues in the Philosophy of Language*. New Haven, Conn.: Yale University Press, 79-91.

——— (1978). "Assertion." In P. Cole, (ed.). *Syntax and Semantics*, Vol.9. New York: Academic Press.

——— (1984), *Inquiry*. Cambridge, Mass.: MIT Press.

——— (1996). "On the Representation of Context." In In T. Galloway and J. Spence (eds.), *Proceedings from Semantics and Linguistic Theory (SALT) VI*. Ithaca: CLC Publications, 279-294.

Stone, Mathew (1992). "*Or* and Anaphora." *SALT* II: 367-385.

Tarski, Alfred (1941). *Introduction to Logic and to the Methodology of the Deductive Sciences*. New York.

Tomioka, Satoshi (1998). "Partition Semantics for Focus." Talk given at Cornell University.

Vainikka, Ann (1987). "Why can *or* mean 'and' or 'or'." *UMOP* 12.

Van der Sandt, Rob (1988). *Context and Presupposition*. London: Croom Helm.

―――― (1992). "Presupposition Projection as Anaphora Resolution." *Journal of Semantics* **9**: 333-377.

―――― and Bart Geurts (1991). "Presupposition, Anaphora and Lexical Content." IBM Deutschland GmbH, Institute for Knowledge Based Systems.

Von Fintel, Kai (1994). *Restrictions on Quantifier Domains*. PhD. Dissertation, UMass. Amherst.

Wilson, George (1991). "Reference and Pronominal Descriptions." *Journal of Philosophy* 88.7: 359-387.

Index

Answers
    context dependency of, 40
    exhaustivity, 72
    indirect, 40-41
    partial vs. complete, 39-40
Antecedent clause, 152
    revised definition, 189

CCP framework, 19-20
    presupposition in, 88-90
Context change
    semantic vs. pragmatic approaches, 9
Context Change Potential (CCP), 20, 88, 99-101
    for conjunction, 20
    for disjunction, 90-92
Context set, 11
Contextual entailment, 29

Definite descriptions
    Fregean/Strawsonian view, 142
    in DRT, 141
    Russellian, 146, 151

Discourse Context (DC), 35, 41-42
    update of, 42-43
Discourse Representation Structure (DRS), 21
Discourse Representation Theory (DRT), 21-22
    external anaphora in, 225-227
    internal anaphora in, 131-134, 136-137
Disjunctive E-type reading, 183
Dynamic Montague Grammar (DMG), 23
    internal anaphora in, 128-130
Dynamic operator, 128

E-type anaphora, 145
    Chapter Five account, 194
    Chapter Four account, 148
    in Cooper (1979), 145
    in Evans (1977), 145
    in Heim (1990), 146
    in Neale (1990), 146, 220
    structural vs. pragmatic accounts, 146

Entailing disjunctions, 29, 46-48
   and presupposition
      projection, 119
   and the Simplicity
      Condition, 34
Exclusive interpretation of
      disjunction
   derived from alternativeness,
      76-77
   derived from exhaustiveness,
      72-76
   semantic account, 64-67
External anaphora, 181
   in DRT, 225-227
   in Rooth and Partee (1982), 224
   in Stone (1992), 228
   narrow scope antecedents, 198-201, 211, 213-217
   to clausal disjunction, 186, 205
   to NP-disjunction, 183, 203

Felicity Conditions
   flouting, 57-58
   summary, 52
File Change Potential, 18
File Change Semantics (FCS), 17-18
   anaphora in, 18

Gazdar, G.
   account of exclusive interpretation, 67-70
   cancellation theory of presupposition projection, 103-105
   on presupposition, 103

Generalized Disjunction operator, 191
Grice, P.
   conversational implicature, 57
   maxims of conversation, 6, 31, 33
   on disjunction, 28-29, 79 fn.7

Heim, I., 83, 113, 144
   CCP framework, 19-20
   File Change Semantics, 17-18
   treatment of presupposition, 88

Inference-based anaphora, 230
Internal anaphora, 125
   anaphora-based accounts, 127-138
   and narrow scope antecedents, 158-159
   felicity-based account, 140-145, 153-157
   in DMG, 128-130
   in DRT, 131-134, 136-137

Logical equivalence proposal, 91-93
Logical Form (LF), 148

Maxim of Manner, 6, 33
Maxim of Quality, 6
Maxim of Quantity, 6, 72
Maxim of Relation, 6, 31, 43
Metalinguistic *or*, 60-63

Index

Narrow scope antecedents, 158, 159, 198-201, 211-216
Neale, S., 144, 159
Non-defective context, 11

Plural pronouns, 166, 230
Presupposition
 elementary, 81
 pragmatic, 10
Presupposition accommodation, 11
 global vs. local, 83
 in DRT, 106-107
 in Stalnakerian framework, 113
Presupposition projection
 accommodation view, 105-112
 cancellation view, 103
 conflicting presuppositions, 94
 in conjunction, 15
 in disjunction, 82, 84-87
Pronoun Rule, 153
 revised, 196

Quantifier Raising (QR), 148
Question Under Discussion (QUD), 31
Questions
 proper, 37
 resolved, 38-39
 semantics of, 35-36

Recoverable predicate, 195
Recoverable property, 195
Relevant Informativity
 Condition, 32-33
 and felicity conditions of disjunction, 43-45, 52
 formal definition, 43

Simplicity Condition, 34
 and felicity conditions of disjunction, 46-48, 50-52
 and Relevant Informativity, 47
Single-antecedent reading, 184, 217
Specific indefinites, 160-164
Stalnaker, R., 82
 Gricean influence, 13
 model of conversation, 7, 10, 30
Supplemented disjunct proposal, 91-93
Symmetry of presupposition projection, 85, 93-94

Translation language, 149
Translation procedure, 149

Update procedure for disjunction, 112

Van der Sandt, R., 120
 on internal anaphora, 138
 on presupposition, 105

For Product Safety Concerns and Information please contact our EU
representative GPSR@taylorandfrancis.com
Taylor & Francis Verlag GmbH, Kaufingerstraße 24, 80331 München, Germany

www.ingramcontent.com/pod-product-compliance
Lightning Source LLC
Chambersburg PA
CBHW070243230426
43664CB00014B/2396